RETHINKING BODY LANGUAGE

Challenging all of our old assumptions, *Rethinking Body Language* builds on the most recent cutting-edge research to offer a new theoretical perspective on this subject that will transform the way we look at other people. In contrast to the traditional view that body language is primarily concerned with the expression of emotions and the negotiation of social relationships, Geoffrey Beattie argues instead that gestures reflect aspects of our thinking but in a different way to verbal language. Critically, the spontaneous hand movements that people make when they talk often communicate a good deal more than they intend.

This ground-breaking book takes body language analysis to a whole new level. Engagingly written by one of the leading experts in the field, it shows how we can detect deception in gesture–speech mismatches and how these unconscious movements can give us real insight into people's underlying implicit attitudes.

Geoffrey Beattie is Professor of Psychology at Edge Hill University. He is the author of 20 books and over 100 journal articles, and was awarded the Spearman Medal by the BPS in recognition of outstanding published work in psychology. He has presented a number of television programmes and was also the resident on-screen psychologist for 11 series of *Big Brother*, specialising in body language and social behaviour.

RETHINKING BODY LANGUAGE

How Hand Movements Reveal Hidden Thoughts

Geoffrey Beattie

Routledge
Taylor & Francis Group

LONDON AND NEW YORK

First published 2016
by Routledge
2 Park Square, Milton Park, Abingdon, Oxon, OX14 4RN

and by Routledge
711 Third Avenue, New York, NY 10017

Routledge is an imprint of the Taylor & Francis Group, an informa business

British Library Cataloguing in Publication Data
A catalogue record for this book is available from the British Library

Library of Congress Cataloging in Publication Data
Beattie, Geoffrey.
 Rethinking body language: how hand movements reveal hidden
 thoughts / Geoffrey Beattie. – 1 Edition.
 pages cm
 Includes bibliographical references and index.
 ISBN 978-0-415-53888-6 (hb) — ISBN 978-0-415-53889-3 (softcover)
 1. Body language. 2. Gesture—Psychological aspects. 3. Hand. I. Title.
 BF637.N66.B4297 2016
 153.6′9—dc23
 2015034712

ISBN: 978-0-415-53888-6 (hbk)
ISBN: 978-0-415-53889-3 (pbk)
ISBN: 978-1-315-88018-1 (ebk)

Typeset in Joanna
by Florence Production, Stoodleigh, Devon, UK
Printed in Great Britain by Ashford Colour Press Ltd

*This book is dedicated to
Emeritus Professor Alan North,
former Vice-President and Dean of
the University of Manchester,
and valued friend.*

CONTENTS

PREFACE AND ACKNOWLEDGEMENTS

This book is a continuation of some ideas which I first developed in *Visible Thought*, published by Routledge in 2003. Since that time I have continued to actively research this area of how gestures articulate our thoughts alongside speech, and this book describes much of this new, and hopefully exciting, research. The book thus necessarily owes a great deal to my fellow researchers, and the co-authors of the various published empirical papers, and I would like to thank very publicly Brian Butterworth (who supervised my PhD at the University of Cambridge), Rima Aboudan (who did a PhD with me at the University of Sheffield), and Jane Coughlan, Heather Shovelton, Judith Holler, Jamie Ross, Kate Webster, Doron Cohen and Laura Sale (all PhD students, research assistants or research fellows at the University of Manchester). Doron and Laura started off as gesture researchers but became experts in deception! I would also particularly like to thank Laura McGuire (working with me now at Edge Hill University) for everything basically. All of my co-researchers have made very significant contributions to the work I report here. I have tried to tie this body of empirical work together, in order to demonstrate why the spontaneous hand movements generated in talk are so significant.

I would also like to single out a number of academics in particular for special thanks. I have been inspired throughout my academic career by the imaginative and creative thinking of David McNeill, now Emeritus Professor at the University of Chicago, whom I regard as both a mentor and a friend. He is the inspiration behind much of the work I do in this area. I would also like to thank Professor Marcel Danesi from the University of Toronto and Editor of *Semiotica*. Both of these academics have been incredibly supportive of my work and this support has been invaluable, especially over the past few years. Alan North (to whom this book is dedicated) and Christine Rogers were there when I needed them, and I owe them an extreme debt of gratitude.

I am fortunate now to be working in a great university (Edge Hill) that encourages fresh thinking and allows important ideas to develop and flourish, and I would like to thank the Pro Vice-Chancellor (Research) and Dean of the Faculty of Arts and Sciences, George Talbot, and the Vice Chancellor, John Cater, for their faith in me from the beginning and their constant, unwavering support. I think that I can help make Edge Hill University what it aspires to be.

1

INTRODUCTION:
A NEW PERSPECTIVE ON
AN OLD PROBLEM

In this book, I am going to present a new theoretical perspective on bodily communication. It will be very new to the vast majority of people; indeed, it may directly challenge what you think you know about body language. Bodily communication is incredibly significant, indeed more significant than we had ever assumed, but not necessarily in the way that we traditionally imagined. Bodily communication does not just reveal our emotions and how we feel about another person, it reveals our hidden thoughts. In the past few years, new research in psychology has made significant progress in understanding what people do when they communicate to one another, and more importantly exactly how they do it, and this new research challenges many of our long-standing beliefs on this subject. You need to be prepared for a few shocks along the way, to have a few core beliefs shaken. I know enough about human communication to warn you in advance.

I say 'bodily communication' but the focus is really on one important component of bodily communication, namely the movements of the hands and arms that people make when speaking. This might seem overly restrictive but believe me, this in itself is a very large domain of research. I will argue that such movements are not part of some system of communication completely divorced from speech, some system of 'body language' vs 'verbal language', as many psychologists of the past seem to have assumed; rather these bodily movements are intimately connected with speaking and with thinking. The late Michael Argyle, one of the leading British social psychologists for many years, and the clinical psychologist Peter Trower once wrote that 'Humans use two quite separate languages, each with its own function' (Argyle and Trower 1979: 22). The separate languages they were referring to here were 'verbal language' and 'body language'. According to this view, verbal language, unlike body language, conveys semantic information – information about the world, be it our very private inner world ('you have caused me so much pain') or the outer world ('I was stuck in the house because it was raining, watching the people walk by'). It also, of course, conveys ideas and plans, it makes accusations and excuses, insults and compliments, and it cajoles, persuades and disciplines. Body language, they argued, does different things, and is separate from the verbal channel. Body language is the social and emotional channel for conveying emotions and relationships; it signals power, liking, attraction, anxiety and confidence. Of course, it should be immediately obvious that verbal language can do all of these social and emotional things as well; after all, we can simply say 'I am really down' (conveying emotion), 'Can I see you again?' (negotiating relationships), 'I told you to sit down' (signalling power), 'I really find you fascinating' (communicating liking), 'I love your hair' (perhaps indicating attraction, depending upon the context), 'I'm incredibly agitated today' (revealing anxiety) or 'That was so easy' (signalling confidence). None of this might be very subtle when it comes to negotiating the intricacies of social relationships or expressing how we feel, but verbal language clearly has a role to play here. However, this new theory argues for the other side of the argument as well; it suggests that hand gesture communicates semantic information (the traditionally accepted domain of verbal language), acting alongside the speech itself. This new theory argues that these movements of the hands and arms reflect our thinking, like language but in a completely different manner, using a different sort of system of communication with very different properties.

There are a number of major differences between how the two systems of communication work, as we will see, but I just want to mention one here. We seem to be much less aware of what our hands are communicating than what we are saying verbally and for that reason the information in the hands can be incredibly important. One might say that hand gestures actually embody our thinking through bodily action with little or no conscious awareness. I will attempt to persuade you that such behaviours provide us with a glimpse of our hidden unarticulated thoughts. Movements of the hands and arms act as a window on the human mind; they make thought visible. The fact that they do this without our conscious awareness makes them particularly interesting for both psychologists and the general public in their everyday lives.

Speech, of course, also reveals our thoughts; that is after all what speech is designed to do. However, as we all know, we sometimes do not say exactly what we mean, we obfuscate and deviate, we avoid the issue, we talk our way around things, we cheat and we lie, and we can do all of this because our speech is conscious and controlled. Sometimes we give the game away, usually through those bits of speech over which we have least control. When we lie, the pitch of our speech sometimes rises when we feel particularly anxious about getting found out (Streeter et al. 1977), certain pauses may lengthen as we plan our lie (Benus et al. 2006), but a lot of the time we get away with it. Hand movements can be more revealing for one very simple reason: most of them are unconsciously produced in everyday life alongside speech and contain information that we, as the speaker, are unaware is actually there. When we are gesturing we are not only unaware of the exact form and trajectory of our gestures, and what our gestures are 'saying', we are usually unaware of the sheer extent of the gestures, and sometimes we are even unaware of whether we are moving our hands at all.

The major challenge for us here is to start thinking afresh about the very nature of everyday communication in which people express their underlying thoughts and ideas.

The starting point of the book is really the very simple observation that when human beings talk, they make many bodily movements, but in particular they make frequent, and I suggest largely unconscious, movements of the hands and arms. They do this in every possible situation – in face-to-face communication, on the telephone, even when the hands are below a desk and thus out of sight of their interlocutor (I have many recordings of these and similar occurrences). It is as if human beings are neurobiologically programmed to make these movements whilst they talk, that these movements are so important, and they would seem to be (in evolutionary terms) a good deal more primitive than speech itself, with language evolving on the back of these visible movements (or alongside these movements according to McNeill 2012). People who have been blind from birth still gesture even though they have never actually seen gestures themselves, and they continue to gesture even when conversing with other blind people that they know are blind (Iverson and Goldin-Meadow 1997). These gestures are often imagistic in form, and the resultant images are closely integrated in time with the speech itself (on other occasions, however, the movements are simpler than this and appear to be timed with the stress points in the speech). The imagistic movements when they refer to concrete objects, events and actions are called 'iconic gestures' because of their mode of representation; the simpler stress-timed movements are called 'beats'. Words have an arbitrary relationship with the things they represent (and thus are 'non-iconic'). Why do we call a particular object a 'shoe' or that large four-legged creature a 'horse'? They could just as well be called something completely different (and, of course, they are called something completely different in other languages). But the unconscious imagistic gestural movements that we generate when we talk do not have this arbitrary relationship with the thing they are representing. The imagistic form of these gestures somehow captures certain aspects of the thing that they are representing (hence they are called 'iconic') and there is often a good deal of cross-cultural similarity in their actual form (as well as some important differences depending upon the structural features of the language).

If you are alone in a room when you are reading this just visualise someone speaking, if you are reading this in public just look around you. What do you see? You see lots of talk and lots of movement in the face, in the eyes, in the body and particularly in the arms and hands. In Figure 1.1 we see just one speaker, but quite a famous speaker at that, who seems pretty engrossed in what he is saying. He was the CEO of a very large and successful multinational, and he is talking in an interview about future developments of the PC and other 'intelligent edge devices'. I have transcribed this speech using some well-known conventions developed by a Conversation Analyst called Gail Jefferson for representing speech and conversational talk (see Table 1.1). I have slightly adapted these for gesture–speech transcription. The idea behind this particular transcription method is that if you understand the symbols used, you should be able to recreate the speech as it was originally said. The square brackets [text] show which words were accompanied by gestures.

Just look at these hand movements, drawing out images in the space in front of his body. I will argue, following the pioneering work of David McNeill and others, that these imagistic gestures do not merely 'illustrate' the content of the speech; rather I will argue that they are a core part of the underlying message. The speaker does not say what he intends to say and then try to make it clearer with a gestural illustration, after a brief pause. Rather he uses both speech and movement simultaneously; the movements and the words both derive from the same underlying mental representation at exactly the same time (actually the beginning of the gestural movement often slightly precedes the speech so that the hands can be in exactly the right

Table 1.1 A glossary of Gail Jefferson's transcription symbols (Jefferson 2004)

(.)	Micro-pause	A brief pause, usually less than 0.2 seconds.
. or down arrow	Period or Down Arrow	Indicates falling pitch or intonation.
? or up arrow	Question Mark or Up Arrow	Indicates rising pitch or intonation.
,	Comma	Indicates a temporary rise or fall in intonation.
!-	Hyphen	Indicates an abrupt halt or interruption in utterance.
>text<	Greater than/Less than symbols	Indicates that the enclosed speech was delivered more rapidly than usual for the speaker.
<text>	Less than/Greater than symbols	Indicates that the enclosed speech was delivered more slowly than usual for the speaker.
°	Degree symbol	Indicates whisper, reduced volume or quiet speech.
ALL CAPS	Capitalised text	Indicates shouted or increased-volume speech.
underline	Underlined text	Indicates the speaker is emphasising or stressing the speech.
:::	Colon(s)	Indicates prolongation of a sound.
hhh		Audible exhalation
.hhh		Audible inhalation
(text)	Parentheses	Speech which is unclear or in doubt in the transcript.
[text]	Square brackets	Speech within square brackets is accompanied by the meaningful part of the gesture – the so-called 'stroke phase'.

position to make the critical movement at the right time). That way the stroke phases of the gestures are perfectly timed with the speech, and together with the speech, they form a complete whole. The two systems are perfectly coordinated. In the words of David McNeill (2012), 'Gestures are components of speech, not accompaniments but actually integral parts of it' (2012: 2), where a gesture here is understood to be 'a manifestly expressive action that enacts imagery . . . and is generated as part of the process of speaking' (2012: 4). Gesture and speech are hypothesised to originate from the same 'growth point' that gives rise to the overall communicative message in both the speech and the hands.

Of course, there are different types of gestures in everyday life, and psychologists use the concept of the 'gesture continuum' (developed by the

```
The PC is an important part of the [overall ecosystem] (.)
```

```
that people are using (0.2)
I think there's gonna be [TWO places of innovation]
```

```
for developers over the next (.) few years.
and I think that [people got very excited] (.)
```

```
appropriately about the interne::t (.) and htm::l and browse::rs.
```

Figure 1.1 The connections between gesture and speech.

psychologist Adam Kendon) to distinguish between them. The kinds of gestures that we will be considering in this book are at one end of the continuum. There are essentially three critical dimensions to this continuum; the position of any category of gesture on this continuum depends upon the answer to the following three questions:

1. Is speech necessary for the generation of the gesture?
2. How similar to language is the gesture?
3. How conventionalised is the gesture?

For example, in the case of the *sign languages of the deaf* the answers to these three questions are:

1. 'No' (speech is not necessary).
2. 'Very similar' (the systems are, of course, designed to be similar).
3. 'Very' (if the signs were not conventionalised the system would not work; you could not have one person making a sign for 'dog' that was totally unlike someone else's sign).

   In the case of *emblems*, which are gestures with a strict verbal translation, for example, the palm-front 'V' sign for 'peace', the answers are:

1. 'No' (speech is not necessary).
2. 'Similar in limited respects'. These gestures can stand as meaningful words or concepts, e.g. 'peace' or 'good', but there are constraints on their possible combination into larger units (the equivalent of phrases in verbal language) to express more complex ideas. The 'peace' sign (palm-front 'V'-sign gesture) followed by the ring gesture (where the hand is held up, palm away from the person gesturing, with the forefinger and thumb touching to form a circle, and the other three fingers extended, see Morris et al. 1979) may potentially communicate 'peace is okay' or 'peace is good', but how would you communicate 'peace is good but difficult to achieve'? The number of possible acceptable combinations of emblems is low and observations of communication in everyday life would suggest that they are actually rarely combined to any degree at all. In other words, emblems do not have the 'combinatoric, hierarchic, recurrent property' (McNeill 2012: 9) that ordinary verbal language possesses.
3. 'Very' (if you reverse the 'V' sign, palm back, it means something completely different, to most people!). As McNeill points out, there are

clear differences between well-formed and not-well-formed ways of making emblems and they also have culturally determined meanings that can sometimes give rise to significant communication difficulties when cultures interact/meet/collide. These meanings have often been conventionalised for significant periods of our history. Thus, in the first century AD the Roman scholar Quintilian describes in his book *Institutio Oratoria* (Book XI, III, 104) how to make the ring gesture: 'If the first finger touch the middle of the right-hand edge of the thumb-nail with its extremity, the other fingers being relaxed, we shall have a graceful gesture well suited to express approval.' Morris *et al.* (1979) make an interesting observation on this description. They say that 'by insisting that the finger-tip touches, not merely the end of the thumb, but "the right-hand edge of the thumb-nail", Quintilian ensures that the precision hold is made in such a way that the two digits are more or less forced to adopt a circular posture. It is possible to bring the fleshy tips together in such a way that the shape created is a "circle" so squashed as to be hardly circular at all. But the details he gives insist on the ring shape and leave no doubt that he was writing about exactly the same gesture that we see today' (Morris *et al.* 1979: 103). In other words, the ring gesture is carefully prescribed in terms of its execution. The circular shape would seem to be crucial to its conventionalised form (although when you watch people make this gesture in everyday life, sometimes they do only approximate that circular shape). The ring sign is recognised as an 'okay' sign across a wide range of European and Mediterranean locations in Morris *et al.*'s field research, except for one location they tested, namely Tunisia, where apparently it is not recognised at all as an 'okay' sign (there it is used as a threat meaning 'you are a zero').

But in the case of the gestures that we will be considering (imagistic gestures that are iconic in nature, and beats) the answers are:

1. 'Yes' (speech is necessary; these gestures are generated only during the act of speaking, or in the planning pauses immediately before speaking).
2. 'Not similar'. These gestures seem to have very different properties to language, for example, the meaning of the individual components of the gesture derive their meaning from the image as a whole rather than vice versa. Look back at the gestures in Figure 1.1 and consider the form of the individual components. They could very well be communicating something very different (e.g. the apparent 'fist' gesture in the second

picture) in the context of a very different overall gestural image. Language works in a 'bottom up' manner – we understand phrases, clauses and sentences by first understanding the meanings of the words that comprise them; these iconic gestures work in the opposite way, a 'top down' manner – we know what the gesture as a whole is alluding to and that allows us to interpret the meanings of the individual gestural movements that comprise it. This is how McNeill (2012) describes this property – 'the elements of the gesture (the handshape, the location, the direction, the tension) are meaningful only as parts of the whole. They are not meaningful in themselves – the meaning determination was from whole to part, not part to whole. "Global" doesn't mean that only the whole is meaningful; it is that the parts of the whole gain meaning from the whole. None of these meanings were attached to the hand properties before this immediate gesture but, within it, they have the meanings described' (2012: 12).

3. 'Not at all' (they are not conventionalised and speakers spontaneously generate images in real time to convey meaning without relying on any lexicon of gestures).

However, there is another critical factor here as I have already indicated: these types of gestures (unlike sign languages of the deaf or emblems) seem to be generated with little, if any, conscious awareness. When people are talking they will often know that their hands have just done something, that they have made some movement, but if you ask them to make exactly the same gesture again they find it very difficult to do this, or if you ask them what exactly the gesture was communicating, they will say 'I have no idea', or something similar. They may even shrug. Many gestures contain a complex of different features, and speakers when asked to repeat the movement may make a stab at repeating one of these. They may know where in front of their body they made the movement, but usually this is about the only thing that they will get exactly right (unlike speech itself, which we are pretty accurate at repeating and reproducing). This makes the spontaneous gestural movements made whilst speaking particularly interesting.

In the words of the psychologist Katherine Nelson writing in 2007, the movements of the hands in everyday talk represent 'a mode of unconscious meaning unconsciously expressed'. They are very common when people speak, particularly in conversation rather than, say, in speeches or monologues, where they still appear but not quite as frequently (see Beattie and Aboudan 1994). Indeed, in the research I conducted with Rima

Aboudan, we found that even when you give participants the same basic task (to tell a story on the basis of a simple cartoon storyboard), the frequency of gesture more than doubles (when you control for the number of words) when you have somebody interacting with the speaker rather than just listening.

The hands articulate ideas that run parallel to those expressed in our speech, and in everyday conversation listeners habitually and effortlessly extract the information from these movements and combine it with the information contained in the speech itself. In the chapters to come I will show conclusively that although this is done without any conscious awareness, the information contained within the gestural movement is crucial to receiving the full message from the speaker (and thus represents part of the original idea). Most often, the two channels of communication, speech and gesture, are congruent and represent a single idea broken down across the verbal and nonverbal modes. The meaning expressed is most often complementary to that expressed in the speech, quite literally 'combining in such a way as to enhance or emphasize each other's qualities' (see Holler and Beattie 2002, 2003a).

In Figure 1.2 is a well-known British journalist and political commentator talking about a recent stroke that had nearly killed him. The focus here is on the gestural movements accompanying the speech after line 14 when he talks about what actually happened to him during the stroke (all made by one hand because of the stroke). In this example, I show how gestures often have a 'preparation' phase where the hands get into position and adapt particular forms to make the meaningful part of the gesture, the so-called stroke phase, which is that part of the gesture that carries the critical meaning.

There are a number of things to note about the gestures here. The first and most obvious thing is the way they connect to the speech. In gesture 1, the slightly wavering hand movement is an abstract gesture (a so-called metaphoric gesture) accompanying 'very strange feeling' (the wavering movement representing 'strangeness'). It is also complementary to the speech because it represents the fact that the very strange feeling was in the head region, in other words it communicates something about the *location* of the experience. After all, intensive exercise can produce a very strange feeling elsewhere in the body (the legs, stomach, arms, etc.), as anyone who engages in intensive exercise will know. But notice how the hand movement seems to anticipate what is about to be said ('very strange feeling') by moving into a position near the head to make the meaningful part of the gesture, the hand moving forward. This anticipatory movement is called the 'preparation phase' of the gesture; the meaningful part of the gesture is called the 'stroke phase'. This shows the connectedness between the speech and the movement. When the speaker says 'very strange feeling', the right hand is exactly in the correct position (the side of his head) to show the location of that feeling. The gesture is complementary to the speech because he does not say in his speech where in his body that strange feeling was. It is only his gesture that tells us this.

Gesture 2 accompanies 'flashes of light'; again there is a preparation phase for the hand to get into position. This is a separate gesture to gesture 1; iconic gestures do not combine into larger structures unlike language which, of course, does combine into phrases, clauses, sentences, etc. The gesture seems to be representing the speed of the flashes of light; it doesn't necessarily add much to the speech here, so there appears to be a degree of overlap or redundancy between the two systems in terms of this meaning (or semantic) feature of 'speed'. However, the gesture also shows the flash crossing the eyes (again showing something about 'location').

Gesture 3 shows the relative position of the carotid artery which had been torn (there are two carotid arteries, the one torn was on the right-hand side of his neck). Note the exact correspondence between the speech ('I'd torn the carotid artery') and the gestural movement, again requiring a preparation phase to get the hand into position. The speaker could have said 'I'd torn the carotid artery on the right-hand side of my neck, the artery runs from the lower part of my neck to the brain', but the iconic gesture represents the relative position and the extent of the artery (or its approximate size), again perfectly coordinated with the speech. It is not as if he says 'I'd torn the carotid artery' and then thought, I had better illustrate this with a gestural movement. Both the speech and the gesture occur simultaneously, indicating that they both emerge at the same time from the underlying mental representation.

Gesture 4 corresponds to 'takes blood into the brain' and signifies the position of the functioning of this artery (and is therefore somewhat redundant with respect to the preceding gesture). Gesture 5, again needing a preparation phase, shows which bit of the brain was 'wiped out' by the stroke, the right-hand side controlling the left-hand side of his body (including, of course, the speaker's left arm and hand) but not any of the speech centres (the main area for speech production, Broca's area, is situated in the left hemisphere).

In each example here the gesture is perfectly coordinated with the accompanying speech and in each case this requires anticipatory movements (the preparation phases of the gesture). The result is a coordinated whole

1. >Well< I had a major stroke

2. I'm frankly lucky to be <alive>

3. Ummm (0.2)

4. <I had> been (0.2) very very heavily overworking

5. mostly my own fault

6. In the year before that (0.2)

7. I've had two minor strokes it turned out (:) in that year

8. which I hadn't noticed (0.2)

9. And then I did the terrible thing of believing what I read in the newspapers (0.2)

10. because the newspapers were saying

11. what we must all do is take <very(:)very> intensive exercise in short bursts (0.4)

12. and that's the way (:) to <health> (0.2)

13. Well I went onto a rowing machine (:)

14. and (:) gave it everything I had (:)

Preparation phase of gesture 1

15. and had a [very strange feeling] afterwards

Stroke phase of gesture 1

16. and then a blinding headache

Preparation phase of gesture 2

17. and [flashes of light] (0.4)

Figure 1.2 The coordination of gesture phases and speech. (I would like to thank Jessica Phillips for doing the preliminary sketches that formed the basis for Figure 1.2.)

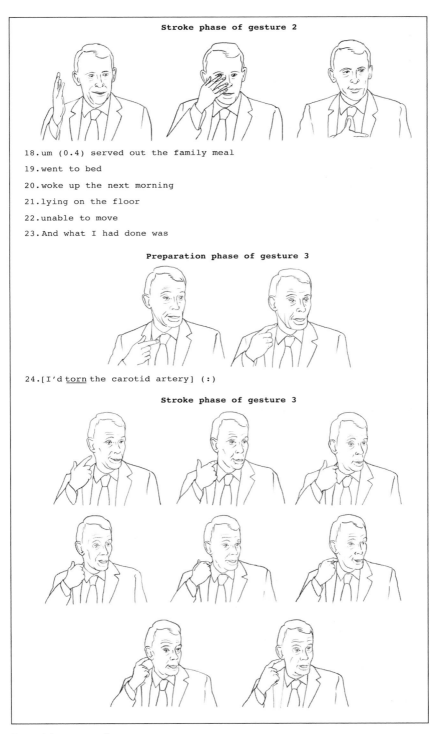

Stroke phase of gesture 2

18. um (0.4) served out the family meal
19. went to bed
20. woke up the next morning
21. lying on the floor
22. unable to move
23. And what I had done was

Preparation phase of gesture 3

24. [I'd <u>torn</u> the carotid artery] (:)

Stroke phase of gesture 3

Figure 1.2 continued

Preparation phase of gesture 4

25.which [takes blood into the brain] (0.4)

Stroke phase of gesture 4

26.and ((had a)) stroke overnight

27.which is basically just (0.2)

Preparation phase of gesture 5

28.[wi – wipes out a bit of your brain]

Stroke phase of gesture 5

29.In my case (0.2) <u>LUCKILY</u> (0.2) not my voice or memory or
   anything like that

30.but (0.4) uh the whole <u>left</u> hand side of my body

31.so I'm <u>still</u> (0.4) uh not able to walk fluently

32.I do a kind of <u>elegant</u> hobble

33.is the best I can manage (0.2)

34.my <u>left</u> arm isn't much good yet (0.2)

35.and uhm so (:) as soon as I'm ready

36.I hope to be back

37.But I've got (0.2) a lot of physio still to do

Figure 1.2 continued

in which both the speech and the movement contribute to the overall meaning. Neither would seem to be sufficient on its own. The degree of coordination is in many ways remarkable, and yet happens effortlessly and without any apparent conscious awareness on the part of the speaker.

This degree of synchrony between the speech and the co-expressive gesture with the gesture often initiated before, but not after, the accompanying speech is very important for how we (as listeners) respond to the message. Habets *et al.* (2011) used EEG recording to measure participants' neuronal responses to various speech–gesture combinations where differences in onset between the speech and the stroke phase of the gesture were systematically manipulated. They found that integration of the information from the speech and the gesture was done most efficiently when the onsets did not exceed a certain very limited time span (360 milliseconds). In other words, the very close temporal relationship between speech and the accompanying gesture is critical to the on-line processing of the information contained within them both. This very close temporal relationship also often requires a preparation phase where the hands need to get into position to make the critical phase of the gesture (the stroke phase) even before the speaker has any conscious thoughts about what they might say next.

The above example supports some of the observations made by some former colleagues at the University of Manchester (Rowbotham *et al.* 2012) who analysed people talking about a variety of recent pain experiences. They found that gestures were produced at a rate of 7.7 gestures per 100 words, which tells us something about how common these are in talk of this kind. In their sample of 757 gestures that they scored as carrying some meaning, they found that the gestures accounted for 57 per cent of all the information conveyed (that is to say, more than half). Significantly more information about the *location* and the *size* of the pain ('small', 'localised pain', 'more widespread pain', etc.) was represented in the gestures than in the speech, whereas the speech tended to represent information about other dimensions, including the intensity, the effects, the duration, the cause and the awareness of the pain. The only category of information that was represented significantly more in gesture and speech together than in either modality alone was the quality of the pain, suggesting in the words of the authors that 'neither modality is sufficiently able to provide a complete representation of the information' (Rowbotham *et al.* 2012: 13). Through these bodily movements the participants in this research were able to externalise meaning about pain and that may be of enormous benefit in helping others understand the internal, bodily experience of pain, and perhaps it also evokes sympathy on the part of others. It might well be interesting to investigate how sympathetic we are when someone uses a lot of gestures to communicate about pain compared to when they do this mainly in the speech modality. It would seem that for the majority of people (at least in the experimental setting the researchers at the University of Manchester used) the sensations and private experiences of pain are communicated via the two modalities simultaneously. How this impacts on the interlocutor was not considered, but it really would be interesting to see if the pain became more 'real' for the other person when they saw the gestures and whether they became more sympathetic as a result of this.

But on occasion, even when the speech and the hands refer to the same basic concept or idea, they do not match and when there is a clash of this kind (or a 'mismatch' as it is called) I will argue that the idea expressed in the hand movement tends to be a much more accurate reflection of our underlying thoughts than the speech itself. And this occurs for one very simple reason, namely that the 'unconscious meaning unconsciously expressed' has not been controlled or edited by the speaker to send a particular type of message. This is a recurrent theme of this book.

This new research on gesture is having a significant influence on the academic discipline of psychology but rather surprisingly it has not had the impact on everyday thinking that it might have had (or should have had). There are many best-selling books on body language that will show static images of people arranged in various postures and explain how to interpret the hidden signals embedded in that picture in front of you. These hidden signals are often thought to concern secret feelings and inclinations, longings and desires, 'who fancies whom' (there is clearly a big market for these sorts of things) and sometimes hidden emotions or power relations. However, one of the first things that strike you when you start studying body language seriously is how much movement there is when people are interacting. If only people spent more time in static configurations, how much easier the interpretation of bodily movement would be! But people are rarely static and many of the movements in everyday interaction are quite fleeting and easy to miss (this is especially true of many facial expressions, of course). The hand gestures that we will be considering are also very dynamic; they map out their meaning in the trajectories of their movement. They may not be as fleeting as some of the briefer facial expressions but they can, on occasion, be very quick indeed (a second or less in total duration), yet imbued with real significance as they work alongside the speech.

Indeed, when you watch people interacting it becomes fairly obvious that a good deal of bodily movement, and not just hand movement but foot movement, facial expression and eye gaze, posture and lean, all seem to connect in apparently significant ways with this speech. These connections are often critical to the meaning of the bodily communication, and yet are seemingly neglected by the vast majority of books on body language. As a PhD student at Cambridge, a number of years ago, I studied such bodily communication. I filmed the kinds of interactions that occur naturally in psychology buildings, mainly staff and students interacting in tutorials and seminars, and there I noticed one thing immediately – much of the bodily communication in conversation is closely integrated with the speech itself, and the psychological processes underpinning it. I noticed, for example, how speakers averted their eye gaze during hesitations in speech when they seemed to be planning what they were going to say, and showed more direct eye gaze when they got to the more fluent sections of their speech (Beattie 1983). It seems to be very difficult to plan what you are going to say and maintain direct eye contact with your interlocutor. It just overloads the cognitive system, the mental planning of the content of speech and the distractions caused by those fast fleeting signals coming back at you, competing for the same cognitive resources. Indeed, I found in my early research that false starts in speech, which are one type of speech error where somebody would start saying something and then stop abruptly, were five times more common in speech when speakers did not avert their eye gaze from their interlocutor when they were planning what they were going to say (Beattie 1983: 64). I had read a lot about the importance of eye gaze and eye contact as a body language signal and what it might mean, but few of the authors of these books started with the premise that if you want to really understand eye gaze as a signal, then you need to recognise that eye gaze is also a channel for receiving information and that because it is a channel it coordinates with the planning requirements of the speech stream. We avert our eye gaze when we are planning speech because otherwise we overload our cognitive capacity. It is simply too demanding to plan fresh ideas in speech and monitor and interpret complex nonverbal signals at the same time (Beattie 1981). So any serious analysis of eye gaze and eye contact should perhaps start with how it is affected by what is being said, in other words the relationship between speech and eye gaze. However, few body language books did this. Instead, we are presented with a host of silent characters, all standing there 'interacting' with each other, without saying a word, showing lots of eye contact or little eye contact, all clear and accessible, with no hint of how the amount of eye contact varies with what is being said or the pauses within the speech that remind us that speech does often require significant amounts of cognitive planning. These encounters look like no interactions we have ever seen or personally experienced (or that we would ever really want to experience). And for that reason, body language books are, to my mind at least, of very limited usefulness.

This is particularly true of any popular body language analyses of hand movements. Quite simply, they miss the point, which is that these movements are intimately connected with speaking and thinking, and this connection may have significant implications for what functions they possess. When you watch someone talk, their hands seem to start moving as they start speaking and there do, at first sight at least, appear to be some important connections between the pattern and the timing of these movements and the content of the speech. And yet people do not seem to be aware of what their hands are doing whilst they are talking, and oddly they make these movements even when they are talking on the telephone (which is always a little strange to behold) as if the deep connection between the speech and the hand movement cannot be broken by the invention of the telephone some 140 years or so ago. These deep connections obviously predate this invention by some time and seem largely undisturbed by this great technological development, which has done much to change the frequency and convenience of interaction without changing some of the most fundamental aspects of it, namely that certain behaviours interconnect.

Our theoretical understanding of the relationship between speech and gesture really does owe a great deal to the pioneering work of the American psychologist David McNeill, but I have taken this theory and tried to understand and test the implications of it in a number of domains where effective communication is critically important, like politics, public speaking, persuasion, advertising and marketing as well as everyday conversations, which, despite being mundane and ordinary, shape all of our lives. I have also been interested in using this theory in reverse, to start with the spontaneous and unconscious actions of the hands to infer the 'real' underlying thoughts of the speaker. I have done research in this area sometimes using tightly controlled psychological experiments, which I do think can be highly revealing, but, in addition, I have studied people talking and analysed in detail when the speech and the movement are congruent and compatible, and when they are not. I will also show how this theory might help us understand why if you just listen to what people say, rather than listening and watching, then you might end up badly deceived by what they are saying.

One area that I have been particularly interested in over the past few years is climate change and whether or not people are prepared to change their behaviour to mitigate its effects. The vast majority of people say that they really do care about environmental issues when they are interviewed on this subject and yet I could not help noticing that *sometimes* there is something about the form and nature of their hand movements when they talk about climate change in these interviews which might suggest otherwise. I do not think that the individuals here are just consciously trying to deceive the interviewer in order to appear 'greener' than they actually are (although some might be); I think that some of these people are deceiving themselves. I think that the hand movements reveal their underlying *implicit* attitude, an attitude which is held quite unconsciously but directs much of their relevant behaviour in this domain (Beattie 2010; Beattie and Sale 2011) and manages to reveal itself in the actions of the hands and arms. I will discuss this hypothesis in detail in Chapter 16. I will also show how this theory might help us to identify the more mundane *deliberate* attempts to deceive in other domains. Here again, the hands portray certain images which are not congruent with what is being said in the speech. We will consider this in detail in Chapter 15. I will show how these movements could potentially allow us to identify when certain politicians, as well as friends, neighbours and partners, are being economical with the truth or downright deceptive. I will show how politicians and others unconsciously inhibit their hand movements on occasion in case they reveal too much, and I will show that when they fail to do this, the form, timing and shape of the gestural movements can reveal a great deal.

As well as many publications in academic books and journal articles, I have used this theoretical perspective on a number of popular TV programmes in the past few years, including *Big Brother* when it was on Channel 4 in its original guise as 'an experiment in human behaviour'. I did this for 11 series. My role was to drill down through the carefully constructed facades of the housemates to identify what was really going on. Many viewers seemed to like the basic idea and agreed that my interpretations of unarticulated thoughts were at least plausible, but what was the value of this new theory that I was using? Where did the theory come from? How had it been tested? Were there other possible explanations for the unconscious movements of the hands and arms as people speak? In a TV show, you are not afforded opportunities to go into these kinds of issues. In this book, I will outline the scientific case for this new theory and explain why movements of the hands and arms are a crucial and an integral part of thinking, and why careful scrutiny of these movements might reveal a great deal about the thinking of the individuals concerned, sometimes much more than they ever intended. Following on from *Big Brother* I was given the opportunity to study a range of people in various situations for other TV programmes, including ITV's *News at Ten*, in the weeks running up to the General Election in 2005 in a slot called 'The Body Politic', and the 2010 General Election for various other TV programmes. Here, of course, it was politicians trained in communication and control who were put under the microscope.

But am I just some other body language 'expert' with a particular take on what bodily communication really means, with even more extravagant claims than the last expert? I think that what might be different about this book is my willingness to detail the new research in this area, some of which I conducted myself, and this research will be the thread that we will follow in trying to understand the revealing actions of people when they talk and what this form of bodily communication really means. As you will discover, I will let the research itself do the talking much of the time and hopefully it may well be eloquent enough on its own.

SUMMARY

- Bodily communication is incredibly significant, indeed more significant than we had ever assumed, but not necessarily in the way that we traditionally thought.

- Bodily communication does not just reveal our emotions and how we feel about another person, it reveals our hidden thoughts.

- In the past few years, new research in psychology has made significant progress in understanding what people do when they communicate to one another, and more importantly, exactly how they do it.

- This new research challenges many of our long-standing beliefs on this subject.

- We seem to be much less aware of what our hands are communicating when they spontaneously accompany speech than what we are saying verbally and for that reason, the information in the hands can be incredibly important.

- Hand gestures actually embody our thinking through bodily action.

- Such behaviours provide us with a glimpse of our hidden unarticulated thoughts.

- Hand movements are unconsciously produced in everyday life alongside speech and contain information that we, as the speaker, are unaware is actually there.

- When we are using spontaneous gestures we are not only unaware of the form and trajectory of the gestures, and what our gestures are 'saying', we are usually unaware of the sheer extent of the gestures, and sometimes we are even unaware of whether we are gesturing or not.

- According to one famous psychologist, the movements of the hands in everyday talk represent 'a mode of unconscious meaning unconsciously expressed'.

- Gestures and speech are coordinated, and many gestures have a 'preparation phase' to allow this coordination to happen.

- People who have been blind from birth still gesture even though they have never actually seen gestures themselves, and they continue to gesture even when conversing with other blind people that they know are blind.

- When the speech and the hands refer to the same basic concept but do not match the idea expressed in the hand movement, this can be a much more accurate reflection of the underlying thoughts than the speech itself.

- This is because the 'unconscious meaning unconsciously expressed' has not been controlled or edited by the speaker to send a particular type of message.

- Movements of the hands and arms can act as a window on the human mind; they make thought visible.

2

TWO SEPARATE LANGUAGES?

The focus on nonverbal behaviour (which is often, it should be said, taken to include both bodily communication and some vocal aspects of speech), as the significant domain through which human emotion is expressed, relationships are built and interpersonal attitudes are negotiated, has a long and distinguished history in psychology and in related disciplines. The argument has always been that language, the verbal channel of communication, is used primarily to convey factual or semantic information about the world, whereas the nonverbal channels have primarily social functions – 'to manage the immediate social relationships – as in animals', according to Oxford psychologist Michael Argyle, writing in 1972.

This functional separation of language and nonverbal behaviour is something of an established orthodoxy in psychology. Again (as we have already seen), the psychologist Michael Argyle, this time writing with Peter Trower in 1979, stated that 'Humans use two quite separate languages [language and nonverbal communication], each with its own function.' This is perhaps the most basic and therefore the clearest statement of how psychologists view language and nonverbal communication and their relationship. In a similar vein, Peter Trower, Bridget Bryant and Michael Argyle in their book *Social Skills and Mental Health* (1978) write: 'In human social behaviour it looks as if the nonverbal channel is used for negotiating interpersonal attitudes while the verbal channel is used primarily for conveying information.'

Language has always been considered to be linked to thought and to communicate information about the world. 'It will rain tomorrow in Manchester, again', is easily conveyed by language, but not at all easily conveyed by nonverbal communication. I have just tried to do this consciously and believe me it is very difficult. It is 'Manchester' that I just can't do and I have a bit of trouble with 'again' (and with 'tomorrow', if I'm being totally honest), although 'rain' is more or less alright (my fingers pitter-patter downwards). Nonverbal communication, it is argued, does other sorts of things than convey information about the world and the weather in Manchester. It conveys information about our emotional state, about whether we like someone or not, about whose turn it is in social interaction. It is verbal language that distinguishes us from other animals (as well as 'drinking when we are not thirsty and making love all year round', as Pierre-Augustin Caron de Beaumarchais notes in *The Marriage of Figaro*); it is nonverbal communication that we share with other animals.

Charles Hockett writing in 1960 identified 13 design features that all human verbal languages possess to convey information about the external environment (and about everything else as well). I will identify some of the most significant here. All languages use the vocal–auditory channel and, given the physics of sound, a linguistic signal can be heard by any auditory system within earshot and the source localised by any hearer, and there is rapid fading of the signal. This has potentially important implications in terms of evolutionary pressures:

> The rapid fading of such a signal means that it does not linger for reception at the hearer's convenience. Animal tracks and spoors, on the other hand, persist for a while; so of course do written records, a product of man's extremely recent cultural evolution.
>
> (Hockett 1960: 90)

In any communicative system the relationship between meaningful messages and their meanings can be either arbitrary or non-arbitrary. In verbal language this relationship is arbitrary, as Hockett writes:

> 'Salt' is not salty or granular. 'Whale' is a small word for a large object; 'microorganism' is the reverse. A picture, on the other hand, looks like what it is a picture of. A bee dances faster if the source of the nectar she is reporting is closer, and slower if it is farther

away. The design feature of 'arbitrariness' has the disadvantage of being arbitrary, but the great advantage that there is no limit to what can be communicated about.

(Hockett 1960: 90)

Human language can also be used to talk about things that are remote in space and time (the design feature of 'displacement') and it is an open system. We can convey an infinite number of messages using a finite number of words or morphemes, and applying a set of rules or principles (the design feature of 'productivity'). Wilhelm von Humboldt's famous dictum was that language provides a finite means for generating an infinite variety of expressive forms. In other words, human language is a very powerful system of communication, which is infinitely flexible and yet immediately comprehensible to all who understand the language.

So, it would seem, verbal language has a number of distinctive characteristics. Nonverbal communication is considered to be quite different to this, different in design and different in function. The traditional view of the function of nonverbal communication is that it does not communicate semantic information about the (inner or outer) world, but signals emotional state and attitudes crucial to the forming and development of interpersonal relationships. Of course, this position intuitively makes some sort of sense. One advantage of interpersonal matters being dealt with nonverbally, as psychologists have noted, is that the expression of such attitudes can be kept vague and flexible. Again, according to Michael Argyle (1972), 'People need not reveal clearly nor commit themselves to what they think about each other.' Once we start using language to communicate our attitudes to another person, then everything is out in the open in quite a different way. We are publicly committed to what we have said and therefore accountable. 'You said that you loved me' is a perfectly reasonable retort. 'You acted like you loved me, there was just something momentary in your facial expression and in your eyes' is much weaker somehow. But that is just one aspect of the process. The anthropologist Gregory Bateson highlights another important aspect:

It seems that the discourse of nonverbal communication is precisely concerned with matters of relationship . . . From an adaptive point of view, it is therefore important that this discourse be carried on by techniques which are relatively unconscious and only imperfectly subject to voluntary control.

(Bateson 1968: 614–15)

We can all say 'I love you', some of us rather too easily. It is quite a different matter to fake love nonverbally, or so Gregory Bateson seems to think. So the argument goes that we express relationships nonverbally because these types of communication are less subject to voluntary control, and therefore presumably more honest, and yet at the same time are more nebulous. We send out signals and yet remain unaccountable for their expression.

These views about the separate functions of language and nonverbal communication are not confined to psychology, as we have already seen. Gregory Bateson also states that 'nonverbal communication serves functions totally different from those of language and performs functions that verbal language is unsuited to perform'. He continues that 'nonverbal communication is precisely concerned with matters of relationship – love, hate, respect, fear, dependency, etc. – between self and vis-à-vis or between self and environment'. He was also concerned with conflicts between these two channels, when the verbal channel says one thing directly but the nonverbal channel says something completely different, and the effects of such conflicts on others. He introduced the concept of the 'double bind' as an aberrant form of self-contradictory communication, which may play a pivotal role in the development of schizophrenia within families, particularly in communication from the mother to the child (an idea taken up by the British psychiatrist R. D. Laing (see Laing and Esterson 1964, and others). The problem with 'double binds' is that there is no rational response permitted to such contradictory communications.

The argument therefore within psychology and other disciplines has been that nonverbal communication performs functions that language is unsuitable to perform and that verbal language, on the other hand (that peculiarly human attribute), is concerned with the world of thinking, abstract ideas and the communication of complex information about the world.

If we are thinking about issues of power and control, especially with regard to the organisation of turn taking in a discussion, then it seems obvious to consider both verbal and nonverbal behaviour, but at other times when we are analysing behaviour it seems natural and equally obvious to focus on either language or nonverbal behaviour, on the assumption that they are quite separate and that people use them for quite different functions. If you are interested in the communication of complex ideas you study language; if you are interested in emotion and relationships you study nonverbal behaviour. That is the established orthodoxy. But what happens if this orthodoxy is wrong? Where does that leave us? What happens if people

use verbal language as much as nonverbal behaviour for the subtle communication of their attitudes towards each other? What happens, and this
idea does seem strange, if nonverbal behaviour is used instead of, or
alongside, language for the communication of complex ideas? What happens
if we do use nonverbal behaviour to communicate ideas like 'it will rain
tomorrow in Manchester, again', despite my conscious efforts a few pages
earlier, which failed miserably? And let me be clear here – I'm not talking
about sign language like British Sign Language or American Sign Language
for the deaf, which are types of verbal language anyway, with a dictionary
and a syntax or set of rules for combining the individual words. They are
types of verbal language transmitted using the body rather than the voice
(although, of course, they do not have Hockett's design feature of use of
the vocal–auditory channel, but they do have the critical design features of
'arbitrariness', 'displacement' and 'productivity' among others). I'm talking
about nonverbal behaviour as we usually think of it – behaviour acquired
through the normal processes of socialisation, without the acquisition
of a dictionary of items and syntax for combining them into meaningful
sentences. I'm talking about nonverbal behaviour where meaning can
be transmitted in a more global and spontaneous fashion than this. I am
talking about a new idea that has arisen principally as a consequence of the
work of an American psychologist called David McNeill (1985, 1992,
2012) who has produced a new theory of how the mind works (but see
also Adam Kendon's extremely important work 1972, 1980, 1988). This
is the idea I will be exploring in this book. I will outline McNeill's theory
and discuss my own research in this particular area. These ideas challenge
the established orthodoxy in psychology and they have potentially enormous
theoretical and practical implications for gaining a much greater insight into
what people are really thinking as they talk.

I will argue that language and some nonverbal behaviour are not separate
in the way that most psychologists have thought. They are not separate in
terms of how they are produced and they are not separate in terms of what
they do. My first shot across the bows of this established orthodoxy will
involve reconsidering some classic research in psychology, which purports
to show that when language and nonverbal communication are both used
explicitly to communicate interpersonal attitudes, the language channel is
virtually ignored. The claim is that language plays virtually no role in such
matters. This is reflected in widely known and widely quoted statements
of the kind that when it comes to the social world and interpersonal
relations 'only 7 per cent of communication is verbal'. Forget verbal
language, it says, concentrate exclusively on the nonverbal bit. The problem

is that the research from which this conclusion derives is really quite weak. We turn first to consider the possible limitations of the classic psychological experiments from which this apparent conclusion is derived.

There are two sets of critical experiments that are crucial here. The first set was carried out by Albert Mehrabian at the University of California in Los Angeles and published in a number of important studies in the late 1960s (Mehrabian and Ferris 1967; Mehrabian and Wiener 1967). Mehrabian investigated the effects of consistencies and inconsistencies between the various channels of communication, including the actual meaning of the words and the tone of voice in which they are spoken and the facial expressions and the tone of voice, on the communication of interpersonal attitudes and in particular on judgements of degrees of liking. In the first study he selected three words judged to convey liking – 'honey', 'thanks' and 'dear'; three words judged to be neutral in this regard – 'maybe', 'really' and 'oh'; and three words that conveyed dislike – 'don't', 'brute' and 'terrible'. Two female speakers read each of the nine selected words using positive, neutral and negative vocal expressions and these communications were then played to sets of judges. In a second study, one neutral word was selected, the word 'maybe'. This time the facial expression was varied: it was positive, neutral or negative. Judges in this second study were presented with an audio recording of the message and a photograph of the person delivering the message. The judges had to rate the overall communication to determine how positive or negative it came across.

From these studies Mehrabian concluded that in the communication of interpersonal attitudes the facial and the vocal channels greatly outweigh the verbal channel and he estimated the relative contributions of the three channels as 55 per cent for the facial channel, 38 per cent for the vocal channel and 7 per cent for the verbal channel. Mehrabian's conclusion was that 'when there is inconsistency between verbally and implicitly expressed attitude, the implicit proportion [the nonverbal component] will dominate in determining the total message'.

This is the first study that attempted to say exactly how much the verbal and nonverbal channels each contribute to the communication of inter-personal attitudes and it produced a set of figures that have been picked up and adopted within popular culture. Most of us have heard things such as nonverbal behaviour is 13 times more powerful than language in the expression of interpersonal attitudes, and that facial expression is 8 times more powerful than language. If you read almost any copy of Cosmopolitan magazine you will see these figures quoted not just by journalists but also by experts, including psychologists. An advert for a credit card from a few years ago begins with the statement that 'only 7 per cent of communication is verbal', which is exactly Mehrabian's estimate, so the advert continues 'make the other 93 per cent count', presumably by using this particular credit card, which is meant to say a lot about you.

But the problem with these psychological studies is that they do not really consider language at all in the expression of interpersonal attitudes; at least not language as we normally understand it, with meaningful sentences used to express how we feel. Only individual words like 'honey', 'brute' and 'maybe' were used. Nobody talks in individual words in the real world for prolonged periods of time, when they can help it. 'Honey' as an expression on its own only gets you so far. Then when Mehrabian considered the effects of facial vs vocal cues, these different cues were not presented together on videotape but merely as a photograph accompanying a single word. In other words, the participants in this study were simply presented with a photograph of a particular facial expression and they heard the single word being said; then they had to integrate these two things in their mind and make their judgement. So this experiment made no real attempt to simulate anything approaching normal social behaviour or normal social judgement. Hence, we have to be a little wary about the conclusions that have been drawn from it.

However, two experiments carried out a bit later at Oxford in the early 1970s by Michael Argyle and his colleagues seem at first sight to address many of these issues. The experiments were published as two import- ant studies, indeed 'citation classics' (Argyle *et al.* 1970; Argyle *et al.* 1971). For a long period of time before his death in 2002, Argyle was a leading British social psychologist, one of the pioneers of the experimental study of human nonverbal behaviour using a series of often ingenious experi- ments. His goal was to lay bare the very basis of our everyday behaviour, as well as among other things attempting to assess what makes people happy using detailed psychological analyses. He was famous at a more personal level for his dry sense of humour, his lifelong interest in Scottish country dancing and his slightly unusual style of social interaction, which made some comment that he was indeed researching something that many, perhaps including himself, found difficult and problematic – social behaviour with all of its layers and hidden depths.

The basic methodology of these experiments is quite ingenious but it does require careful scrutiny. Very briefly, three verbal messages, paragraphs this time rather than individual words (hostile, neutral or friendly in one experiment; superior, neutral or inferior in another), were delivered in each of three different nonverbal styles (the friendly style being 'warm, soft tone of voice, open posture, smiling face', the neutral style being 'expressionless voice, blank face', the hostile style being 'harsh voice, closed posture, frown with teeth showing'). Care was taken at the outset to ensure that the verbal message and the nonverbal style had approximately the same effects on listener evaluation on certain specific dimensions. Here is an example of the types of message used in this experiment. This is the hostile message: 'I don't much enjoy meeting the subjects who take part in these experiments. I often find them rather boring and difficult to deal with. Please don't hang around too long afterwards and talk about the experiment. Some people who come as subjects are really rather disagreeable.'

The combined communications, with the three verbal messages delivered in each of the three verbal styles, were then rated by judges to see how friendly or hostile the resultant messages were perceived as being. The results again apparently demonstrate quite clearly that the nonverbal channel greatly outweighs the verbal channel in the communication of interpersonal attitudes. For example, on a seven-point scale, where '7' means extremely friendly and '1' means extremely hostile, the hostile verbal message delivered in a friendly nonverbal style was rated as 5.17; in other words it was perceived as being towards the friendly end of the scale and higher than the mid-point of 4. When the nonverbal style was friendly it didn't really seem to matter what was actually said; the overall communication was perceived as friendly. Similarly, when the nonverbal style was hostile, again it didn't really seem to matter what was said. The difference in perception of the friendly and hostile verbal messages delivered in the hostile nonverbal style was trivial, the scores being 1.60 and 1.80 respectively. Indeed the hostile verbal message delivered in the hostile style was perceived as slightly friendlier than the friendly message in the hostile style. This latter form of communication is, of course, essentially a conflicting commun-ication of the type Bateson termed a 'double bind'.

These results led Michael Argyle to the conclusion that nonverbal communication is 12.5 times more powerful than language in the com-munication of interpersonal attitudes, specifically on the friendliness–hostility dimension, and over ten times more powerful in the communi-cation of a different interpersonal attitude, namely superiority–inferiority.

These figures are very similar to those of Mehrabian and have become an important part of our everyday culture. This series of studies obviously struck a chord with the public and gave those who wished to discuss the importance of nonverbal communication precise figures to work with. The studies demonstrate that nonverbal communication is not just highly significant, but also that we can virtually dismiss verbal language if we want to understand how interpersonal attitudes are signalled, and interpersonal relations are built, in everyday life. It also means that we can ignore the connections between language and nonverbal communication because the judges in this experiment seem to do just that. Much is built on these two sets of studies. But in my view these pioneering and very influential studies have fundamental weaknesses that really do limit the conclusions that can be drawn. Let's consider what these might be.

The Oxford studies involve judges having to watch a set of nine successive communications on videotape, all from the same person, tapes in which the language and nonverbal communication are systematically varied. Therefore, the whole point of the experiment would be immediately obvious to anyone who took part. Participants could quickly work out what the experimenter was getting at and therefore might decide to play along with him or her. This sometimes happens in psychological research and is called the 'demand characteristics' of the experiment. (Sometimes the opposite occurs: the participants work out what the experimenter wants and deliberately do not go along with it. This is known rather more colloquially as the 'f . . . you' effect.) This is always a problem for psychological research where the point of the experiment is as obvious as it was here.

Second, in order to try to measure the relative importance of language and nonverbal communication, the strength of the two channels had to be both measured and equated at the outset. They had to be equal in strength when measured independently. These studies therefore, at best, tell us about people's perceptions of a certain class of communication with the range of the strength of the components artificially set. The studies do not tell us anything about the range of effects produced by language and nonverbal communication in the world at large. Perhaps in the real world people do not use such explicitly friendly or unfriendly messages. Consider that hostile verbal statement again: 'I don't much enjoy meeting the subjects who take part in these experiments. I often find them rather boring and difficult to deal with.' Is that ever likely to be said directly to someone apart from as a joke? And when it is accompanied by a friendly verbal style ('warm, soft tone of voice, open posture, smiling face') how else is this supposed to be understood apart from as some sort of joke, with the verbal statement to be dismissed? Don't forget that this is exactly what was found to happen in this experiment.

What would happen if we did not make the message quite as explicit as this? What would happen if we made the verbal message slightly more real and then used the same basic pattern of delivery? How would it then be perceived? Would the nonverbal component still make the verbal component seem completely unimportant? Let's do a quick mind experiment. Let's start with something pretty explicit but (in my experience) quite plausible: 'Would you mind leaving?' This is delivered in the:

1. friendly nonverbal style, 'warm, soft tone of voice, open posture, smiling face', or the
2. hostile nonverbal style, 'harsh voice, closed posture, frown with teeth showing'.

You have to imagine both. Perhaps you could try delivering both messages in front of a mirror, or better still try delivering them to a friend. I am afraid that in both cases I think that I would get the message and go. The first message I imagine being delivered by 'the hostess with the mostest', you know the kind of person I mean. She is asking me to leave a posh party. The second I imagine being delivered by a nightclub bouncer. Both are clearly hostile but 'the hostess with the mostest', whilst hostile, is keeping it under control mainly for the benefit of the other guests (hence the friendly nonverbal style). The verbal message is, however, significantly more important in communicating her basic unfriendly attitude here than any accompanying behaviours. It may be explicit but it is a real request, heard many times, I would imagine, at many dinner parties (or is this just me?).

Or what about something that is a statement rather than a request or a command, something as basic as: 'You used to be such a nice person'? Again this is delivered in the:

3. friendly nonverbal style, 'warm, soft tone of voice, open posture, smiling face', or the
4. hostile nonverbal style, 'harsh voice, closed posture, frown with teeth showing'.

My guess is that the nonverbal behaviour in message style 3 will neither transform nor soften the basic message. It is not a friendly statement and the fact that it is being delivered in this style could make it even less friendly because it is as if the speaker is still trying to be understanding and yet, despite being understanding, she can still make the basic statement. In message style 4 the person has started to lose control.

The point to be made here is that psychologists have never really been able to quantify the relative importance of language and nonverbal communication in interpersonal communication. It would be an extremely difficult and time-consuming experiment to do. I have made it seem easy with a few examples, but think of the generality of the conclusions that people are trying to draw from such an experiment. We would need a representative sample of an enormous variety of utterances, sampling all of the kinds of things that language can do and sampling different contexts as well. I have sketched in a few contexts above, but I am sure you can imagine some different contexts that might affect the basic interpretation of the utterances. Utterances after all only make sense in context.

If you don't believe me let's return to the first utterance, this time imagining slightly different contexts for the utterance: 'Would you mind leaving?' Imagine this being delivered at the very end of the evening by a bouncer in a nightclub and delivered in that friendly style, 'warm, soft tone of voice, open posture, smiling face'. Suddenly, it's quite friendly. Everyone has to leave, it's just that time of night. The bouncer is, after all, asking in a very friendly manner. I tried this experiment, believe it or not. I asked a doorman I knew to ask people to leave using this style of nonverbal behaviour. I then asked the poor innocent punter how he perceived the message. At the end of the night the punter said: 'Everything was fine, the bouncer was polite and friendly. Are you doing some research into customer satisfaction?' I also asked the doorman to say exactly the same thing in the same friendly manner early in the evening to a different punter. This second punter looked confused. He thought that it was a case of mistaken identity; bouncers don't just ask you to leave for no good reason. But how did the new punter perceive the overall message – the 'hostile' message in the 'friendly' style (at this point I really do need to rely on inverted commas)? Actually, he perceived it as very threatening. 'It was the understated way that he asked me,' the second punter explained. 'He was really hostile, as if he was looking forward to giving me a good thump if I didn't go immediately. But I hadn't done anything,' he added, 'that was really the annoying thing.' He smiled when he was told that this was just a little test.

The picture is, as you can see, becoming a little more complicated. The conclusions, which are that interpersonal attitudes are signalled almost exclusively by nonverbal behaviour, are looking a little more shaky. The general conclusion that 'humans use two quite separate languages, each with its own function', is looking somewhat less secure.

But to return to the studies of Michael Argyle, how could we make them more convincing? As a starting point we would want to make sure that the behaviours studied in the laboratory mirrored the kinds of behaviours shown in the real world. We can all be hostile using language without being quite as explicit as the speaker was in these experiments. When verbal statements become less explicit and more plausible, and more like the things that are said in everyday life, do they then become more powerful and significant as a consequence, and not so readily dismissed as some sort of joke in an experiment of this kind? The important point is that we do not know because unfortunately this experiment has never been carried out.

At this point you might be wondering how verbal language would function to signal friendliness in subtle and less direct ways in everyday life. (I came up with a couple of quite hostile utterances off the top of my head; again I wonder what this tells you about me). Here are a few suggestions. You can perhaps add your own here because the range of ways verbal language might do this is potentially quite large. But I would suggest that opening up a conversation in the first place, the use of first names, compliments, disclosure, reciprocated disclosure, the asking of personal questions, verbal engagement, shared perspectives, sharing of childhood memories, offers of help, offers of support, all play some role in the communication of certain interpersonal attitudes by language itself.

How important are each of these verbal strategies compared with the appropriate forms of nonverbal communication like facial expressions, postures, smiles and frowns in the overall communication of interpersonal attitudes? We simply do not know, but my guess is that the verbal statements would not be dismissed quite so readily as they were in those pioneering but somewhat transparent experiments of the early 1970s. Again this is not to argue against the incredible significance of nonverbal communication, but merely represents an attempt to reinstate ordinary language and the connections between ordinary language and nonverbal communication in the heart of social relationships and the study of human communication.

Let me also add that there are other rather more specific criticisms of these studies that are necessary given the incredible cultural weight which has come to rest on their conclusions. Only one person was used in these Oxford experiments to deliver the nine messages in the first place and she was described as 'an attractive female student'. In other words we know nothing about the generality of the results. How do we know that the results were not specific to this one individual? Would the results have generalised to male students, to less attractive students or to the population at large? We do not know. But a number of years ago I tried to replicate the original study using a male speaker, and the results were altogether a good deal less clear-cut. For example, the friendly verbal message in a hostile nonverbal style was rated as 3.90, essentially perceived as neutral rather than as very hostile, as in the original study (see Beattie 1983: 9).

There is another very important point to make. In the original study the judges were watching the combinations of verbal and nonverbal communication on a video screen and were specifically requested to attend to the video clips. In real life, however, when we are engaged in social interaction we sometimes look at the other person, sometimes we do not. This shifting pattern of eye gaze depends upon interpersonal distance, relative status, seating or standing position, the content of what we are saying, the structure of what we are saying and emotions like shame, embarrassment, guilt, etc. In real life we may miss a number of critical nonverbal signals for a variety of reasons. In the classic experiments by Michael Argyle there was never this possibility. Again, these experiments failed to simulate the complexities and patterns of everyday social life. For this and for the other reasons outlined we need to be extremely careful about how we interpret the results of these classic experiments.

There are a number of lessons to be learnt here. We live in a world where body language is now understood to be of extraordinary importance in everyday social life. We are all becoming that bit more aware of the layers and complexities of human communication, including the nonverbal aspects of the whole process. This, of course, I approve of, but popular books always work somehow within the established orthodoxy. When it comes to human communication, unfortunately or fortunately depending upon your point of view, the established orthodoxy may now need to be challenged. The claim that 'humans use two quite separate languages, each with its own function' may simply not be correct. First, the two languages may not be in any sense really separate; indeed I will argue in this book that they may be part of the same basic process. Second, language is almost certainly crucial to the communication of interpersonal attitudes, and classic experimental studies which suggest otherwise are themselves fundamentally flawed. Third and perhaps most important of all, the assumption that language functions to express thinking and abstract ideas and that nonverbal communication does not, and indeed cannot be used for this sort of thing, may also be incorrect. The old adage that no animal, armed only with nonverbal communication, could ever hope to express the idea that his or her family was poor but honest may have to be reconsidered in the light of the most recent theoretical research in psychology. This is what I am going to explore in this book.

I always justified my involvement in *Big Brother* and other popular shows by arguing that we are all intuitive psychologists, interested in observing and interpreting the behaviour of the people around us. I always thought that part of my job in *Big Brother* was to assist people in this process. But it seems to me that we also have to become psychologists in quite a different sense. We all have to learn to evaluate the evidence on which many psychological claims are based. We can see the shortcomings of the classic studies by Albert Mehrabian and Michael Argyle when we have some of the details in front of us. In this book I want to challenge the established orthodoxy on the functional separation of language and nonverbal communication and I want you, the reader, to understand the strength of the evidence. I want to challenge the very notion that some nonverbal behaviour is in any sense separate from language – the nonverbal behaviour in question being hand movements or gesture. I want to suggest instead, following the pioneering work of Adam Kendon and David McNeill, that gestures are closely linked to speech and 'yet present meaning in a form fundamentally different from that of speech', and that through hand movements 'people unwittingly display their inner thoughts and ways of understanding events of the world'. I want to argue that gestures open up a new way of regarding thinking and speech and the connections between them. Such gestures can be a window on the human mind and allow us to see thoughts and images that would otherwise be quite invisible.

But let me end this chapter with a word of caution. I am an experimental psychologist. I do not want you just to accept the ideas that I am going to present here as a new orthodoxy. I do not want these new ideas to go unchallenged. I want you to understand where the ideas come from. The experiments from which the ideas derive are all very simple. They can be followed and understood by individuals with no background in psychology; an interest in understanding human social behaviour will suffice. But I think that it is worth learning about some of this research because in my opinion the new ideas that emerge from it may change forever how you think about human behaviour in general, and nonverbal communication in particular. You may also learn to read minds in a very real and in a very scientific sense.

SUMMARY

- It has been argued that 'In human social behaviour it looks as if the nonverbal channel is used for negotiating interpersonal relations while the verbal channel is used primarily for conveying information'. This view is wrong on both counts.
- The verbal channel is critical for negotiating interpersonal relations.

- The nonverbal channel is critical for conveying semantic information.
- Some classic research in psychology claims to show that when we use language and nonverbal communication to communicate interpersonal attitudes, we can virtually ignore the language channel. This research is very restricted in scope and does not allow such general conclusions.
- Some have argued that 'only 7 per cent of communication is verbal'. This is a serious misreading of these original studies.
- Psychologists have never really been able to quantify the relative importance of language and nonverbal communication in interpersonal communication. It would be an extremely difficult and time-consuming experiment to do in any sensible way. It would probably be impossible.

3

WHERE THE ACTION IS

The form of nonverbal behaviour that I will be focusing on in this book is movement of the hands and arms. Psychologists call these hand and arm movements 'gestures'. 'Gestures' is really quite a confusing term here because, as I said in Chapter 1, when we think of gestures we often think of things like the palm-front 'V' sign for 'peace' or 'victor', or the palm-back 'V' sign, the so-called 'Harvey Smith', which has quite a different meaning in the UK. These very special types of gesture are called 'emblems'. They substitute for words and are defined as gestures with a direct verbal translation. The palm-front 'V' sign means peace or victory; the palm-back 'V' sign means . . . well, you can translate the Harvey Smith for yourself. Emblems are gestures that are consciously sent and consciously received (see Ekman and Friesen 1969). If someone has just used an emblem and is asked to repeat it then they can reproduce the gesture quite easily. The vast majority of gestures are not, however, like emblems. They have no direct verbal translation. They do not substitute for words; rather they are produced alongside words. There is another major difference as well in that they are produced quite unconsciously as individuals speak. They are almost impossible to inhibit. Just watch someone gesturing with their free hand as they speak on the telephone, when the person that they are talking to clearly cannot see the hand movements being produced. I have a number of videotapes of people speaking in a variety of types of conversation, where their hands are clearly out of sight of their interlocutors – for example, below the level of a table but nevertheless visible to the video-camera – and yet their hands still display an intricate and complex pattern. If you interrupt speakers while they are talking and ask them to reproduce these types of gesture they find it much more difficult to do so and sometimes quite impossible, depending on the type of gesture concerned. Now many psychologists consider these gestures to be a form of body language whose function is primarily to do with the expression of emotion or the signalling of interpersonal attitudes in social interaction. Occasionally, hand gestures do indeed have these functions. As I was driving to work one morning I saw a motorist in a silver BMW cut up another motorist on a notorious stretch of road where two lanes suddenly become one as you drive into Manchester. The second driver stopped abruptly and I noticed that his right hand formed a fist and made one staccato movement in the direction of the BMW driver. It seems that on occasion people don't so much shake their fist in anger, which is how we colloquially describe it, as thrust the fist forward. This was a hand movement that no doubt reflected intense emotion. Later when I was in work I noticed two colleagues displaying the same hand movement as each other. It was not just that the timing of their hand movements was perfectly synchronised, what we call interactional synchrony, but the precise form of the gesture and posture was also copied. My interpretation is that these behaviours reflect something about the relationship between the two people, although I would not dare to point this out to them. Sometimes hand gestures do seem to be part of body language and perform the functions traditionally assumed to be associated with it – the expression of emotions and the sometimes unconscious signalling of interpersonal relationships. But these were two isolated examples from a very long day. In between I witnessed literally thousands of other gestures about which many psychologists and all popular body language books have nothing substantial to say.

A female student was late with a course essay. She was discussing why she was unable to work in her student house. It was too noisy, too cold, too draughty, etc., etc. Her housemates were all English students, a little Byronic in their attitude. They sat around all night talking. She could not get to sleep. She sat in front of me with her hands tightly folded. Then as she started to talk her hands unfurled and started moving. She talked for about 15 minutes and my guess is that her hands were in perpetual motion for about 12 of those minutes. Unfortunately, I could not time the behaviour exactly. Nowhere in those 12 minutes did I detect a shaking fist or any interactional synchrony, just the hands moving alongside the speech, doing something – but what exactly?

Then my secretary came in to tell me about some important meetings that I must not miss ('The Dean wants to see you. . . The VC's secretary rang, he wants to know. . .') and this time I watched my secretary's hands moving in perfect synchrony with her speech, but again there did not appear to be much about emotion in these hand movements, nor much signalling of relationships. So it went on all through that day – hand movement after hand movement, gesture after gesture, all unconscious, all doing something. But it was not nonverbal communication, at least not in the traditional functional sense, as far as I could tell and, perhaps just as important, the movements did not appear to be separate from the speech (remember Argyle and Trower's claim that 'humans use two quite separate languages, each with its own function'). The gestures seemed to be somehow connected with the speech itself. Where did that leave all the popular books on the subject?

I went home that night; I really did need a break, but there was no escape. I switched on the TV. The presenter started by introducing the programme and I reached for the button on my video-recorder. This is what she said. Note that I have split the complex behaviour into separate movements so that you can see how the movement closely integrates with the speech itself. The boundaries of each movement are marked by the [ ] brackets. You might like to try the movements yourself and consider why they might be relevant to what the presenter was saying.

'Welcome to _Better Homes_. This week we're in Leicester to give [a huge helping hand] [to some newly weds] [and a new mum].'

Movement 1. Hands are spread far apart with the palms facing downwards, the fingers are spread.

Movement 2. The thumb of the right hand points upwards, the fingers are clenched.

Movement 3. The index finger on the right hand is extended outwards, the thumb is pointing up. The other fingers are clenched.

She then met the builder that she was to be working with, and even in this short command the hands moved:

'Carry on, [young man].'

Movement 1. Right arm is lifted to about head height and the palm of the right hand faces up, as if throwing something over the right shoulder.

Next she met the designer and again the hands were spontaneously called into action:

'Dave said, [I just want a shower] [that's all].'

Movement 1. The right hand is at chest height, the fingers are together and the palm faces the designer. The right hand moves up and down, the left hand rests on her hip.

Movement 2. The palm of the right hand faces downwards with the fingers together. There is a sharp, sweeping movement of the hand from left to right.

I had had enough. I put on a nature programme, but there in front of me stood David Attenborough talking straight to the camera. I had to video-record it.

'[This is the acorn of a white oak] [and this a red oak] [only this] one is just slightly darker, [but the acorns] [of the white oak germinate almost immediately] [using up] their food supply. [The red oaks] on the other hand [don't germinate until next spring]. [The squirrels recognise the difference between the two] and treat them differently.'

There were nine distinguishable movements in this short extract, the boundaries of each marked by the square brackets. Just note how little of the speech was not accompanied by hand movement: 16 out of 59 words. That is, only 27.1 per cent of the words were *not* accompanied by hand movement.

Movement 1. The right hand is raised to just below shoulder level. The acorn is gripped between the index finger and the thumb; the other fingers are clenched.

Movement 2. The left hand is raised to mirror the right hand.

Movement 3. The hands are moved closer together until the acorns are almost touching. The little finger on the right hand is extended to point to the acorn in the left hand.

Movement 4. The left hand is lowered, the index finger and thumb of the right hand rotate the acorn so that it is closer to the face.

Movement 5. The right hand then moves up and down.

Movement 6. The left hand is raised up and the three remaining fingers are extended towards the acorn in the right hand.

Movement 7. Both hands are moved together to just below shoulder height. The little finger of the right hand points to the acorn in the left hand. The remaining fingers of the left hand extend upwards.

Movement 8. Both hands are lowered slightly and spread apart, the fingers are together. The hands move up and down simultaneously.

Movement 9. The left hand is lowered out of shot and the right hand makes sharp up and down movements.

I went to make a cup of tea and came back to find David Attenborough crouching now and talking to the camera, but still moving his hands.

'And once [that has] gone the acorn will never germinate.'

Movement 1. The elbow of the left arm rests on the knee, the left hand then extends upwards with the fingers spread apart and pointing upwards.

Next he was sitting in a boat.

'[A pool of] [deep] cold water like this.'

Movement 1. The left arm extends out at just above waist height over the water. The palm of the left hand faces down with the fingers spread apart.

Movement 2. The left arm moves back slightly and the first gesture is repeated.

These movements of the hands and arms are gestures and you can see that these individual movements are closely integrated with the content of the speech itself. They are nearly always unconscious movements, even for experienced TV presenters like David Attenborough. I will argue later in the book that we can potentially discriminate between unconscious movements produced naturally by the brain and those that are used consciously and deliberately by TV presenters or people 'acting' in everyday life.

But the main point is clear – hand movement is a ubiquitous feature of everyday life. Those psychologists and body language popularisers who tell us that such movements are separate from language and perform essentially social functions are really missing the point. Some (and I mean a very small number) hand movements might reflect emotional state. The vast majority do no such thing and if you read almost any book with body language in the title, you would be at a complete loss as to what they actually do. This book will hopefully explain exactly what they do and why they are uniquely important in reading another person.

SUMMARY

- Hand movement is a ubiquitous feature of everyday life as a natural accompaniment of speaking.

- Those psychologists and body language popularisers who tell us that such movements are separate from language and perform essentially social functions are really missing the point.

- Some hand movements might reflect emotional state. The vast majority do no such thing.

- If you read almost any book with body language in the title, you would be at a complete loss as to what such hand movements actually do.

- These movements are uniquely important in reading another person's underlying thoughts.

- These hand movements are therefore uniquely important.

4

'A REMARKABLE BIOLOGICAL MIRACLE'

I keep talking about a new theory of bodily communication and yet in a sense some of the ideas about the importance of gesture in communication and as a medium for representing thought are far from new (see Kendon 1982 for a review of some of the historical issues). The first writings about gesture and speech and their connection are to be found in antiquity in Greek and Roman times. For Demosthenes, the Athenian statesman, military leader and orator, the delivery of a speech was at the very heart of oratory. Such delivery involved the whole body, but in particular it involved the hands working alongside the speech. According to the Roman statesman and philosopher Cicero, the 'action of the body' expresses 'the sentiments and passions of the soul'. In fact, the Latin word *actio* was Cicero's term for delivery. Cicero stated that 'nature has assigned to every emotion a particular look and tone of voice and bearing of its own; and the whole of a person's frame and every look on his face and utterance of his voice are like the strings of a harp, and sound according as they are struck by each successive emotion'. The body, according to Cicero, is like a musical instrument with the delivery or action being 'a sort of eloquence of the body, since it consists in gesticulation as well as speech' (see Kennedy 1972).

The Greeks and Romans attempted to master this eloquence by studying and then prescribing the actions or movements to be made during the delivery of a speech. These prescribed actions or movements were quite exaggerated and would probably look quite alien to us today. This focus on gesture (and exaggeration of the form in terms of oratory) may have derived from the fact that, according to some scholars, the ancient Greeks and Romans relied more on gestures in everyday life and were somewhat better at reading them than we are today. For example, Wundt writes:

> The ancients were more familiar with the pleasure of gestures in casual communication than we are today. In fact, conventions actually demanded a superfluity of affective expression, whereas now we tend to suppress it. So the ancients had a more lively feel for the meaning of gestures, not because theirs was a more primitive culture, but simply because it differed from ours, and especially because the ability to discern outer signs of inner feeling was more developed.
>
> (Wundt 1921/1973: 66)

Condillac offers a wonderful commentary on the work of the ancient Greeks and Romans on gesture and rhetoric and how it might be viewed from a contemporary perspective (at least from the contemporary perspective of eighteenth-century France):

> We do not value an actor except so far as he commands the art of expressing all the emotions of the soul by a slight variation of gestures, and find him unnatural if he deviates too much from our usual gesticulation. For that reason we can no longer have fixed principles to regulate all the attitudes and movements that are used in declamation.
>
> (Condillac 1756/2001: 133)

For Cicero, the attitudes and movements of actors could be regulated for maximum effect but, according to Condillac, in Greek and Roman times they went even further than this

> by dividing the chant and the gestures between two actors. This practice may seem extraordinary, but we see how one actor, by a measured movement, could appropriately vary his attitudes to make them agree with the narrative of the other who did the declamation, and why they would be as shocked by a gesture out of measure as we are by the steps of a dancer who does not keep time.
>
> (Condillac 1756/2001: 133)

Condillac also points out that it was only in scenes of dialogue that a comic actor would continue to do both gesture and narration, otherwise the narration and gesture would be split between two actors. The reason for this, according to Condillac, is that 'his action gained in liveliness because his energies were not divided'. In other words, in antiquity the natural association between speech and gesture was split. The practice of dividing communication in this way led to the discovery of the art of mime and to the continued exaggeration and prescription of the movements to be used in communication with gesture.

Quintilian in the first century AD discusses gesture in his work *Institutio Oratoria*. One section of his work involved specifying the kinds of gestures to be used by orators as they gave their speeches; detailed instructions were provided as to how the gestures should be used by orators to achieve the maximum effect (see Kendon 1982: 46). Quintilian stresses the similarities, including similarities in function, between gestures and speech when he states: 'For other portions of the body merely help the speaker, whereas the hands may almost be said to speak. Do we not use them to demand, promise, summon, dismiss, threaten, supplicate, express aversion or fear, question or deny?' (100/1902: 85–6).

The kinds of gestures being discussed here, while still being hand movements used to accompany talk, are really quite different from those we shall consider in this book in that they are, like language itself, to be carefully, intentionally and consciously produced. We are concerned with the *spontaneous* gestures produced without careful consideration and therefore much more revealing of a speaker's thoughts.

It was in the seventeenth century that the first academic works exclusively on the use of gesture started to appear. The earliest work in English was a book by Bulwer (1644/1974) entitled *Chirologia–Chironomia*. The first part is a descriptive glossary of 64 gestures of the hand and 25 gestures of the fingers. Bulwer not only describes each gesture in considerable detail but also the affective, cognitive or physiological state associated with that gesture. He outlines one or two variants of the gesture and then offers an interpretation of each one. The second part of the book is a prescriptive guide that outlines the proper usage of an additional 81 gestures during well-delivered discourse, with Bulwer cautioning against the improper use of 'manual rhetoricke' (see Morrel-Samuels 1990 for a review of Bulwer).

The next major work on gesture, written in English, is Austin's *Chironomia* (1806/1966). This book includes a detailed consideration of gestures and their effects on an audience, with examples to practise appropriate delivery.

This book had a significant impact on the textbooks written over the next century designed for instruction in the art of elocution in schools.

In addition to such practical interest in gesture there was also a bourgeoning philosophical interest, which recognised the importance of gesture in our understanding of human beings and the human mind, and this is evident in, amongst other works, Bacon's *Advancement of Learning* (1605/1952). Bacon argues that gestures provide an indication of the state of the mind of the speaker and of the will: 'As the tongue speaketh to the ear, so the gesture speaketh to the eye' (1605/1952: 49). In fact Bulwer explicitly acknowledges that it is Bacon's exact words here that inspired him to produce his own great work on gesture. A major reason why Bulwer found gesture of such interest was because he thought of it as a 'natural' language in sharp contrast to the artificiality and arbitrariness of ordinary verbal language. He states that 'gesture is the only speech and general language of the human nature. It speaks all languages, and as a universal character of reason, is generally understood and known by all nations' (1644/1974: 3).

The idea that gesture should be studied because it is a natural form of human action and expression which may throw light on the origin of language, and ultimately on the content of the human soul, was introduced by Etienne Bonnot de Condillac (1756/2001). His classic text argues against the seventeenth-century Cartesian view that human reason and knowledge are innate, given by God himself. As Aarsleff (2001) states: 'In the Cartesian view, innateness owes no debt to social intercourse. Right reason and knowledge are private achievements, for in the Augustinian sense we do not truly learn anything from anybody. God alone is the teacher. Communication is risky' (2001: xii). Condillac, on the other hand – while still believing that 'Adam and Eve did not owe the exercise of the operations of their soul to experience. As they came from the hands of God, they were able, by special assistance, to reflect and communicate their thoughts to each other. But I am assuming that two children, one of either sex, sometime after the deluge, had gotten lost in the desert before they would have known the use of any sign' (1756/2001: 113) – held that communication derives from action and experience and that the mimes found in performance in the time of Emperor Augustus had brought their art to such perfection that they could perform whole plays by gesture alone, thus unawares creating 'a language which had been the first that mankind spoke'. Human language, after the deluge, came about as an exchange of natural gestures to which vocalisations later became associated and Condillac attempted to describe how this process might have proceeded.

Diderot believed that the original nature of language might be understood through the study of the expressions of deaf-mutes. Indeed, he states that

> a man born deaf and dumb has no prejudices with regard to the manner of communicating his thoughts. Consider that inversions have not passed into his language from another, and that if he uses them it is nature alone which suggests their use.
>
> (Diderot 1751/1916: 166–7)

This philosophical position meant that the sign language of the deaf would be of considerable interest. In 1774 Abbe L'Epee began his important work with the use of sign language in the education of the deaf. He taught them French by focusing on the use of manual signs, rather than by attempting to force them to produce any vocal output.

However, this was not the approach used elsewhere. For example, in England at this time people who could not speak were not that sympathetically treated, and were seen as not fully functioning in God's image. Methods of instruction for deaf people in England focused on the vocal–auditory channels rather than the manual channel.

In the nineteenth century interest grew in both scientific and philosophical aspects of gesture and what gestures may reveal (see Kendon 1982 for a review). Tylor (1878), one of the founders of contemporary anthropology, explicitly focused on 'gesture language' and considered what variations in gestures across cultures might tell us about the characteristics of the human mind. His conclusion was that gesture language 'tends to prove that the mind of the uncultured man works in much the same way at all times everywhere' (1878: 88).

Wundt, regarded by many as the 'father of experimental psychology', was another leading scientific figure to consider gesture. Indeed his volume *The Language of Gestures* is a classic in the field. In this monograph he anticipates many of the core theoretical questions that we will consider in this book. He is explicitly concerned with the relationship between gestures and thinking:

> It is customary to define gestural communication as an 'expression of thought through visible but not audible movements' and, accordingly, to allot this gestural means of expression a place between script and speech. Like the former, it depicts concepts by means of visible signs, although signs pass quickly, as speech sounds do. Thus gestures appear as pictorial script, or letters, with

which its symbols are sketched in the air by means of transitory
signs, rather than on a solid material which could preserve them.

(Wundt 1921/1973: 55)

Wundt was solely concerned with gestures that become conventionalised
among various people or communities, including Indian tribes, Cistercian
monks, Neapolitan society or deaf-mutes. He examines how particular
gestures come to represent specific properties of the world and how some
gestures, through 'intervening associative links', come to represent more
abstract categories; for example:

> Moving the finger from the eye of the person communicating
> toward that of another person or from heart to heart signifies
> agreement of disposition or view among the Indians; and there is
> the sign for 'anger', as used by the Cistercians: moving both hands
> quickly away from the heart to stimulate the welling up and
> overflowing of feeling.
>
> (Wundt 1921/1973: 91)

One interesting point is that Wundt held that 'the primary cause of natural
gestures does not lie in the motivation to communicate a concept, but rather
in the expression of an emotion' (1921/1973: 146), a view that you could
say has held sway for more than a century in terms of general work in
nonverbal communication. Wundt is fascinating on gesture and, as I have
already stated, he anticipates many of the issues raised by more contemporary writers, but what he ignores (except in the most general terms) are
the rich, spontaneous gestures that people generate in their everyday lives,
as they create meaning with their hands. He was interested in the gestures
that all members of a community would recognise and be able to interpret
correctly and in the syntax, in terms of word order, which would allow
them to do this efficiently and effectively. His conclusions certainly do have
a contemporary ring about them: 'Language, and before that, gestural
communication, is a faithful mirror of man in the totality of his psychic
achievements' (1921/1973: 148–9). In this book, we will consider some
of the psychic achievements of mankind in their *spontaneous* use of speech
and gesture *simultaneously*.

Other scholars have commented on the fact that the movement of the
hands, whether in the form of gesture or not, can be highly revealing in
everyday life. Such scholars include both Sigmund Freud and the anthropologist and linguist Edward Sapir. Freud famously suggests: 'He that has

eyes to see and ears to hear may convince himself that no mortal can keep a secret. If his lips are silent, he chatters with his fingertips' (1905/1953: 77–8). Sapir argues for the existence of a collective 'unconscious', that is, a set of rules or a grammar which everyone applies in bodily expression without being able to make the rules explicit: 'We respond to gestures with an extreme alertness and, one might almost say, in accordance with an elaborate and secret code that is written nowhere, known by none, and understood by all' (1927/1949: 556).

The study of gesture is by no means new, but the majority of systematic work on the subject has been either from the perspective of oratory, in which gesture is to be regarded as a resource to be used deliberately and intentionally in the delivery of a speech, or from the perspective of the language of the deaf where gesture is to be regarded as the only resource that can be used in communication. Many influential figures have commented on gestures but have not necessarily studied them in their natural, spontaneous state – i.e. in terms of their close natural connections with the underlying verbal channel – in sufficient detail really to understand them; except perhaps in the case of Wundt, although he restricted himself to gestures that have become conventionalised. The early observations of Cicero and Quintilian to some extent led to the gestural system becoming disembodied from its natural speech context (and only extraordinarily being reintegrated in time by different speakers in a performance). Rather surprisingly, over the past two millennia the gesture–speech connection has been largely neglected in the case of *spontaneous* gesture, despite the huge growth of recent interest in spontaneous nonverbal communication.

Writing in 1982 Adam Kendon presents an interesting argument for the relative neglect of the study of gesture generally, and spontaneous gesture in particular, despite the enormous interest in nonverbal communication. His argument quite simply is that gesture was never considered a very good example of 'nonverbal communication' and therefore it was left to one side. 'Nonverbal communication' was a concept that relied heavily on the work of Jurgen Ruesch in a number of important papers published in the 1950s (1953, 1955), in which he applied information theory and cybernetics to the analysis of human social interaction. As Kendon says:

> Once human action was conceived of as if it were a code in an information transmission system, the question of the nature of the coding system came under scrutiny. Much was made of the distinction between analogical codes and digital codes. Aspects of behaviour such as facial expression and bodily movement, which

appeared to vary in a continuous fashion, were said to encode information analogically. This included gesture, insofar as it was thought of as 'pictoral' and the indexical character of much gesturing was also clearly of an analogical nature. The sharp dichotomy that this distinction between the two kinds of encoding in human behaviour proposed gave rise to the concept of 'nonverbal communication'. Such communication was seen as employing devices quite different from those of spoken language and it was regarded as having sharply different functions. 'Nonverbal communication' was seen as having to do with the processes by which interpersonal relations are established and maintained, whereas the digital codes of spoken language were concerned with conveying propositional information.

(Kendon 1982: 53)

As I have already pointed out, the anthropologist Gregory Bateson developed this notion. But what about gesture? Well, Ruesch himself was not particularly clear as to what to do with gesture, sometimes considering it to be like language and at other times including it with other forms of 'nonverbal codification'. According to Kendon:

In the expansion of research that followed, attention was directed in the main, to aspects of behaviour that clearly did not have the functions of spoken language. Gesture, though often referred to, was little investigated in the tradition because, as Ruesch himself seemed to be aware, it was less clearly involved in the functions that had been postulated for 'nonverbal communication' and it seemed to have a close association with verbal expression.

(Kendon 1982: 54)

In the years following the work of Ruesch and Bateson there was a huge explosion in research in linguistics and psychology on both written and spoken language and in psychology on nonverbal communication, but gesture, as Kendon puts it, 'fell between two stools'. There it lay relatively neglected and under-researched but invariably categorised as part of nonverbal communication – body language – with implications about its possible function. It remained quite neglected until a number of things happened.

First, a linguist called Noam Chomsky (1957) developed new ideas about the nature of human language, arguing that human language has certain identifiable characteristics which make it essentially and uniquely human and qualitatively different from communication in any other species. Chomsky stressed the creativity of language (Hockett's design feature of 'productivity'). The majority of utterances we produce are ones we have never spoken in precisely that form before and the majority of utterances we hear and comprehend without difficulty are ones we have never heard before.

'Geoff Beattie, psychologist, falls off his chair in his dingy, dusty attic as he reached for the red pencil on the left of his desk as he wrote this book' is a wonderfully creative (and accurate) utterance; wonderfully creative at least in the technical sense we are discussing here, probably generated for the first time in the history of mankind. I generated it effortlessly and you probably understood it without any trouble. You can see me now lying on that floor, trying to pick myself up, covered in dust. Chomsky put great emphasis on the creativity of language and argued that such creativity can only be explained if we credit speakers not with a repertoire of learned responses, which was how behavioural psychologists up to that point were attempting to explain it, but with a repertoire of linguistic rules used to generate or interpret sentences. Chomsky also argued that any theory of language must also explain why some speakers feel some sentences to be 'related' and others 'unrelated'. The following four sentences are all rather different in form, yet speakers accept them as closely related:

1. 'That psychologist who dabbles a bit with TV started work on a new book.'
2. 'Did that psychologist who dabbles a bit with TV start work on a new book?'
3. 'A new book was started by that psychologist who dabbles a bit with TV.'
4. 'Was a new book started by that psychologist who dabbles a bit with TV?'

In contrast, two sentences may be identical in form yet feel very different, for example:

5. 'My son is difficult to wash.'
6. 'My son is reluctant to wash.'

In (5) my son is on the receiving end of the washing whereas in (6) he is the one doing the washing. Similarly, to use one of Chomsky's oft-quoted examples, 'William is easy to please' and 'William is eager to please' have similar surface structures but do not feel closely related because in the former William is the one being pleased, whereas in the latter he is the one doing the pleasing. Chomsky's solution to this dilemma is to propose that every sentence can be described at two levels – at a surface structure level, i.e. how it actually is produced, and at a deep or underlying structure level. Sentences (1) to (4) concerning that psychologist and the book have different surface structures but the same deep structure. According to Chomsky, that is why these sentences are felt to be closely related. In contrast, sentences (5) and (6) about my son's attitude to washing have the same surface structure but different deep structures and are therefore felt to be distantly related (like the two sentences about pleasing William).

Take an ambiguous sentence like 'Striking miners can be dangerous'. This sentence can be interpreted in at least three different ways (and in three additional ways in spoken English if we include the homophone 'minor' as well), namely:

1. Miners who are on strike can be dangerous.
2. It can be dangerous to strike miners.
3. Miners who are striking (in appearance) can be dangerous.

For Chomsky, ambiguous sentences are ambiguous because they permit two or more different deep structures from the same surface structure, one deep structure related to each interpretation. The deep structure is a description of the sentence's underlying grammatical or syntactical structure (in the above example 'striking' can be either an adjective or a verb and is therefore connected in different ways to the underlying grammatical structure of the sentence). This deep structure clearly affects its meaning (for further discussion see Ellis and Beattie 1986).

Chomsky also claims that we can move between related sentences to form different types of sentence. Such moves are called transformations; for example, we can move from sentence (1) to (2) to form a question using a specific type of operation, but the important point here is that this operation recognises the underlying grammatical structure of the sentence. Chomsky calls these types of operation 'structure-dependent' operations, where each structure-dependent operation 'considers not merely the sequence of elements that constitute the sentence, but also their structure' (1972: 29); in this case the sequence 'that psychologist who dabbles a bit in TV' is a particular type of phrase called a noun phrase. Chomsky argues that all human languages use such structure-dependent operations. Although children make certain kinds of error in the course of language learning, they do not make the mistake of applying rules other than the structure-dependent one. His conclusion is that structure-dependent rules 'are a priori for the species' and therefore innate. Such rules, he argues, do not derive from experience. This theory, of course, is a form of neo-Cartesianism and contrasts markedly with the views of anti-Cartesians like Condillac, whom we met earlier, and the views of the empiricists of today. According to Chomsky, we may all speak with different tongues but we have one uniquely human mind, and that mind is to be understood through the analysis and description of these linguistic rules if we are to understand what aspects of knowledge are innate.

The theoretical work of Noam Chomsky transformed psychology. It led to the rejection of behaviourism as a serious framework for the study of complex mental functions like language and heralded a new era in the search for the rules and principles that underpin all human cognitive activity. It led to the birth of cognitive psychology, to use one metaphor, or the cognitive revolution, to use another. Somewhat paradoxically, it also led other researchers to attempt to determine if other species could develop language with the same unique properties as human language. Were we human beings really quite alone, as Chomsky thought? Could, for example, chimpanzees learn some form of human language and display creativity in the use of that language, just like human beings? We already knew that chimpanzees in the wild are capable of displaying a wide range of communicative signals, including a range of calls and facial expressions (Marler and Tenaza 1977; van Lawick-Goodall 1971), with each signal communicating something of the internal state of the animal. A soft barking noise indicates annoyance or mild aggressiveness towards another, while a 'grin' with the mouth closed or only slightly open indicates submission or fright. But these were limited forms of communication. Given the right circumstances, could chimpanzees use language creatively? Could they learn rules to combine words into new sentences just like human beings? The answer was yes and no (see Gardner and Gardner 1978). They did display some degree of creativity, but not quite like human beings, and the theoretical import of the work has been hotly contested (see Chomsky 1976).

Washoe was a young chimp reared by Allen and Beatrice Gardner in as 'childlike' a manner as possible, where her caretakers used a sign language based on the American Sign Language of the US deaf community.

In Washoe's case the acquisition of the basic language took about four years. Her 'words', like the words of sign language, were gestural signs; for example, holding the fingertips of one hand together and touching the nose with them meant 'flower', while repeatedly touching the fingertips together meant 'more'. By the age of around 6 years Washoe was credited with some 160 signs, which she would combine into communicative utterances such as 'gimme flower', 'more fruit', 'tickle Washoe', 'comb black' or 'baby mine'. The Gardners also noted that Washoe learned signs that involved touching parts of her own body quicker than signs which were merely traced in the air, possibly because of the tactile reinforcement from the skin touched. Washoe's achievements were considerable. Kortlandt writing in 1973 comments:

> The Gardners generously allowed me to watch Washoe in some experimental sessions at an age when, according to them, she had already 'spoken' more than 100 different gestural words. I was deeply impressed by what I saw. Perhaps the most convincing of all was to watch Washoe 'reading' an illustrated magazine. When, for example, a Vermouth advertisement appeared, she spontaneously made the gesture for 'drink'; when, on the next page, a picture of a tiger appeared, she signed 'cat'. It was fascinating to see a chimpanzee 'thinking aloud' in gestural language, but in perfect silence, and without being rewarded for her performance in such a situation.
>
> (Kortlandt 1973/1992: 74)

Gardner and Gardner (1978) themselves did not underestimate what they had managed to achieve through their intensive coaching of a young chimpanzee; nor were they inclined to underestimate the theoretical significance of what had occurred:

> The results of Project Washoe present the first serious challenge to the traditional doctrine that only human beings could have language . . . [Washoe] learned a natural human language and her early utterances were highly similar to, perhaps indistinguishable from, the early utterances of human children. Now, the categorical question, can a nonhuman being use a human language must be replaced with quantitative questions; how much language, how soon, or how far can they go.
>
> (Gardner and Gardner 1978: 73)

The claims of the Gardners and other ape language researchers have not, however, gone unchallenged (e.g. Seidenberg and Petitto 1979; Terrace 1979). As Andrew Ellis and I have written in the past, no one seriously doubts that chimps can associate together meanings and arbitrary signs both in comprehension and in production, but most people would want to say that there is more to language than naming. Language orders its words into structures − rule-governed sentences. Sentence structure indicates how named concepts relate one to another. English uses word order for this purpose, so that 'The psychologist teases the chimp' means something different from 'The chimp teases the psychologist'. There is no strong evidence for consistent, productive use of word order or any similar grammatical device by any of the signing chimps. Terrace's (1979) chimp Nim Chimpsky (a name with obvious connections to Noam Chomsky) had a preference for putting certain signs in certain positions (e.g. 'more' at the beginning of sign sequences, and his own name at the end), but otherwise his choice of sign order was quite random.

A feature of animal displays in the wild is their extreme repetitiveness. Wilson writes:

> If a zoologist were required to select just one word that characterizes animal communication systems, he might well settle on 'redun-dancy'. Animal displays as they really occur in nature tend to be very repetitious, in extreme cases approaching the point of what seems like inanity to the human observer.
>
> (Wilson 1975: 200)

Such repetition (e.g. 'Me banana you banana me give you') was characteristic of Washoe and other signing apes, though it is largely absent from the language of young deaf or hearing children. Ape signing is also highly imitative. Close analysis of Nim's signing at the age of 2 years revealed that 38 per cent of his signs were imitations of signs recently used by his caretakers. Unlike the imitations of children, which are far fewer than this and decline with age, Nim's imitative signs reached 54 per cent in words by the age of 4 years. Further, only 12 per cent of Nim's utterances initiated interactions; the remainder were produced in response to prodding by his teachers.

Other criticisms levelled at the chimp research include an excessive reliance on a small number of oft-repeated anecdotes; somewhat generous criteria for what constituted a correct response in formalised naming experiments, the possible contribution of natural, unlearned gestures and the lack of extensive, 'raw' transcripts of chimpanzee conversation. Perhaps the most intriguing criticism is the paradox by Chomsky himself when he writes:

> In some ill-considered popularizations of interesting current research, it is virtually argued that higher apes have the capacity for language but have never put it to use – a remarkable biological miracle, given the enormous selectional advantage of even minimal linguistic skills, rather like discovering that some animal has wings but has never thought to fly.
>
> (Chomsky 1976: 40)

If chimps are capable of acquiring language, why have they not done so of their own accord? The only viable counter to this argument is to propose that the natural lifestyle of chimps is one that does not require language. Hewes (1973a, 1973b) and Kortlandt (1973/1992) have suggested that only with the switch from fruit picking to hunting did language become advantageous to man because of the group coordination needed. Put quite simply, Kortlandt claims that fruit pickers 'have less to discuss with one another than cooperative big game hunters'. But this is just one view as to how verbal language developed in man. Darwin in *The Expression of the Emotions in Man and Animals* suggests that verbal language has developed using 'sound-producing organs . . . first developed for sexual purposes, in order that one sex might call or charm the other' (1872/1955: 355).

So we can see that this work with chimpanzees had one other direct effect – it led to serious speculation about the origins of language for the first time in perhaps a century. (In 1866 the Societet de Linguistique de Paris had banned papers speculating about the origins of language. These papers were very much prompted by Darwin's convincing case made in *The Origin of Species* (1859/1971) for the evolution of man from more primitive species.) But now it was no longer the case that, as Charles Hockett (1978) put it, 'one person's whimsy was as good as another's'.

In a seminal paper Gordon Hewes (1973a/1992) presents a coherent argument that the first form of language must have been gestural in form and the chimpanzee research by the Gardners is critical to his argument. He suggests that some early precursors of man, the australopithecines, had similar brain size and cultural accomplishment to existing chimpanzees and gorillas and therefore 'it is reasonable to credit the australopithecines with at least the cognitive capacities of existing chimpanzees or gorillas' (1992: 66). Existing chimpanzees could acquire a creative gestural language (with considerable effort it should be said); therefore, early man probably had the capacity for a gestural language. Speech, on the other hand, would have required a good deal of brain reorganisation before it could become dominant. Therefore, Hewes argued that 'a preexisting gestural language system would have provided an easier pathway to vocal language than a direct outgrowth of the "emotional" use of vocalization characteristic of non-human primates' (1992: 72). His argument is that speech as a system of communication (Hockett's design feature of 'use of the vocal–auditory channel') had a number of significant evolutionary advantages over manual gesture and that is why it became predominant:

> the vocal–auditory channel is practically a clear channel for communication, whereas the visual channel, as the prime modality for human and all higher primate perception of the external world, is subject to continual interference from nonlanguage sources. Unambiguous decoding of gestural messages requires a fairly neutral background, good illumination, absence of intervening objects (including foliage), relatively short distance between trans- mitter and receiver, and frontal orientation. Making manual gestures is slower than speaking, requires more energy, and prevents the use of the hands for any other activity while the message is being transmitted; decoding sign-language message is also slower, even among trained deaf persons.
>
> (Hewes 1992: 70)

Hewes also presents a further interesting argument, that gesture

> did not merely persist as a kind of older, retarded brother of speech, but gained a new lease of life in the Upper Paleolithic period and thereafter, with the birth of drawing, painting and sculpture, as Leroi-Gourhan (1964–5) and others have observed. Such art forms can be regarded as 'frozen gestures', akin to the air-pictures of sign language, but traced or formed in durable media.
>
> (Hewes 1992: 71)

This old visual–gestural channel, Hewes argues, became

> the preferred mode for advanced propositional communication in higher mathematics, physics, chemistry, biology and other sciences and technology, in the familiar forms of algebraic signs, molecular

structure diagrams, flow-charts, maps, symbolic logic, wiring or circuit diagrams, and all the other ways we represent complex variables, far beyond the capacity of the linear bursts of speech sounds.

(Hewes 1992: 71)

According to Hewes, this is where gesture ended up – as a system to be used in more complex and more specialised communication but not in everyday communication where speech was triumphant: 'The vocal–auditory channel continues to serve the needs of close, interpersonal, face-to-face communication, in song, poetry, drama, religious ritual, or persuasive political discourse.' He draws attention to the somewhat sparse literature on how gesture and speech relate in everyday talk and argues:

Gesture did not wither away, but persisted as a common accompaniment of speech, either as a kinesic paralanguage for conveying nuances, emphasis or even contradiction of the spoken message (Birdwhistell, 1970, La Barre, 1964, Hall, 1959) or in situations where spoken language fails because of inaudibility in noisy places or, more often, where there is no common tongue.

(Hewes 1992: 71)

But just look at the terms he uses when he describes the use of gesture in everyday talk – 'not wither away', 'common accompaniment of speech', 'where spoken language fails'; gesture here is very much second best.

Thus because of developments elsewhere, the system that had not 'withered away' became interesting and important, all because of a young American linguist called Noam Chomsky (he was only 29 years old when his first major book, *Syntactic Structures*, was published in 1957) and those determined to prove him wrong with a couple of chimpanzees and several years of intensive tuition. This new research into hand gestures revealed a great deal more than could have been imagined at that time. It was not just about nuance or about communication in noisy places, but an essential and integral part of all communication; indeed some might say as much a biological miracle as language itself. And David McNeill (2012) recently has used this new theory of speech and gesture to challenge all of the prevailing models of how and why language originated in the way it did.

SUMMARY

- According to Cicero, the 'action of the body' expresses 'the sentiments and passions of the soul'.

- Wundt claimed that 'The ancients were more familiar with the pleasure of gestures in casual communication than we are today'.

- Francis Bacon suggested that gestures provide an indication of the state of the mind of the speaker and of the will: 'As the tongue speaketh to the ear, so the gesture speaketh to the eye'.

- Edward Sapir argued for the existence of a collective 'unconscious', that is, a set of rules or a grammar which everyone applies in bodily expression without being able to make the rules explicit: 'We respond to gestures with an extreme alertness and, one might almost say, in accordance with an elaborate and secret code that is written nowhere, known by none, and understood by all'.

- Hewes speculated on the importance of gesture in the evolution of language. He wrote that 'a preexisting gestural language system would have provided an easier pathway to vocal language than a direct outgrowth of the "emotional" use of vocalization characteristic of non-human primates'.

5

IMAGES IN THE HANDS, IMAGES IN THE MIND

There are a number of different types of gesture that are produced quite unconsciously and appear commonly with everyday speech.

Iconic gestures

The first type are called *iconic* gestures, which we came across in Chapter 1. These are gestures whose particular form displays a close relationship to the meaning of the accompanying speech. For example, when describing a scene from a comic book story in which a character bends a tree back to the ground, the speaker appears to grip something and pull it back. This is called an iconic gesture because it refers to the same act mentioned in the speech; the gesture seems to be connected to the words 'and he bends it way back'. This particular example comes from David McNeill's seminal book *Hand and Mind* (1992: 12). I should point out before showing this example that (following the conventions introduced by McNeill) throughout this chapter and those that follow the speech is underlined in the text. The boundaries of the meaningful part of the gesture (the so-called 'stroke' phase of the gesture), unless otherwise stated, are shown by enclosing the concurrent segments of speech in square brackets, like this [ ]. The gesture accompanying the clause 'and he bends it way back' was as follows; the brackets indicate where the meaningful bit of the gesture occurred:

and he [bends it way back]

Iconic: Hand appears to grip something and pull it from the upper front space back and down near to the shoulder.

This example illustrates the close connection that exists between speech and gesture, the close connection between language and this form of nonverbal communication, which are clearly not separate as many psychologists have assumed. These iconic gestures only occur during the act of speaking itself, although they are sometimes initiated during the brief silent or planning pauses in the speech; they are not made by listeners except very occasionally. The example shows how what is depicted in the gesture should be incorporated into a complete picture of a person's thought process. The sentence describes the tree being bent 'way back'; the gesture at the same time depicts a bending-back image. The gesture clearly adds meaning here because it shows how the bending back is accomplished and it shows it from the point of view of the agent, the person doing the bending back. The gesture shows that the tree is fastened at one end, which is not made explicit in the accompanying speech.

As David McNeill himself says: 'Speech and gesture refer to the same event and are partially overlapping, but the pictures they present are different. Jointly, speech and gesture give a more complete insight.' Notice also that the gesture is produced at exactly the same time as the speech. It is not that the speaker says the words and then decides to illustrate them with a gesture; the two forms of communication are generated simultaneously by the human brain. Also notice that there is no problem in generating the speech; it is not the case that the speaker is trying to compensate for some defect in the linguistic communication.

What is interesting about this iconic gesture is that not only does it reveal the speaker's mental image about the event in question, but it also reveals the particular point of view that he has taken towards it. The speaker had the choice of depicting the event from the viewpoint of the agent or of the tree itself. In performing this particular gesture the speaker was clearly 'seeing' the event from the viewpoint of the agent because otherwise his hand would not have taken the form of a grip. If the speaker had been taking the viewpoint of the tree, the hand would have simply depicted the bend backwards without the grip.

Consider another example of an iconic gesture, also from McNeill (1992: 13):

<u>And she [chases him out again]</u>

Iconic: Hand appears to swing an object through the air.

Again the speech and gesture refer to the same event and are partially overlapping but again the pictures they present are different. The speech conveys the idea of pursuit ('chases') and repetition ('again') but the speech does not mention what she is chasing him with. The iconic gesture conveys that some form of weapon is being used here because the iconic gesture depicts something being swung through the air. The iconic gesture does not tell us exactly what the object is at this point but we can see quite clearly what kind of object it is. The gesture shows that it is a long object, which can be gripped by a hand, and it is something that can be swung through the air. It is in fact an umbrella. The significant point is that if we were to focus exclusively on the speech, as we do on the telephone, for example, or only on the gesture, then we would have an incomplete picture of the speaker's mental representation of the scene. It is only through a consideration of both forms of communication that we see all of the elements depicted: the agent, the type of action, the repetition of the action, the type of weapon used and how the weapon was actually being used – swung through the air to frighten the other character.

Below is an example from my own corpus of speech and gestures, where I used a similar task to that of McNeill, asking participants to narrate cartoon stories to a listener, without mentioning that the focus of the research was gestures. The advantage of asking people to narrate stories such as cartoons is that we can compare their gesture–speech combinations with what was in the original story to see exactly what was included in their communication and what was left out. Cartoon stories have the additional advantage that depicted in them are a lot of interesting characters doing a wide variety of complex actions.

<u>[she's eating the food]</u>

Iconic: Fingers on left hand are close together, palm is facing body and thumb is directly behind index finger. Hand moves from waist level towards mouth.

The speech here tells us that the agent is female. It also conveys the nature of the action involved ('eating') and what is being eaten ('the food'), but it does not tell us how this action is being accomplished. There are after all many different ways of eating food. She could be just chewing the food, which is already in her mouth, or using a knife and fork to eat the food from a plate, but she is not. In this cartoon story she was bringing the food with her left hand up towards her mouth. That is how the action was depicted in the original cartoon and that is how the narrator depicts it in his gesture. The iconic gesture again is critical to communication here because it shows the method of eating – bringing the food to the mouth with the hand. Again, the image depicted was from the point of view of the agent; the hand of the speaker is acting as the hand of the character in the cartoon.

When you consider all of this, it is extraordinary that people have tried to dismiss the movements of the hands and arms which people make when they speak as merely coincidental movements – virtually random flicks and twirls that are merely used for emphasis, merely used to make a point and barely worthy of serious consideration. Alternatively they are thought of as a relatively minor form of nonverbal communication with a fairly insignificant role in the communication of emotion or interpersonal attitudes. Many psychologists argue that this is the main point of nonverbal communication, and quite inferior to the more obvious forms of nonverbal communication such as bodily posture, facial expression or eye gaze, which are clearly more important in this regard.

But these movements are not insignificant, and they are not merely poor forms of communication about emotion or interpersonal attitudes. They are closely integrated with speech and may provide a unique insight into how speakers are actually thinking.

Let us consider the issue of the integration of speech and gesture in a little more detail. A prototypical iconic gesture involves three phases: first, the preparation phase, where the hand rises from its resting place and moves to the front of the body and away from the speaker in preparation to make the gesture; second, there is the main part of the gesture, the 'stroke' phase, where the gesture exhibits its meaning; third, there is the retraction phase, where the hand moves back to its resting position. Some gestures, however, have just two phases and some possess just a stroke phase. The example below, from McNeill (1992: 25), shows the preparation and the stroke phase of this gesture:

he grabs a big oak tree and he [bends it way back]
        (1)   (2)

(1) *Preparation phase*: hand rises from armrest of chair and moves up and forward at eye level, assuming a grip shape at the same time.

(2) *Stroke phase*: hand appears to pull something backwards and downwards, ending up near the shoulder.

Gestures in their preparation phase anticipate that part of the speech which refers to the same event. Indeed, this observation led another pioneer in the gesture area, Brian Butterworth, now Emeritus Professor of Neuro-psychology at the University of London, to suggest that we can actually distinguish iconic gestures that are used alongside speech for intentional effect rather than being used spontaneously by the fact that the preparation phase of intentional gestures does not anticipate the speech in this natural manner. An example he was fond of using was archive footage of Harold Macmillan, former UK Prime Minister, who sometimes made iconic gestures when he spoke in his early TV broadcasts to suggest, presumably, informality and spontaneity, but these gestures did not display the necessary degree of anticipation of the verbal content. In some research I carried out with Brian Butterworth as a student at Cambridge, we found that the average amount of time that spontaneous gestures precede the noun or verb with which they are most closely associated is in the order of 800 milliseconds (see Beattie 1983). Harold Macmillan's gestures did not show this degree of anticipation, or indeed any degree of anticipation. Consequently, they looked false and almost certainly were false, owing more to Quintilian and work on classic rhetoric than the human mind in spontaneous action.

The anticipation of the verbal content by a spontaneous iconic gesture can be seen in the example below (see Beattie and Aboudan 1994 for related examples). Here the narrator is telling a cartoon story about the exploits of 'Headless Harry', who goes fishing in a river with a rod but has no luck, so the head decides to frighten the fish out of the water. But the head then falls into the water and has to swim along back to the body. This particular gesture has a preparation phase, a stroke phase and a retraction phase as follows:

the head starts [swimming] along
(1)   (2)   (3)

(1) *Preparation phase*: index finger of right hand originally touching temple, hand moves forward with fingers opening, palm facing downwards at level of shoulder.

(2) *Stroke phase*: right hand indicates the way that the head is swimming in the water, focusing on forward motion, with splayed fingers representing the head.

(3) *Retraction phase*: right hand moves back to temple, to exactly the same start point, index finger straightens up.

The preparation phase of this iconic gesture in which the hand takes on the shape to represent a head swimming was 440 milliseconds in duration. The stroke phase during which the hand shows how the head was swimming along was 240 milliseconds long. The retraction phase during which the hand returns to the original start position was the longest phase at 600 milliseconds. In all, there was just over a second's worth of complex hand movement during which the mind unconsciously portrayed how the head of a ghost propelled itself in a river before returning the hand to exactly the same resting position that it had started from just over a second earlier.

The analysis of the phases of gesture and how they relate to speech demonstrates the close integration of these two channels of communication. They are not separate and they are also not separate in terms of their sequence of development in childhood or in terms of how they break down together with the brain damage that produces a type of speech disorder called aphasia. Iconic gestures develop alongside language when children are learning to talk, with iconic gestures developing at the same time as the early phrases in speech are used. As Susan Goldin-Meadow notes:

> At a time in their development when children are limited in what they can say, there is another avenue of expression open to them, one that can extend the range of ideas they are able to express. In addition to speaking, the child can also gesture (Bates 1976; Bates et al. 1979; Petitto 1988).
>
> (Goldin-Meadow 1999: 118)

Children usually begin gesturing at around 10 months of age, using pointing gestures (called 'deictics') whose meaning is given by the context rather than by their precise form – the child may point to an object to draw the adult's attention to it. It is only later that children begin to use iconic gestures, which capture aspects of the form of the object or action and are thus less reliant on specific context to give meaning to the particular gesture. Goldin-Meadow argues that the integration of gesture and speech can be identified in the very earliest stages of linguistic development, that is, at the one-word stage:

> Over time, children become proficient users of their spoken language. At the same time, rather than dropping out of children's communicative repertoires, gesture itself continues to develop and play an important role in communication. Older children frequently use hand gestures as they speak (Jancovic, Devoe and Wiener

1975), gesturing, for example, when asked to narrate a story (McNeill 1992) or when asked to explain their reasoning on a series of problems (Church and Goldin-Meadow 1986).

(Goldin-Meadow 1999: 120–1)

This integration continues until adulthood. When communication starts to break down with the brain damage that produces different types of aphasia, the two channels break down in strikingly similar ways. For example, in Wernicke's aphasia, patients produce fluent speech that has little appropriate semantic content; such individuals are also found to use few iconic gestures. In Broca's aphasia there is appropriate semantic content but little overall structure or fluency and iconic gestures are preserved.

Iconic gestures are not separate from thinking and speech but part of it. Potentially they allow us an enormous insight into the way people think because they offer an insight into thinking through a completely different medium from that of language; a medium that is iconic rather than verbal. Such gestures may indeed offer a window into the human mind and how it represents our thinking about events in the world; they may also tell us, through an analysis of the degree of temporal asynchrony of the gesture and accompanying speech, which utterances are really spontaneous and which are being deliberately sent for effect. Politicians who want to be well prepared in terms of the delivery of their message and in total control at all times, and yet at the same time want to look informal and spontaneous, might like to take note at this point.

Metaphoric gestures

The second type of gesture is called a *metaphoric* gesture. These gestures are similar to iconic gestures in that they are essentially pictorial, but the content depicted here is an abstract idea rather than a concrete object or event. In the words of David McNeill: 'The gesture presents an image of the invisible – an image of an abstraction.' McNeill (1992: 14) uses the following example to illustrate the concept of a metaphoric gesture:

It [was a Sylves]ter and Tweety cartoon

Metaphoric: Hands rise up and offer listener an 'object'.

According to McNeill, here the speaker makes the genre of the cartoon, which is an abstract concept, concrete in the form of a gestural image of a bounded object supported in the hands and presented to the listener. In McNeill's words, 'the gesture creates and displays this object and places it into an act of offering'. Borrowing the terminology of the late I. A. Richards (1936) on the nature of metaphor, McNeill argues that the *topic* of the metaphor, the abstract concept that the metaphor is presenting, is the genre of the story (a cartoon) and the *vehicle* of the metaphor, the gestural image, is a bounded, supportable, spatially localisable physical object. The *ground* here, the common ground of meaning on which the vehicle and topic are linked, is that genres of story, meaning and knowledge are like physical containers with physical properties (evidence for this is also found in language itself with expressions such as 'a deep understanding', 'shallow insight', 'broad knowledge', etc.).

Here are a couple of examples of metaphoric gestures from my own corpus. 'Blue', a now-defunct English pop group that were appearing on the *Lorraine Kelly Show* on Sky TV a number of years ago, were discussing with Lorraine Kelly when the band would be touring again. Lee is one of the members of the band.

LEE: For us it's like [we was there] last year.

Metaphoric: Fingers on left hand curled up, but thumb is stretched out. Hand moves upwards in front of left-hand side of chest and thumb points towards the top of the left shoulder.

This is a metaphoric gesture, the topic being the abstract concept, which is time, the *vehicle* being the gestural image, which critically involves the use of the gestural space around the body, and the *ground* is that the future can be thought of as the area in front of the body and the past as the area behind the body.

Here is another example from my corpus. The Appleton sisters were celebrities in Britain and at one time part of the group 'All Saints'. They were being interviewed on TV in a public location. Nicole was describing how she got her figure back so quickly after having a baby.

NICOLE: Working, moving house and lots of stress. It works. It's the [new diet].

Metaphoric: Fingers on right hand are straight and slightly apart, hand rises to a position next to the right-hand side of the face. Hand rotates slightly to its left and then to its right three times.

A 'diet' can be a fairly abstract concept. Some diets involve cutting down on food or eating only certain types of food; others involve graded exercise in conjunction with restrictions on eating. Few diets involve just the stresses associated with work and moving house. In this metaphoric gesture, Nicole makes the abstract concept of a 'diet' quite concrete; she is saying that this was a diet based primarily on activity rather than food intake, and it was a particular type of activity – repetitive, constant and vigorous, all depicted in the metaphoric gesture.

The beat

The third main type of gesture is the *beat*. These are movements that look as if they are beating out musical time. Beats tend to have the same form regardless of the content of the speech that they are accompanying. The typical beat, according to McNeill, is the 'simple flick of the hand or fingers up and down, or back and forth; the movement is short and quick and the space [in which the gesture is made] may be the periphery of the gesture space (the lap, an armrest of the chair etc.)' (1992: 15). Beats look like the most insignificant of all gestures but the simplicity of their form belies their real importance. They accompany the most significant parts of the speech; not necessarily particular words, which are important merely because of their content, but the most significant words in the discourse from the speaker's point of view. Thus, even beats with their regular and simple form may provide a clue as to the inner workings of the mind of the speaker. They demarcate those parts of the discourse that speakers themselves consider most significant, regardless of what anybody else might think.

SUMMARY

- David McNeill argues that 'Speech and gesture [often] refer to the same event and are partially overlapping, but the pictures they present are different. Jointly, speech and gesture give a more complete insight'.

- If we were to focus exclusively on the speech, then we would have an incomplete picture of the speaker's mental representation of an event.

- A prototypical iconic gesture involves three phases: first, the preparation phase, where the hand prepares to make the gesture; second, the main part of the gesture, the 'stroke' phase, where the gesture exhibits its meaning; third, the retraction phase, where the hand moves back to its resting position. Some gestures, however, have just two phases and some possess just a stroke phase.

- Gestures and speech are not separate in terms of their sequence of development in childhood or in terms of how they break down together with the brain damage that produces aphasia.

- In Wernicke's aphasia, patients produce fluent speech that has little appropriate semantic content and such individuals are also found to use few iconic gestures.

- In Broca's aphasia there is appropriate semantic content but little overall structure or fluency and iconic gestures are preserved.

- There are three main types of spontaneous gestures that accompany speech – *iconic* gestures depict concrete objects or events, *metaphoric* gestures depict abstract ideas, and finally, *beats*, which are simpler stress-timed movements.

- Iconic and metaphoric gestures can reveal unarticulated aspects of thinking.

- Even beats may provide a clue as to the inner workings of the mind of the speaker. They demarcate those parts of the discourse that speakers themselves at the moment of production consider most significant.

6

DIFFERENT VEHICLES
OF MEANING

David McNeill argues that the method by which gestures convey meaning is fundamentally different to the way language does this. Language acts by segmenting meaning so that an instantaneous thought is divided up into its component parts and strung out through time. Consider the following example from my own corpus, which again derives from someone telling a cartoon story:

the table can be [raised up towards the ceiling]

Iconic: Hands are resting on knee; hands move upwards, palms pointing down, forming a large gesture; hands continue moving until the hands reach the area just above shoulder level.

The single event here is being described both by language and by the accompanying iconic gesture. The speech does this in a linear and segmented fashion, first identifying what is being raised ('the table'), then describing the action ('can be raised up') and then describing the direction of the action ('towards the ceiling'). The linguist de Saussure (1916/1959) argued that this linear–segmented character of language arises because language is essentially one-dimensional whereas meaning is essentially multi-dimensional. Language can only vary along the single dimension of time with regard to the units out of which it is comprised. As the psychologist Susan Goldin-Meadow and her colleagues noted in 1996: 'This restriction forces language to break meaning complexes into segments and to reconstruct multidimensional meanings by combining the segments in time.' But the gestures that accompany language do not convey meaning in a linear and segmented manner; rather they can convey a number of aspects of meaning at the same time in a single multidimensional gesture. This gesture depicts the table (and its size), the movement (and its speed) and the direction of the movement, all simultaneously. The important point is that, as Goldin-Meadow notes, the iconic gestures which accompany speech 'are themselves free to vary on dimensions of space, time, form, trajectory, and so forth and can present meaning complexes without undergoing segmentation or linearization'.

According to David McNeill (1992), gestures are also different from speech in terms of how they convey meaning. Speech relies on 'bottom-up' processing, in that the meanings of the words are combined to create the meaning of the sentence. To understand a sentence you have to start with the lower-level words (hence 'bottom-up'), whereas in gestures we start with the overall concept portrayed by the gesture. It is this concept which gives rise to the meaning of the individual parts (hence 'top-down'). McNeill provides the following example:

> The gesture is a symbol in that it represents something other than itself – the hand is not a hand but a character, the movement is not a hand in motion but the character in motion, the space is not the physical space of the narrator but a narrative space, the wiggling fingers are not fingers but running feet. The gesture is thus a symbol, but the symbol is of a fundamentally different type from the symbols of speech.
>
> This gesture–symbol is global in that the whole is not composed out of separately meaningful parts. Rather, the parts gain meaning because of the meaning of the whole. The wiggling fingers mean running only because we know that the gesture, as a whole, depicts someone running.
>
> (McNeill 1992: 20)

The important point to remember here is that when produced by this same speaker, this wiggling finger gesture may well have a different meaning (McNeill points out, for example, that it was also used for 'indecision between two alternatives'). In order to argue that gestures are processed like language in a bottom-up fashion, you would need to be able to demonstrate that the three components which comprise the running gesture – the 'V' hand shape, the wiggling motion and the forward movement – have relatively stable meanings in the person's communicational repertoire, which can be recognised and interpreted wherever they are used. But this is not the case.

Another important difference between speech and gesture is that different gestures do not combine together to form more complex gestures:

> With gestures, each symbol is a complete expression of meaning unto itself. Most of the time gestures are one to a clause but occasionally more than one gesture occurs within a single clause. Even then the several gestures don't combine into a more complex gesture. Each gesture depicts the content from a different angle, bringing out a different aspect or temporal phase, and each is a complete expression of meaning by itself.
>
> (McNeill 1992: 21)

Gestures also convey meaning in a different way because there are no standards of form with gestures. Standards of form are a defining feature of all languages. All linguistic systems have standards of well-formedness to which all utterances that fall within it must conform, or be dismissed as not proper or not grammatical. Gestures have no such standards of form. Thus, different speakers display the same meaning in idiosyncratic but nevertheless recognisable ways. As McNeill (1992: 41) says: 'Lacking standards of form, individuals create their own gesture symbols for the same event, each incorporating a core meaning but adding details that seem salient, and these are different from speaker to speaker.' This non-standardisation of form is very important for theoretical reasons:

> Precisely because gestures are not obliged to meet standards of form, they are free to present just those aspects of meaning that are relevant and salient to the speaker and leave out aspects that language may require but are not relevant to the situation.
>
> (McNeill 1992: 22)

In the following example from my corpus, which has been chosen because of its obvious simplicity, each of the three speakers creates the spinning movement of the table, but they do this differently. One uses one finger, two use both arms, two use clockwise movements, one makes an

Table 6.1 Iconic representation in gesture

Actual speech and gestures produced by three different narrators	Event referred to
[It like spins round] Iconic: left index finger makes three rapid, small clockwise movements.	Billy Whizz causes a table to spin around
The table went [spinning] Iconic: right arm moves in two large clockwise circles, while the left hand moves away from and then towards the right arm.	
Wrecks everything [spinning round and round and round and round and round] Iconic: both arms make two large, rapid anti-clockwise movements.	

anti-clockwise movement, two make two movements, one makes three movements (Beattie and Shovelton 2002a). The point of this particular picture in the cartoon story is to show the chaos caused when Billy gets on a chair that now spins, causing a table to spin. One of the gestures seems to focus specifically on the rapid speed of the spinning, one specifically on the extent of the spinning and the third depicts both aspects simultaneously.

This is one major difference between the kinds of iconic gestures that we are discussing here and the sign languages of the deaf. The gestural languages of the deaf have the same fundamental properties as verbal language and are quite different from the spontaneous iconic gestures that people create while they are talking. Sign languages have to be able to split complex meanings into their component parts and then to reconstitute the meaning through combinations of signs. This necessitates a lexicon and therefore standards of well-formedness and a syntax, or a set of rules for combining signs that includes word order, to form meaningful sentences. The gestures that accompany speech have no such lexicon and no such syntax.

The iconic gestures that accompany speech also depend upon their iconicity to convey meaning. The gesture as a whole spontaneously created by the individual in conversation must be a good representation of the thing to which it is referring. The movements of the fingers or hands described here are obviously a good iconic representation of the concept of spinning. If something that is being depicted is moving very slowly, the spontaneous iconic gesture that is depicting it must also be very slow. This is different from sign languages, where in American Sign Language the sign for 'very slow' is the sign for 'slow' made more rapidly. This speeding up of the sign is quite arbitrary, and quite unlike what happens with spontaneous iconic gestures, which are not arbitrary in this way. This dimension of arbitrariness (discussed by Hockett and others) found in sign languages is what, of course, characterises ordinary verbal language. In ordinary verbal language we don't assume that 'head' and 'lead' or 'hedge' and 'ledge' will be similar in meaning. As Shakespeare wrote:

> What's in a name? that which we call a rose
> By any other name would smell as sweet

The point that Shakespeare is making is that the concept of a rose could quite well be called something else. The name is arbitrary. But this is not the case for the spontaneous iconic gestures that accompany speech. These would have to represent a rose in a non-arbitrary way: perhaps by illustrating the bloom (hands opening to form a circular shape); perhaps illustrating the thorns on the stem (hands iconically portraying the sharp inverted 'V' shape of the thorn); or perhaps even depicting the expression of a lover presented with one (hands opening with awe and gratitude).

Therefore, iconic gestures and speech convey meaning in radically different ways, with speech relying on a lexicon for breaking meaning down into its component parts and a syntax for combining these various elements into meaningful sentences, whereas iconic gestures represent multi-dimensional meanings simultaneously in one complex image. Each speaker creates the iconic gestures spontaneously without relying on a lexicon with defined standards of form, and even consecutive iconic gestures do not combine into higher-order units. Each gesture is complete in itself, and the overall meaning of what is being portrayed gives the meaning to the individual components. It is also important to emphasise that the meaning in the gesture may, on occasion, never be represented in the speech itself and thus may carry powerful new information about what the speaker is thinking.

McNeill also suggests that 'the gestures of people speaking different languages are no more different than the gestures of different people speaking the same language. While their speech moves in different directions to meet linguistic standards, their gestures remain close together'. This is an extraordinary suggestion because when we think of the gestures of people who speak different languages we think of difference and diversity; we think of the extravagant gesticulations of the Italian compared to the rather more inhibited gesticulation of the English. Indeed, it has been recognised since

the seventeenth century that those from southern Italy make more use of
the hands when talking than those from northern Europe, but that both the
frequency and form of the gestures change with cultural assimilation. The
classic study into the effects of cultural assimilation on gestures was carried
out by David Efron during the 1930s in New York City. He found that both
the number and type of gestures used by assimilated eastern Jews and
assimilated southern Italians differed greatly from their traditional cultures
and had started resembling each other. His research emphasised both
cultural differences in gesture and the effects of the intermingling of
different cultures on the nature of the gestures used (1941/1972). Others
have focused on cultural differences in gesture and this process of cultural
assimilation in different languages and cultures. In describing Arabic gesture,
Robert Barakat writes:

> Arabs . . . make extensive use of a vast variety of gestures and body
> movements to register reactions to events and peoples, or to
> communicate messages silently . . . the Arab is often accused of
> speaking with his hands and body as well as his mouth. So
> intimately related are speech, gesture and culture, that to tie an Arab's
> hands while he is speaking is tantamount to tying his tongue.
>
> (Barakat 1973: 751)

Barakat also outlines how Arabic gestures change with the process of
cultural assimilation in that Arab students living in the USA attempt to inhibit
some of the more conscious gestures that would normally be interpreted
as peculiarly Arabic. Gestures, for example, that involve bodily contact
between males, which would be perfectly acceptable in Arabic culture but
taboo in Western cultures, tend to be inhibited. When we think of people
speaking different languages we tend to be aware of how different the
gestures are, while sometimes recognising the influence of cultural assimilation on the process. We also think of how emblems, those gestures which
are used consciously and intentionally to replace speech, can be misunder-
stood in different places; the palm-back and the palm-front 'V' signs mean
quite different things in the UK, whereas in the rest of Europe they have
exactly the same meaning, that of 'victory'. Although interestingly I do have
a photograph of the late Mrs Thatcher from the early 1980s giving the palm-
back 'V' sign to a group of devoted Tory supporters, the particular smile
on her face makes this an unusual photograph in many respects.

According to the theory that is being discussed here, differences in
gesture use (excluding emblems, of course) in different languages and

in different cultures are relatively trivial compared to the underlying similarities in their use.

I explored this in a study with a PhD student, Rima Aboudan, in which we asked native Arabic speakers to narrate the same basic cartoons used with our English speakers (see Aboudan and Beattie 1996). One story concerned a ghostly, disembodied hand starting an old-fashioned car with a starting handle while the owner, an upper-class elderly man in tweeds and a bow tie, was trying to push it to get it started. In other words, the ghostly hand was helping the elderly man out. One English-speaking narrator used the following speech–gesture combination. Here, by the way, we are interested in the whole gesture and not just the stroke phase, so the brackets indicate the boundaries of the whole gesture. This also applies to all the examples in the rest of this chapter and in Chapter 7.

so [the hand is now trying to start the car]

Iconic: Hand forms a fist and performs four circular movements in front of body.

Another said the following with the accompanying gesture:

[starting it at the front with the] winder thing

Iconic: Hand forms a fist and performs four circular movements in front of body.

One Arabic speaker with a particular Syrian dialect, on the other hand, used the following speech–gesture combination to refer to the same event:

تَشْغَلُو السَّيارة، يظهر على الموديل القديم [بالمانيول هاندل]

The idiomatic English translation of this Arabic sentence is:

Trying to start the car in an old-fashioned way by using [a manual handle]

Iconic: Hand forms a fist and performs three circular movements in front of body.

The similarities were striking from speakers from two different cultures which use very different languages. In each of the three examples, exactly the same gesture was used with almost identical preparation, stroke and retraction phases. Even the basic timings were similar. The first English speaker had a preparation phase of 200 milliseconds during which the fist was formed, followed by a stroke phase of 1,320 milliseconds during which the winding movements were performed, followed by a retraction phase of 280 milliseconds where the fingers of the fist uncurled. The second English speaker displayed essentially the same movements in a preparation phase of 120 milliseconds, followed by a stroke phase of 1,080 milliseconds, followed by a retraction phase of 360 milliseconds.

The Arabic speaker again performed the same movements in a preparation phase of 160 milliseconds, followed by a stroke phase of 1,000 milliseconds, followed by a retraction phase of 480 milliseconds. The overall duration of the gesture varied from 1,560 milliseconds to 1,800 milliseconds; both English speakers were at the extremes, with the gesture of the Arabic speaker falling somewhere in between. So in approximately one and a half seconds of animated talk, an Arabic speaker and a number of English speakers demonstrated some striking similarities in the types of unconscious iconic gesture they were generating alongside their speech.

There were some interesting differences in the speech used. The speech of the Arabic speaker seems to be the most explicit, leaving least for the gesture to communicate. The speech here made it clear that the car was being started in 'an old-fashioned way' and that 'a manual handle' was being used. But nevertheless, the gesture still showed exactly how the manual handle was used. The speech does not, after all, explicitly state that it was 'a starting handle'; 'a manual handle' is a somewhat vaguer term. Neither of the two English speakers in their speech mentioned how the car was being started. One didn't mention it at all; the other merely stated that 'a winder thing' was being used. The iconic gesture was necessary to show how the car was being started.

There appear to be differences in those parts of speech accompanied by the gestures in the two languages. In the two English examples the gesture accompanies the verb phrase, whereas in Arabic it accompanies a noun phrase. But in other English examples where the speaker is more explicit in terms of the linguistic channel and includes a mention of 'the starting handle', the iconic gesture is found on some occasions to accompany at least part of this noun phrase rather than the verb phrase as in some of the examples provided earlier. For example:

by turning [the starting] handle

Iconic: Hand forms a fist and performs five circular movements in front of body.

Another set of examples from the same experiment again demonstrates the close similarities in iconic gesture across different cultures and language groups in how events are represented unconsciously. Here one Arabic-speaking narrator used the following gesture–speech combination to describe how the ghostly hand manages to keep an irate policeman down a manhole:

ضاغطه عليه] بحيث انه ما يقدر يطلع

This translates as:

[pushing him down] so that he cannot get out

Iconic: Right hand rises up from resting position with palm facing down, fingers extended, downward motion as if pressing down on something.

One English speaker used the following gesture–speech combination:

the hand is [pushing down] on the policeman's head

Iconic: Right hand rises up from resting position with palm facing down, fingers extended, downward motion as if pressing down on something. Repeated twice.

Another English speaker said:

by [pushing down] on his head

Iconic: Left hand rises upwards with palm facing down, fingers extended, downward motion as if pressing down on something. Repeated three times.

The gestures in both English and Arabic show how the pushing down was accomplished, i.e. it was done with the hand rather than with anything else, that the hand had to be extended in order to do this and finally that the palm had to be facing downwards. The iconic gesture also conveyed something about the resistance that the ghostly hand had to overcome in order to keep the policeman in the manhole. In Arabic, the verb comes first in the sentence and it was here that the iconic gesture occurred (the Arabic has to be read from right to left). In English, the subject comes before the verb but the gesture accompanied the appropriate action part of the sentence.

The duration of the gesture, including the very similar preparation, stroke and retraction phases, was 1,360 milliseconds for the Arabic speaker, 1,480 milliseconds for the first English speaker and 1,720 milliseconds for the second English speaker; less than half a second difference between the longest and the shortest.

These similarities are all the more surprising not just given the focus in the published literature on differences in gesticulation between cultures, although previous research has not focused on the detailed micro-analysis of individual unconscious gestures like those being studied here, but also given the enormous linguistic differences between Arabic and English. The standard sentence structure in English is the subject–verb–object pattern, but the standard pattern in Arabic is verb–subject–object. Arabic is also read from right to left, not from left to right. The iconic gesture accompanied the appropriate part of the utterance in the two languages even though the surface forms of the utterances were very different. The similarity of the gestures across languages thus suggests an essential similarity of thought in the development of utterances irrespective of the specific language used (interested readers might like to consult Aboudan and Beattie 1996 for further detail on this point).

To summarise, the fundamental idea here is that the images depicted in the hand gesture and the verbal utterance emerge together from the same underlying idea or representation. It is not that the gesture is a translation of the sentence or an independent visual display simply shown at the same time as the verbal utterance; the real division of meaning between the gesture and the speech argues against that idea, as would the close integration of the various phases of the gesture with the utterance. The fact that gestures convey meaning in a totally different way to speech with its linear segmented nature would suggest that the gesture does not arise from some advanced verbal plan of the utterance, but rather that the two forms of communication arise from some underlying primitive idea. Analysis of the iconic gesture allows us potentially a great deal of insight into the nature of that primitive idea.

SUMMARY

- Speech operates in a linear and segmented fashion; gesture operates in terms of multidimensional images.

- The linguist de Saussure (1916) argued that this linear–segmented character of language arises because language is essentially one-dimensional whereas meaning is essentially multidimensional.

- In speech, the various elements of language can combine to form larger units – words combine into phrases, clauses into sentences, etc. – but different gestures do not combine together to form more complex gestures.

- Traditional sign languages have a lexicon, standards of well-formedness and a syntax, or a set of rules for combining signs that includes word order, to form meaningful sentences.

- The spontaneous gestures that accompany speech have no such lexicon, no such standards of form and no such syntax.

- The images depicted in the hand gesture and the verbal utterances emerge together from the same underlying idea or representation.

- A spontaneous gesture is not a translation of a word, concept or sentence, or an independent visual display shown at the same time as the verbal utterance; rather it is a part of the verbal utterance.

- Given that gestures convey meaning in a totally different way to speech would suggest that the gesture does not arise from some advanced verbal plan of the utterance.

- Rather the two forms of communication arise from some underlying primitive idea.

- Analysis of the spontaneous, unconscious gesture can allow us a great deal of insight into the nature of that primitive idea.

7

GESTURES AND THE FRUSTRATIONS OF EVERYDAY LIFE

Imagine a dinner party where old friends have met to discuss their schooldays. They are sitting around a long oak table lit by candles in silver candlestick holders. Life has been good to them. Each one has been something of a success in life and they are now looking back fondly, the way that you do when you can afford to. One has just told the story of how he was habitually late for school assembly. 'But it never did me any harm,' he says with a slight wry smile, very pleased with himself now that he runs a successful advertising agency. 'Go to work without an egg, eat a snack happy bar instead, nothing inside but pure white sugar' was unfortunately one of his efforts. 'My lateness is seen as a power trip these days; my clients have come to expect it,' he says. 'Lateness is a semiotic extension of power, they know the rules and rituals of everyday life.'

One has been discussing the French teacher, Mr Snowball, whom they used to call Monsieur Bal Neige. 'Well he told us to use French for everything in class,' she explains with a laugh, 'but he hated being called that – Bal Neige, it even sounds revolting.' The third is just about to describe how she flicked some note across the classroom using a protractor, but Monsieur Bal Neige intercepted the note and she was given detention, where she met her future husband, later to become the chief executive of some PR agency. That at least was her intention. There was only one slight problem, however.

She couldn't remember the name for that plastic object which measures angles in geometry, that plastic thing which was once so important in her maths class.

She began the story quite successfully. 'Do you remember that French class where I flicked the note across the room with the . . . what's it called, you know, the . . . what's it?' The faces around the table looked at her face encased in a wince. 'Oh God,' she says. 'What's it called?' She taps her foot on the floor repeatedly; she puts both hands up to her head.

'A set square,' the ever-late advertising executive who is deeply into semiotic extension says helpfully.

'No, no, no,' she replies, 'not one of those, the other thing, the . . . what's it?' And at this point we must all step back from the immediacy of her language to consider her body language and particularly her iconic gestures as she tries to find the word.

> Oh it's a type of circumference thing, I know what it is, it's that [bloody arc thing. Oh no, what's the word], it's on the tip of my tongue. It's

Iconic: Right hand makes a semi-circular movement, moving quickly up and down twice with index finger pointing outwards. Right hand and left hand then move quickly round each other five times in circular fashion.

> [erm circumferential]

Iconic: Hands move in and out three times touching at fingertips and base of palm in a curved fashion.

> [Oh shit, excuse me]. It's driving me crazy.

Iconic: Right hand makes a semi-circle shape.

> [Erm] It's an arc, no it's an arch, it's a ro- something. It's an, oh God, something arc . . . arch . . . rotor . . . arc.

Iconic: Right hand makes a semi-circle shape.

'Please won't somebody help me?' she says.

'Is it a protractor?' suggests the tormentor of Monsieur Bal Neige, and a new expression sweeps across the face of the tormented one. She had only meant to tell a brief and amusing story about how chance and fate determine all our lives, and instead she was locked into a frustrating and highly public situation of complete failure where she was unable to locate the right word in her mental dictionary, the failure no doubt occasioned by the fact that she had not used or discussed a protractor since she left school (or even mentioned it in previous versions of the story), plus she had been drinking a lot of Pinot Noir.

There are a number of interesting things to comment on here: our response to routine cognitive failures of this type, others' reaction to us, the willingness of others to help us out, a sort of cognitive midwifery, our demands that they should assist us in this way; but the most interesting things in the present context are the iconic hand gestures that are generated during this failure, iconic gestures that seem to map out significant features of the word being searched for – the fact that a protractor is curved, and indeed semi-circular, unlike a set square, which might have seemed like a reasonable alternative.

This example has been made up – the dinner party never occurred, the advertising executive never existed, although Mr Snowball did – but the phenomenon, this tip-of-the-tongue (TOT) state with the accompanying iconic gestures, did occur, although the words have been changed slightly to make it more comprehensible. We will see the actual words shortly and learn something of the context in which this TOT state really did occur. But such occurrences have led some psychologists to argue that this is the real function of iconic gestures, to help us find the words that we are looking for in everyday speech.

Having got thus far in the overall argument it is useful to pause and consider whether iconic gestures could actually have quite a different function to that suggested by David McNeill. Some psychologists have argued that iconic gesture and speech are clearly not separate, which is also the starting point for McNeill's argument. Also if you watch speakers who have difficulty in finding the word that they are looking for in everyday speech, often in their frustration they produce an iconic gesture. This gesture is clearly connected to the word that they are looking for, as if (and this is the critical bit) this gesture might somehow be helping them find the word. Furthermore, those who suffer from aphasia, who have an impairment of language abilities following brain damage, often have word-finding difficulties and appear to gesture more as a result. Could this be the main function of iconic gestures – that is, could iconic gestures really be used by speakers to help them locate words in their mental dictionary, the mental store of intuitive knowledge of words and their meanings? Is this why we gesture so much on the telephone? Even though we know that listeners cannot see our gestures, do we still gesture because we are really using them for our own benefit in our effort to produce meaningful and interesting speech?

This is an intriguing idea. Word finding in everyday speech, accessed from the mental dictionary in our brains, is something that we tend to take for granted, except when it goes wrong, as in the imaginary dinner party, and fails to happen quite as it should, as in aphasia or when we find ourselves stuck momentarily for a word during routine conversation. Then perhaps for the first time we think of how complicated this process actually is.

The rate of such word finding in speech is very impressive. It has been estimated at between 120 and 250 words per minute on average (Maclay and Osgood 1959), but with bursts of up to twice this rate. The rate during actual articulation (that is, ignoring all those unfilled pauses, those brief silent pauses which in the case of speech involving spontaneous thinking can comprise half or even more of all speaking time) is nearer the top end of this estimate rather than the bottom. So just imagine, therefore, how frequently we have to delve into that mental store to pull out the required items to produce coherent and fluent sentences. This is clearly a very rapid process but how complex a task is it really? Well, there are a lot of words in our mental dictionary and also a lot of words to choose from that may be appropriate for any given slot in an utterance. How many words exactly do we have in this mental store? The answer is that nobody really knows. The Dutch psychologist Willem Levelt (1993) has pointed out that there are fairly reliable ways of estimating the size of our word-*recognition* lexicon (for example, showing a sample to people and seeing what proportion they recognise). This word-recognition lexicon has been estimated as consisting of approximately 75,000 items for Oxford undergraduates by Oldfield (1963), but there are no comparable methods for estimating the size of the *production* lexicon, i.e. the words that we actually employ ourselves rather than just recognise. Levelt has suggested that we have around 30,000 words in our production lexicon, but he notes that this estimate could be out by a factor of two, with perhaps as many as 60,000 words available. So just imagine people in their everyday conversations producing coherent speech, with all the right words in the right places, chosen from all of these alternatives, at this sort of rate. It is also an extremely efficient cognitive skill because we can access this huge database at such high rates, over long stretches of time and without any obvious signs of fatigue. The skill is also characterised by a very low error rate. It has been reported that there were only 86 errors of word choice in a spoken corpus of 200,000 words, with 105 other slips of the tongue.

So just try to imagine this process in action, that is, finding the right words at the right time in everyday talk. It's like consulting the *Concise Oxford Dictionary*, which has 75,000 entries, up to four times a second and getting it right almost every time for hours and hours on end.

There have been a number of different approaches by psychologists to the question of how word finding operates in speech. Some researchers have studied natural spontaneous speech, examining where the brief unfilled or silent pauses actually occur. These sometimes reflect the delay in finding certain words and tell us where speakers have most difficulty in accessing certain words or types of word. Unfilled pauses occur before categories of words like nouns and verbs, which have the lowest frequency in the language as a whole.

Iconic gestures have been implicated in the process of word selection for two main reasons. First, the words that iconic gestures are most clearly associated with in everyday speech are nouns and verbs – the main content words that tend to be associated with pauses in speech and seem hardest to access. Second, because the preparation phase of a gesture precedes the associated word, the gesture might be thought to be mapping out some core parts of the meaning of the word, perhaps to help the speaker find the right word in the mental dictionary. In other words, iconic gestures may be involved in (and also able to reveal some of the processes behind) the generation of speech, a process that is otherwise notoriously difficult to study.

Detailed analysis of a small corpus of natural speech taken from a variety of academic interactions, which I carried out as a student at Cambridge, then revealed a strong association between the presence of iconic gestures and particular form classes of words, particularly nouns, verbs and adjectives – the classes which contain the words most difficult to retrieve in speech. These observations led Brian Butterworth and me to the tentative conclusion that certain types of gesture are products of word-finding processes and indicate that speakers know in advance some aspects of the meaning of words before the words themselves are actually uttered (see Beattie 1983). Brian Butterworth and Uri Hadar (1989) attempted to develop a model of this process to show why such iconic gestures might assist in this process of locating words in the mental dictionary. They suggested that the visual image in the iconic gesture displays certain core parts of the meaning of the word that is being searched for because

> word finding is delayed by the slow build-up of activation [in the brain] in the searched for word. By raising the overall activation in

the system through the production of a motor movement, the word
will reach a firing level more quickly.

(Butterworth and Hadar 1989: 173)

In the previous section of this book we saw some examples of different
speakers describing the same event from the story 'The Haunts of Headless
Harry', where a ghostly hand started an old-fashioned car with a starting
handle. What is interesting is that some of the examples from this
experiment seem to fit into one theory, that of David McNeill, and other
examples fit into the alternative theory, that of Butterworth and Hadar. For
example:

so [the hand is now trying to start the car]

Iconic: Hand moves in a winding movement.

This first example seems to fit directly into McNeill's theory, which holds
that iconic gestures do not assist in word finding; rather they operate in
conjunction with the speech itself to communicate the speaker's thinking.
In McNeill's words: 'To get the full cognitive representation that the speaker
had in mind, both the sentence and the gesture must be taken into account.'
In this example, the speech conveys only part of the overall message, the
iconic gesture conveys another complementary part, i.e. how the car is
actually being started, and to get the full cognitive representation of what
the speaker had in mind both the sentence and the gesture must be taken
into account. The sentence is also well formed and the iconic gesture is clearly
not a repair, or an attempt to fix the sentence in any way. Furthermore, the
sentence appears extremely fluent even when the unfilled pauses in speech
(as brief as 200 milliseconds) are analysed.

Now consider a second example, which comes from a different speaker
narrating the same cartoon:

(pause) [starting it at the front with the (pause)] winder thing

Iconic: Hand moves in a winding movement.

Here, the iconic gesture starts and finishes before its associated words
('winder thing'). There are also brief silent pauses in this segment of
speech and the gesture starts and terminates in two of these pauses. Here
the gesture boundaries include the preparation and retraction phases of

the gesture. The speaker does not find 'starting handle' and settles instead for 'the winder thing'. This example, it could be argued, fits more clearly into Butterworth and Hadar's theory and one could imagine a possible role for the iconic gesture in word finding here. The iconic gesture is mapping out the actions involved in using a starting handle and this aspect of its use may help find the location in the brain where the word is actually stored.

In the third example we find more hesitations – both silent and filled ('ah', 'er', 'um', etc. – pauses with some sound). Again, there is a gap between the start of the preparation phase of the iconic gesture and the generation of the word with which the gesture is most clearly associated, although the correct word is eventually found in this particular case after a number of pauses.

by (pause) [turning the eh] (pause) starting handle

Iconic: Hand moves in a winding movement.

However, the problem here is that even such detailed analyses of the precise relationship between speech and iconic gesture cannot really answer the question of the possible functional role of iconic gesture in word finding. Mere associations of this kind cannot prove causality; the results are always going to be too inconclusive. Some examples seem to go along with Butterworth and Hadar's theory, while some do not. Even when they do and it looks as if there is evidence of word-finding difficulty and the iconic gestures precede the word, mapping out some relevant features, then McNeill's theory can still explain the results because he says that people communicate in gesture–speech combinations. If people have trouble in finding a word in the linguistic channel, it would be appropriate for the gesture still to carry information about that word. Where he differs from Butterworth and Hadar is that he would say that iconic gestures should not in any way help us find the word because that is not what they are designed to do.

I reasoned that what we needed to do was to test experimentally the Butterworth and Hadar theory that iconic gestures have a functional role in word finding. So along with Jane Coughlan I asked participants to narrate cartoon stories, as I had done on a number of occasions before, but this time they were asked to repeat their stories to a number of different listeners on a series of consecutive trials. This was done so that there would be a gradual shift from hesitant spontaneous speech to fluent, well-rehearsed speech. This was based on some early research by a psychologist called Frieda

Goldman-Eisler (1968), who had discovered that the more times you repeat a story or a sentence, the more fluent it becomes until the pausing starts to level off. To begin with the pauses are all over the place, as the speaker searches the mental dictionary at many different points in the story for difficult words. But once these difficult words have been found (for example, words like 'starting handle' in the type of story that I was using, which is not in everyday use), on the next occasion that the story is told a shorter pause or no pause at all is necessary to retrieve this word. The speaker has already found 'starting handle' in the first telling of the story. Now it can be found quite quickly when the story is told again. After a number of repetitions of the story, the pauses end up being restricted to mainly grammatical junctures; for example, at the ends of sentences, where they occur even when people are reading text and where they are now being used just to segment the story for the listener.

I wanted to use this method because it seemed to me that if Butterworth and Hadar were correct that iconic gestures are mainly used to help speakers find certain words in the mental dictionary, then you would predict that when words have been found once and used fluently, the possible role of iconic gestures in all subsequent retrieval processes should diminish. Therefore, the frequency of iconic gestures should decrease across trials when speakers are telling the same story again and again.

So we asked eight participants to tell the same story six times each, resulting in 48 stories overall. They displayed 694 gestures in total, 403 of which were iconic gestures and 291 were beats. Our results showed that the frequency of iconic gestures did not significantly decrease across trials but rather remained remarkably stable from trial two onwards. By the sixth and final trial, participants were gesturing, on average, 91 per cent as much as they did on the very first trial. Even, for example, when 'starting handle' had been used by participants, whenever they came to use the word subsequently in the repetition of the story, the iconic gesture still occurred, suggesting that whatever the function of the gesture it was not solely being used to generate an image that would help speakers access that part of their mental dictionary where the word was stored (Beattie and Coughlan 1998).

I then tried a different approach to answer this question of whether iconic gestures are primarily concerned with helping us access our mental dictionaries. I used one of the better-known experimental techniques, which has been successfully employed to probe other aspects of the mechanism of word finding. The technique involves studying something called the TOT state. The TOT state is a particular type of word-finding problem. If you provide a definition of a word to a set of individuals and they try to give you the word, sometimes they do not know it and are certain that they don't know it; sometimes they tell you the word immediately; sometimes they are sure that they know the word but just cannot say it at that precise moment in time. This can be a very frustrating experience for the individuals concerned, which I am sure everybody recognises.

This state can be a very useful phenomenon for the experimental psychologist because here, in the words of Harvard psychologist Roger Brown, 'the mind swims excitingly close to the surface'. As A. S. Brown notes:

> Because word retrieval is usually so rapid, examining, in a temporary 'holding pattern' imposed by the TOT, has the potential to reveal subtleties of normal retrieval functions, similar to how slow-motion photography clarifies the dimensions of a humming-bird's flight.
>
> (Brown 1991: 204)

The study of this phenomenon has a long history in psychology. William James, one of the founders of modern psychology, was also intensely interested in the phenomenon and he describes the TOT experience in the following terms:

> The state of our consciousness is peculiar. There is a gap therein, but no mere gap. It is a gap that is intensely active. A sort of wraith of the name is in it, beckoning us in a given direction, making us at moments tingle with the sense of our closeness and then, letting us sink back without the longed-for term.
>
> (James 1893: 251)

Diary studies have revealed that TOT states are really quite common in everyday life. In the TOT state individuals may know certain things about the word. They may know certain parts of the word like the first letter or they may know a particular syllable in the word. They may even be able to suggest similar sounding words with the same first letter, which makes the whole thing that much more frustrating. As Roger Brown (1966) describes: 'It is like fumbling in a filing cabinet for a particular card when you know the approximate, but not the exact, location. You come up with a fistful of cards – all wrong but all obviously out of the right drawer' (1966: 274).

The information that they do know about the target word may hold a clue as to how the mental dictionary is organised and accessed.

Roger Brown and David McNeill carried out the first really systematic experimental investigation of the TOT state in 1966 (the same McNeill who later turned his attention to gestures, although he never studied the relationship between iconic gestures and the TOT state). In their laboratory, participants were read definitions of rare words from which they had to recall the target. Brown and McNeill define the TOT experience in the following way: 'If you are unable to think of the word but feel sure that you know it and it is on the verge of coming back to you then you are in a TOT state.' They also felt that there were often visible signs of a TOT state. For example, in 57 out of 360 instances, participants 'would appear to be in a mild torment, something like the brink of a sneeze, and if he found the word his relief was considerable'. In this experiment, they found that participants in the TOT state could often provide the initial letter and number of syllables of the target word, even when they could not retrieve the word itself. Overall, TOT states were experienced in 13 per cent of retrieval attempts in this study.

In my laboratory we investigated whether permitting participants to use gestures in the TOT state affects the rate at which they resolve the state, and thus whether iconic gestures function effectively in finding words in the mental dictionary. My reasoning was that if gestures are associated with word finding, as some psychologists suggest, then when participants are free to gesture (whether in a TOT state or not), they should be able to find the correct word significantly more frequently than those who have their arms folded and are therefore unable to gesture (assuming comparable vocabulary sizes in two randomly chosen groups). Second, if iconic gestures do have a functional role in finding words in the mental dictionary, then they should be involved significantly more in resolved TOT states, those in which they find the word having been in a TOT state, than unresolved TOT states. After all, participants may resolve more TOT states when they are free to gesture but this may, of course, have nothing to do with the occurrence of iconic gestures per se.

We induced a TOT state by reading participants a set of 25 definitions of target words, for example: 'A man's soft felt hat with an indented crown' – trilby; 'A material for starting a fire, such as dry wood or straw' – kindling; 'The open main court of a Roman house' – atrium. When each definition was read out, the participant was told they would have 30 seconds in which to say the word. If they couldn't immediately recall the word, they were then told to keep thinking and to offer any suggestions they might have. If they didn't say the word after 30 seconds, they were given a clue – the initial letter of the target word – in order to increase the number of TOT states further. Some participants didn't have a TOT state until they were given this first letter. They were then allowed a further 15 seconds to say what the target word was. If they didn't get it in the time allowed, they were told it and we moved on to the next word on the list. Half the participants (totalling 30) were instructed to fold their arms and keep them folded throughout so as to prevent any gesturing, while the rest were left free to gesture.

In this experiment we succeeded in eliciting 112 TOT states (in 1,500 trials); the TOT states tended to be accompanied by the following types of behaviour (and these behaviours were important in identifying the TOT state):

1. Verbal statements, like 'Oh, God I know it!' or 'Oh, what are they called?' Our participants also sometimes got the initial letter of the word or said words (or non-words!) similar to the target, e.g. 'quiff' or 'quin' for the target word 'quill'.
2. Certain types of facial expression, such as wincing.
3. Certain types of bodily movement, for example, leaning forward and holding their head in their hands.
4. Characteristic head movements, for example, the head falling back, dropping forward or turning to the side.
5. Characteristic foot and leg movements, for example, excessive tapping and jigging about.

Here is an example of one female participant in a TOT state. You may recognise the example from earlier at the dinner party. The imaginary dinner party scene was based on this example. The definition that had been read to her was 'a semi-circular instrument for measuring angles on paper'. The participant was a university undergraduate, who had obviously some difficulty in recalling the names of those things that she had kept in her pencil case a few years earlier. Most of the behaviours described above were shown here. She felt extremely frustrated that she couldn't find the word. In the 30 seconds before the first letter was provided, she also generated four iconic gestures plus two self-touching movements and one beat, but only the iconic gestures are included in the transcript below. In other words, word-finding problems are clearly associated with the generation of iconic gestures, but do these iconic gestures actually help us find the words? This is the question that this experiment attempts to answer. But first let us see what she actually did during her TOT state.

> Oh ts ts circumf circumference thing, I know what it is, it's that [bloody arc thing, oh no what's the word], it's on the tip of my tongue ts

Iconic: Right hand makes a semi-circular movement, moving quickly up and down twice with index finger pointing outwards. Right hand and left hand then move quickly round each other five times in circular fashion.

> [erm circumferential]

Iconic: Hands move in and out three times touching at fingertips and base of palm in a curved fashion.

> [oh shit, excuse me] ts

Iconic: Right hand makes a semi-circle shape.

> [Erm] arc arch ro ro, it is r oh God, something arc arch rotor arc

Iconic: Right hand makes a semi-circle shape.

> don't you really want to give me a clue?

The correct answer, of course, was 'protractor' (anyone who has seen or imagined the iconic gesture should have got that). The iconic gestures that accompanied the TOT state tended to illustrate either the shape of the target word (as in the case of the target word 'protractor' above, and also in the case of target words like 'set square' and 'palette') or the function of the target word, for target words like 'stethoscope', 'trowel' or 'castanets'. Sometimes the iconic gesture illustrated both the function of the target word and its shape, as in the case of words like 'accordion' and 'metronome'.

The first prediction tested in this experiment was that if gestures are associated with word finding, then participants who are free to gesture should be able to find the correct word significantly more frequently than those who have their arms folded. Contrary to prediction, we found that the group with arms folded were the more successful in the recall of words (72.4 per cent compared to 66.8 per cent), although this difference was not statistically significant. Nevertheless, this result is clearly at odds with the theory that using iconic gestures helps us find the words we are looking for.

The second prediction was that if iconic gestures do help us find words in our mental dictionary, then they should be involved significantly more in resolved than unresolved TOT states. This was the critical prediction. Although more TOT states were resolved when participants were free to gesture, iconic gestures were not significantly associated with this resolution: 69 per cent of TOT states were resolved when iconic gestures were present and 72.9 per cent when they were absent. Furthermore, the resolution rate for TOT states when participants were free to gesture and iconic gestures were present was not significantly different from the resolution rate for TOT states when participants had their arms folded (Beattie and Coughlan 1999).

In other words, this experimental study failed to find any evidence that iconic gestures actually play a significant role in word finding and therefore goes against the Butterworth and Hadar theory. As I stated earlier, the fact that iconic gestures do occur when speakers have trouble finding words is not incompatible with McNeill's basic theory. He argues that speech and gestures originate from a single process of utterance formation with meaning divided between the two channels. The fact that on occasion there may be a problem in finding a word in the linguistic channel does not interfere with the meaning that is being generated in the gestural channel. He has always maintained that the fact that the preparation phase of the gesture precedes the associated speech is important evidence for the fact that both gesture and speech arise from the same common representation, with the more primitive visual image, depicted in the gesture, arising first.

The evidence from the TOT experiment and related studies (see Beattie and Shovelton 2000) greatly weakens one of the most powerful opposing theories to that of McNeill. Iconic gestures are common in everyday speech. They do not seem to assist the speaker in retrieving words from the mental dictionary, although they are common when speakers are having word-finding difficulties. They often appear to convey aspects of meaning that are not present in the speech itself. Having carried out the TOT and related experiments, I therefore turned my attention back to the work of McNeill, whose theory I was now starting to believe provided us with a powerful incentive for studying iconic gestures as a way of seeing how the mind really works in everyday life.

SUMMARY

- Word finding in speech is a routine but complex part of our everyday life.

- There appears to be a strong association between the presence of iconic gestures and particular form classes of words, particularly nouns, verbs and adjectives – the classes which contain the words most difficult to retrieve in speech.

- This led a number of psychologists to suggest that one of the main functions of the gestures was the mapping out of images to help with word finding.

- If you put people in a TOT state, where people are sure that they know a word but just cannot say it, allowing them to gesture does not make this word retrieval any easier.

- Iconic gestures (arguably) do not seem to assist the speaker in retrieving words from the mental dictionary, although they are common when speakers are having word-finding difficulties.

8

SPEECH IS ONLY
HALF THE STORY

McNeill's theory of speech and gesture is extremely interesting, but in my opinion it had one fundamental flaw. He never actually demonstrated that listeners extract the information contained within naturally occurring gestures to combine with the information in the speech channel. This is a major shortcoming of a theory that maintains that such gestures are actually *communicative*. All of his analyses are based on whether information appears to be present in the gesture–speech combination. McNeill carried out very few experiments to determine how listeners deal with the information contained within speech and within gestures. He did demonstrate that *staged* gestures and speech that *did not match* in their gesture–speech combinations were combined by listeners in their memory of the event. For example, in the case of a narrator describing a Sylvester and Tweety cartoon who said 'and he came out the pipe', performing an up-and-down bouncing gestural movement at the same time, their utterance was recalled by listeners as the character emerging from the pipe in a particular bouncing manner. McNeill also argued that this process of resolution was done quite unconsciously by listeners and occurred with mismatches of 'form' like the above and 'space', where a particular space identifies one character but the narrator suddenly changes the space in the mismatch in his or her story.

But this experiment was based solely on staged combinations. How do listeners deal with information in the gestural and linguistic channels when they occur naturally? There might be a variety of both theoretical and practical reasons why listeners are unable to use the information from both natural sources. They may not, for example, be attuned to the gesture, except when there is a mismatch. The information contained within the natural gesture might be too vague or too hard to interpret, or listeners might be overcome by the sheer complexity of combining information from linguistic and non-linguistic sources.

A number of other psychologists had attempted to determine if iconic gestures were communicative, but they had all used similar and, in my opinion, unsuitable methods. For example, Krauss *et al.* (1991) tried to see if people could match gestures with the words that they accompanied and concluded that the relationship between gesture and speech is relatively imprecise and unreliable. However, the Krauss *et al.* study only investigated semantic relationships between speech and gesture, the semantic relation-ships between the two channels of communication. There were no questions designed to ask about the relationship between gestures and the 'world out there'.

Another experiment that again considered only the semantic relationships between speech and gesture was conducted by Hadar. Here participants had to choose, in a forced choice condition, that word which best described the meaning of a gesture clip shown to them. Hadar concluded that 'although the shaping of gestures is clearly related to the conceptual and semantic aspects of the accompanying speech, gestures cannot be interpreted well by naive listeners' (2001: 294).

It could be argued, however, that this type of approach is in principle unable to answer the question as to the possible communicational function of gestures. If gestures are designed to communicate, then they should provide critical information about the semantic domain to be encoded, the world out there or that part of it involved in the experiment, rather than about the accompanying speech.

In a series of studies conducted with Heather Shovelton we decided to tackle this issue. In our first study (Beattie and Shovelton 1999a; see also 1998) we video-recorded participants narrating cartoon stories and then played just the speech segments or the gesture–speech combinations to another set of participants whom we subsequently questioned about details of the original stories. For example, some participants just heard:

Billy going sliding along and causing all sorts of mayhem

The other set of participants were presented with the following gesture–speech combination:

<u>Billy going [sliding along] and causing all sorts of mayhem</u>

Iconic: Left hand moves upwards to position in front of chest (preparation phase). Fingers of left hand are straight and close together, palm is pointing downwards. Hand makes a rapid movement to the left (stroke phase in brackets above) then returns to original position (retraction phase).

In this experiment, we studied 34 iconic gestures and 60 participants – 30 participants just heard the speech segments, another 30 were presented with the gesture–speech combinations. After each extract was presented the participant was asked (via a questionnaire) two questions relating to what was happening in the original cartoon. We generated the questions on the basis of what we as the experimenters thought might be being depicted in the gesture. For example, in the extract above we thought that the iconic gesture could have told the listener something about the direction of movement and perhaps also something about the speed of the movement. So we asked two very straightforward questions after each extract was presented. The questions were to be answered by a simple 'yes' or 'no' to make the scoring easy and unambiguous:

'Does Billy slide to his left?'

'Does Billy slide slowly?'

The questions were different for each and every gesture. We asked things like: 'Does the table move in a circular motion as it is rising?' 'Does the boy spin around in a clockwise direction?' 'Is the net very low down?' 'Is the pole very large in relation to the table?' Of these questions, 31 related primarily to properties of actions and 37 related to properties of objects. They covered such things as the identity of any people or objects that were talked about, the size of the people or objects, the shape of the people or objects, the number of people or objects discussed, the relative position of the people and objects, the nature of the action in the extract, the speed of any action, the direction of any action and whether the action involved upward movement, rotation or contact, plus we enquired about the location of any action.

The highest possible mean score for each participant for each gesture was 2.00, corresponding to getting both questions correct; the chance probability in answering two yes/no questions correctly was of course 1.00.

We found that those participants who were presented with the gesture–speech combinations got an average of 1.67 questions correct, whereas those who heard only the speech extracts got 1.42 questions correct. The percentage correct in each case was 83.5 per cent and 71 per cent, respectively. In other words, this study demonstrated that those participants who were presented with gesture–speech combinations got significantly more information about the original story than those who only heard the speech. This was an important discovery.

At first sight in purely quantitative terms, this might not seem like much of a difference – an overall increase from 1.42 to 1.67 out of a possible 2.00 – but there is something very important which must be considered here. This study was based on yes/no questions, and the chance probability where a participant got absolutely no information from the speech or the gesture–speech combination was 1.00, which represents 50 per cent of 2.00. From the speech alone participants got an additional 0.42 units of information, and from the gesture–speech combinations they received an additional 0.67 units of information. Therefore, from the gesture–speech combinations they received 0.25/0.42 more information, which as a percentage is approximately 60 per cent more information. These iconic gestures, in other words, are crucial to the overall message and in purely quantitative terms carry over half as much again as the verbal part of the message.

The iconic gestures also seem to carry information about a whole raft of things, including the speed and direction of the action, whether the action involved rotation or upward movement or not, the relative position of the people and objects depicted, and the size and shape of the people and objects depicted. Clearly, these results were very much in line with McNeill's basic theory: if you want to get the full meaning behind a communication you need to take both the iconic gesture and the speech into consideration. Those who either fail to notice or ignore the iconic gestures are clearly missing a source of much potential information.

The next study (Beattie and Shovelton 1999b) tried to be more precise about exactly what information listeners pick up from the iconic gestures that accompany speech. The first study only asked two questions about each iconic gesture, but there was always the possibility that each iconic gesture contained a good deal more information than we were measuring. So in this second study, after each participant heard just the speech or saw just the iconic gesture on its own or was presented with the gesture–speech combination, we asked eight general questions that we felt explored the 14 relevant types of information with which the iconic gestures were associated:

1. What object(s) are identified here? (*identity*)
2. What are the object(s) doing? (*description of action, manner*)
3. What shape are the object(s)? (*shape*)
4. How big is each of the object(s) identified? (*size*)
5. Are any object(s) moving? (*movement*)
6. If so, in what direction are they moving? (*direction, rotation, upward movement*)
7. At what speed are they moving? (*speed*)
8. What is the position of the [moving/stationary] object(s) relative to something else? (*relative position, location of action, orientation, contact*)

Participants in this experiment were presented with 18 clips (six containing only speech, six containing only iconic gestures and six containing gesture–speech combinations). After the clip was played the interviewer asked the participant half of the questions. The same clip was then played again, and the remaining questions were asked to see what information about the original cartoon they had managed to glean. These interviews, it should be added, were very intensive and lasted up to two hours. Each participant also had to give a confidence rating on each of their judgements on a scale from 1 to 3, where 1 meant 'not confident', 2 meant 'moderately confident' and 3 meant 'very confident'.

The experiment showed that when participants were presented with the gesture–speech combination they were significantly better at answering questions about the original cartoon story than when they heard just the speech extracts. The speech on its own, perhaps not that surprisingly, was significantly better than the iconic gestures on their own. We estimated the mean percentage accuracy for the gesture–speech combinations to be 62.1 per cent, for the speech only to be 51.3 per cent and for the iconic gestures only to be 20.4 per cent (averaging across all of the different categories).

The estimate of how much the iconic gesture adds to the speech is much lower here because all semantic dimensions were considered for every iconic gesture (and we cannot consider the chance probability in the way that we did in the first study). Nevertheless, critical information was clearly carried by the gestures. Even when the iconic gestures are presented in isolation from speech, they still convey a great deal of important information.

There is another very important observation in this study. McNeill had always argued that iconic gestures convey meaning in a 'top-down' rather than a 'bottom-up' fashion; that is, you have to have some understanding of the overall image portrayed in the hand movement before you can understand what the component actions are representing. McNeill says that the individual parts of iconic gestures only convey meaning 'because of the meaning of the whole'. He says: 'The wiggling fingers mean running only because we know that the gesture as a whole depicts someone running.' But this experiment means that we have to add an important proviso to this statement. We found that an iconic gesture can convey the speed of movement, the direction of movement and also information about the size of the entity depicted in the gesture, even when people watching the iconic gesture in isolation could not determine exactly what the entity actually was. You only had to know that something was sliding along in a particular direction and at a certain speed to get certain questions correct, but you didn't have to be able to say with any confidence what that something actually was. So iconic gestures may operate in a 'top-down' fashion, but that does not mean that you have to get the full meaning at the highest level before any information is transmitted via the gesture. The meaning of the gesture is still global, with the meaning of the individual parts given their meaning by the meaning of the gesture as a whole, but the process can operate even when there is some ambiguity at the highest level.

One of the most extraordinary results in this experiment emerges when you consider the performance of individual participants. Although all the participants gleaned some additional meaning from the iconic gestures, the percentage increase in accuracy in moving from the speech only to the gesture–speech combinations ranged from 0.9 per cent to 27.6 per cent. In fact the analysis also revealed that the participant with the lowest percentage increase in accuracy in moving from the speech only to the gesture–speech combination was also very poor at obtaining information from the iconic gestures on their own, whereas the participant who showed the highest increase in accuracy going from speech only to gesture–speech combinations was very good at obtaining information from the iconic gestures on their own. There was, in fact, a statistically significant correlation between these two things. In other words, those participants who obtained most information about aspects of the original cartoon depicted in the clips in the iconic gestures also tended to get the most additional information when they saw the iconic gestures in addition to hearing the speech. Clearly some people are neglecting this very important channel of iconic gesture in their everyday life and are therefore missing out on a lot of important information that is clearly available, but is not being picked up by them.

Here are the responses of two participants who watched the same iconic gesture but did not hear the corresponding segment of speech. The first participant, who happened to be male, was good at picking up information from iconic gestures generally and obtained an overall accuracy score of 75 per cent for this particular gesture. The second participant, a female, despite trying very hard, did not display much evidence of having obtained significant amounts of information from iconic gestures generally. In this particular case, she obtained an overall accuracy score of 12.5 per cent.

[Bubbles start coming out of her mouth]

Iconic: Fingers on left hand are spread out and hand moves backwards and forwards in front of mouth.

Example 1, the male participant

EXPERIMENTER [E]: Do you know what object or objects are identified there?
PARTICIPANT [P]: It looks as if someone has eaten something hot and steam
    is coming out of their mouth. So I think I'll say 'steam'.
E: And how confident are you about that?
P: Not very – I'll go with two.
E: So what's being done with it or what's it doing?
P: I think it is coming out of someone's mouth.
E: How confident are you about that?
P: Two again.
E: Do you know what shape the object is?
P: Kind of longish – like steam is. It's really difficult to describe what shape
    steam is, isn't it?
E: Yeah. So how confident are you there?
P: One.

Clip is then played for the second time.

E: Do you know how big the object is?
P: Well, it starts off being small enough to come out of someone's mouth.
    It might get a bit bigger after, but I'll stick with small.
E: How confident are you about that?
P: One.
E: And is this object moving?
P: Yes. My confidence is three.
E: In what direction and at what speed is it moving?
P: The steam would probably be moving slightly upwards and it would
    be moving quite quickly. My confidence for both of those is only one.

E: So what do you think the position of the object is, relative to anything else?

P: I think it is moving away from someone's mouth.

E: How confident are you about that?

P: Two.

Example 2, the female participant

E: Have you any idea what object or objects are identified there?

P: A hot drink.

E: OK. And how confident are you about that?

P: Two.

E: And what's being done with it or what's it doing?

P: Kind of waving it, someone is waving it, to make it cool down.

E: How confident are you?

P: One.

E: Do you know what shape the object is?

P: Well, it's in a mug, so the liquid is mug shaped. Yeah.

E: How confident are you about that?

P: Two.

Clip is then played for the second time.

E: OK. Do you know how big the object is?

P: Smallish. Normal mug-type size. Confident – two.

E: OK. Is the object moving?

P: No.

E: How confident are you?

P: Three.

E: Do you know what the position of the object is, relative to anything else?

P: It's in someone's hands, on their knee.

E: How confident are you?

P: Three.

This experiment using this interview technique managed to uncover the kinds of information that participants retrieve from iconic gestures, both in isolation from speech and when they are working alongside speech. Consider the following example:

[she's eating the food]

Iconic: Fingers on left hand are close together, palm is facing body and thumb is directly behind index finger. Hand moves from waist level towards mouth.

Using McNeill's general line of argument, you would probably say that the sentence conveys the action involved ('eating'), but not how it is accomplished. The iconic gesture is critical to communication here because it shows the method of eating – bringing the food to the mouth with the hand. McNeill would also presumably point out that the sentence in the example above is well formed and therefore the gesture cannot be considered as a repair or some other transformation of the sentence. The speech and gesture appear to cooperate to present a single cognitive representation.

Unlike McNeill, we determined, through interviewing three sets of participants who either saw the gesture with or without speech, or did not see the gesture but just heard the speech, what information they *actually* received from the iconic gesture. What we discovered was that they received a wider range of additional information than McNeill's typical argument would suggest. For example, in this particular case all four participants who saw the iconic gesture, in addition to hearing the speech, knew that the food was moving towards the mouth (*relative position*) in the original cartoon, whereas only one out of three participants who did not see the gesture reported this. The other two thought that the food was 'below the character', presumably on a plate. Without hearing the speech (gesture only), one out of three participants got the *description of action* right. All four participants in the video condition (gesture–speech combination) got the *direction* of the movement correct – food was being drawn upwards towards the mouth (only one out of three participants in the speech-only condition got this right). None of the participants in the video condition (gesture–speech combination) or the speech-only condition got the *shape* of the food correct. The correct answer here, by the way, was a triangular sandwich shape (either triangular or sandwich shaped would have been considered sufficient in the scoring). Very interestingly, one participant in the gesture-only condition said the food was sandwich shaped. With only one participant, of course, it might have been a lucky guess, but since there are so many possibilities here, it was really some guess.

Consider now a second example:

[by squeezing his nose]

Iconic: Fingers on left hand are quite straight and only slightly apart; thumb is pointing away from the fingers. Fingers and thumb then move further away from each other before moving towards each other so that hand becomes closed.

Here the sentence conveys the action involved ('squeezing') and the object involved ('nose'), and in both the video condition (gesture–speech combination) and the speech-only condition all participants reported this information correctly. However, the gesture seemed to convey information about the *shape* of the nose (oblong shaped) being squeezed. It also conveyed information about the *relative position* of the nose with respect to the hand that is squeezing it and whether the nose was *moving*. The gesture conveyed information about the *size* of the nose and to a much lesser extent the *speed* of the movement.

On the basis of these and similar examples, it could be argued that McNeill had, if anything, underestimated the amount and nature of information conveyed by these seemingly slight and apparently insignificant iconic gestures which accompany everyday speech. Having investigated what information participants actually pick up from such gestures, one can look again at McNeill's examples and analyses, and suggest that even in these examples McNeill was underestimating the full extent of the communication via this gestural channel. Thus, consider again his classic example:

she [chases him out again]

Iconic: Hand, gripping an object, swings from left to right.

McNeill argued that the sentence conveys the concepts of pursuit ('chases') and recurrence ('again'), but not the means of pursuit. The iconic gesture, he says, is critical to communication here because it shows the method of pursuit – swinging an umbrella. But one could argue, in the light of this new research (Beattie and Shovelton 1999b), that the gesture here may potentially convey much more information than McNeill allowed for. It may convey other attributes like the *direction* of the swinging (from left to right), the *speed* of the swinging, the *size* of the umbrella and the *relative position* of the umbrella with respect to the hand (vertical, horizontal, etc.). Multiply this example by hundreds of others and it can be seen that there is the possibility that even McNeill may have underestimated the range and types of information conveyed by the iconic gestures which accompany spontaneous speech.

In summary, the experiments that I have just described reveal something of the nature, depth and range of information conveyed by iconic gestures. At one level, it lends considerable support to McNeill's basic idea that such iconic gestures are crucial to meaning. However, this study goes beyond this. It not only tells us that such gestures do convey meaning, but it gives the first glimpse of the range of information conveyed by them, and which particular types of information are best captured by them. In this particular study, attributes like the *relative position* of people and objects and the *size* of the people and objects depicted were significant right across the sample of gestures. With respect to these particular types of information it is also interesting to note that it was found that in the gesture-only condition participants were significantly more confident that the answers they were giving were correct than they were when answering questions about *identity*, *description of action*, *shape*, *movement*, *direction* and *speed*. It is not just that participants were receiving more information in these particular categories right across the board, but they also knew that they were.

These experiments have shown the considerable power of those spontaneous iconic hand gestures that go along with the talk found in everyday life. One question they do not answer is which particular iconic gestures are the most communicative and why. This is the question that we turn to in the next set of experiments where we delve a little deeper into this whole issue.

One final point is that critics (or careful thinkers) might say that the viewing conditions in this study were highly contrived, with the viewing of gestures confined to gestures presented on a video screen. One could argue that these results might not generalise to actual face-to-face conditions. In 2009, however, we published evidence that iconic gestures are at least as effective and in some cases even more effective at communicating relative position and size information when they occurred in the face-to-face compared to video condition (see Holler *et al.* 2009).

SUMMARY

- Participants who were presented with clips of gesture–speech combinations from a speaker telling a story based on a storyboard got significantly more information about the original story than those who only heard the speech.

- Some gestures were more communicative than others.

- Attributes like the *relative position* of the people and objects and the *size* of the people and objects depicted were significantly communicated right across the sample of gestures.

- Some people were better at decoding the information in the gestures than others.

- Those participants who obtained most information about aspects of the original stories depicted in the clips in the iconic gestures also tended to get the most *additional* information when they saw the iconic gestures in addition to hearing the speech.

- Some people seem to be more sensitive than others to this form of behaviour.

9

WHO OR WHAT THE HANDS PORTRAY

The experiments described in the previous chapter tell us that iconic gestures convey significant amounts of information, either on their own or combined with speech. David McNeill appears to have been right. But the research described so far does not, of course, mean that every single gesture carries information over and above the speech. Also some iconic gestures appear to carry much more information than others, but what affects this?

There is one absolutely fundamental property of gestures that was not considered in these early studies, but which may well turn out to be critical, because the way that information is depicted in gestures varies greatly depending upon this one property: that is, the *viewpoint* from which the gesture is generated.

McNeill (1992) points out that two different viewpoints appear in the gestures people perform during narratives: observer viewpoint and character viewpoint. A gesture is said to have an observer viewpoint when it appears to display an event from the viewpoint of an observer. McNeill says: 'With this viewpoint, the narrator keeps some distance from the story.' An observer viewpoint gesture 'excludes the speaker's body from the gesture space and his hands play the part of the character as a whole'.

Below there is an example of a gesture produced from an observer viewpoint:

[runs out of his house] again

Iconic gesture: Thumb of right hand is pointing upwards, other fingers are curled together. Hand moves upwards slightly and then to the right in a rapid movement.

Here the speaker's hand represents the whole cartoon character. The character is in front of the narrator and the character is running, from right to left, but the narrator is not part of the scene.

The other viewpoint that appears when people narrate stories is character viewpoint. Here McNeill (1992) says that with character viewpoint 'we feel that the narrator is inside the story', in that a character viewpoint gesture 'incorporates the speaker's body into the gesture space, and the speaker's hands represent the hands (paws, etc.) of the character'. The running event mentioned earlier could have been conveyed by a gesture produced from a character viewpoint. Thus:

[runs out of his house] again

Iconic: Arms bent at elbows, pump backwards and forwards moving from the shoulders.

In this case, the narrator would be moving his arms as if he were actually running himself. The narrator would therefore be imagining himself playing the part of the character rather than external to it, as in the observer viewpoint gesture described earlier.

McNeill's research has suggested that character viewpoint gestures are strongly associated with verbs that take a grammatical object (e.g. 'he hit the ball', where 'ball' is the grammatical object). Observer viewpoint gestures are strongly associated with verbs that do not take an obligatory grammatical object, so-called intransitive verbs (e.g. 'she is jumping', a verb that cannot take a grammatical object; you cannot say 'she is jumping ball', as it is quite simply ungrammatical). The viewpoint from which a gesture is generated is a critical variable in the conceptual understanding of gesture and may also have an important influence on the communicative power of individual gestures simply because the hands are being used very differently in these two types of gesture.

Let us have a look at some of the iconic gestures that we have already encountered and consider the viewpoint from which they have been generated so that the distinction becomes completely clear.

and he [bends it way back]

Iconic: Hand appears to grip something and pull it from the upper front space back and down near to the shoulder.

This is clearly a character viewpoint gesture. The hands of the speaker act as the hands of the person that he is discussing. The hands show how the object ['the big oak tree' identified in the previous clause] is gripped and pulled back. The clause is transitive; there is a grammatical object, 'it'.

And she [chases him out again]

Iconic: Hand appears to swing an object through the air.

This is another character viewpoint gesture. The hands of the speaker are again acting as the hands of the character being discussed. The hands show how the object, 'the umbrella', which is not mentioned in the speech, is being held. This is also a transitive clause, with the grammatical object being 'him'.

[she's eating the food]

Iconic: Fingers on left hand are close together, palm is facing body and thumb is directly behind index finger. Hand moves from waist level towards mouth.

Again another character viewpoint gesture – the hands of the speaker are acting as the hands of the character in the story, showing how she eats the food by drawing it up to the mouth. The speech is again another transitive clause, with the grammatical object being 'the food'.

the head starts [swimming] along

Iconic: Right hand indicates the way that the head is swimming in the water, focusing on forward motion with splayed fingers representing the head.

This one is an observer viewpoint gesture where the hands play the part of the character as a whole, in this case the whole head, which has a life of its own. The speaker takes an observer's perspective on the action; the head is swimming away from the stationary observer, the speaker himself. The speech, in this case, consists of an intransitive clause with no grammatical object. You cannot say 'the head starts swimming it'; it is simply ungrammatical.

But do character viewpoint gestures and observer viewpoint gestures convey different amounts of information, and if so why? How do the hands operate from each of these two different viewpoints? I tested this in another set of experiments (reported in more detail in Beattie and Shovelton 2001a, 2001b, 2002b).

We asked 21 participants to narrate a number of cartoon stories and in this task they displayed a total of 513 identifiable hand and arm movements, 103 of which were identified as iconic gestures. Of these gestures 30 were selected for presentation to a set of participants. These 30 gestures were selected on the basis that first, the gesture's span did not stretch out of view of the camera and second, they depicted different events from the cartoons. There was actually considerable overlap in what the gestures referred to in the cartoon narratives in this particular sample. Of these 30 iconic gestures, 15 were generated from a character viewpoint and 15 from an observer viewpoint.

The speech sample to be played to participants was restricted to the clausal unit in the immediate vicinity of the gesture, again following McNeill's logic that gestures usually do not cross clause boundaries. (However, one of the iconic gestures did cross a clause boundary, so in this case a slightly larger speech unit was used.) The accompanying 30 speech clauses were then classified regarding their transitivity. Transitive verbs, as I have explained, take obligatory direct objects, while intransitive verbs do not.

It was found that all of the character viewpoint gestures in our corpus were associated with transitive clauses and all of the observer viewpoint gestures were associated with intransitive clauses. These gestures produced from different viewpoints were randomly ordered onto the presentation tape. Each gesture, without its corresponding speech, was played twice and then the participants had 30 seconds to write down their answer to the following question: 'Please give as much information as possible about any actions and any objects depicted in the following gesture.' We expected the overall accuracy to be lower in this experiment than in the previous study because participants were not interviewed here in the intensive way used earlier.

Again, we used eight broad semantic categories to break the meaning down into its parts, namely identity, description of action, shape, size, movement, direction, *speed* and *relative position*, to determine what individual types of information the participants received from gestures.

It is perhaps worthwhile providing a little bit of detail as to how the individual semantic categories were scored in this experiment to illustrate some of the issues involved in this process. After all, if the reader is convinced of the care that went into this process, the final conclusions will seem all that more convincing.

Identity

This semantic category reflects whether or not the participant correctly specified the main entity (person, animal or thing) associated with the iconic gesture. The number of entities contained (or assumed) in each of the clauses varies from one to three. The mean number of entities for intransitive clauses was 1.60 whereas it was 2.27 for transitive clauses. Here is an example of an intransitive clause containing just one entity:

and the [roof starts cracking]

Iconic: Index finger of left hand points vertically upwards, other fingers and thumb are slightly curled. Index finger moves to his left and then to his right.

Here the entity is 'roof' and the iconic gesture illustrates the roof cracking.

Below is an example of a transitive clause containing two explicit entities (ball and ground) and one assumed entity (the dog that was actually bouncing the ball):

bouncing the ball [on the ground]

Iconic: Palm of right hand points downwards; hand moves rapidly downwards and upwards three times.

Here the gesture mainly illustrates the 'ball' bouncing rather than the nature of the dog doing the bouncing or the nature of the ground on which it is bouncing. We could have attempted to score identity by taking into account all of the entities referred to explicitly or assumed in the linguistic clause, but we chose instead to focus on the main entity associated with the iconic gesture, in other words, the gesture's principal lexical affiliate ('the ball'). One advantage of scoring it this way was that it allowed for a direct statistical comparison of character viewpoint and observer viewpoint gestures, which do differ in terms of the number of entities in their associated clauses. The alternative strategy would have been to attempt to consider all of the entities in the clause, even those entities that did not appear to be connected to the gesture and indeed those entities that were poorly specified either linguistically or gesturally. We decided that this latter approach was not quite as appropriate.

So the identity category involved the participant correctly specifying the one main entity associated with the iconic gesture. In terms of the categorisation, if a participant only used a pronoun in their answer, then we reasoned that this did not provide enough information for identity to be scored as correct. For example, if a participant wrote 'he', then this could refer to a number of male entities including a boy, a dog, etc., so for identity to be scored as correct a participant had to specify more precisely what they were referring to. The main entity in five of the clauses was a person or an animal and the other 25 main entities were things like 'a rope', 'a microphone', 'a trolley', 'a pole', 'a nose', 'a tie', etc. In all cases the entity in the participant's answer had to be judged as equivalent in meaning to the specified entity in the clause, before the identity category could be classed as correct.

Shape

This category reflects whether or not the participant correctly specified the shape of the main entity. In the case of one-third of the clips there was only one possible shape for the entity involved and therefore if a participant provided correct information about identity, then the shape category was also scored as being correct. For example, bubbles are, by definition, round. Therefore, if a participant wrote about bubbles in their answer it could be assumed that they knew that these were round.

In the case of the remaining two-thirds of the clips the shape of the entity had to be explicitly mentioned; for example, a participant would have to explain what shape a table was because it could be a number of different shapes – round, square, etc. Other shapes associated with these clips included 'triangular', 'oblong', 'long and thin', etc.

Size

This category reflects whether or not the participant correctly specified the size of the main entity. Participants had to mention explicitly the correct size of the entity before this category was considered to be correct. The argument that the size of an entity is implicit within the identity category is rejected here because the size of entities in cartoons can vary dramatically. For example, in a cartoon story a 'drink' can be bigger than a boy's body and a 'ball' can contain three kittens but nevertheless fit snugly into a basketball hoop. When the participants' answers were scored, any explicit size information that had been provided was placed into the following four categories: 'big', 'medium', 'small', 'varying sizes'.

Movement

This category reflects whether or not the participant correctly specified whether the main entity was moving or not – it was therefore a straightforward dichotomous category. Movement, in this current study, was only scored as correct if there was movement in the original scene and in the participant's answer. In the case of 13.3 per cent of the clips there was no movement, for example 'it's a circular table', and thus this movement category did not apply to these clips.

Description of action

This category reflects whether or not the participant correctly specified what was being done or what was happening in the clip. The description of action in the participant's answer had to be judged as equivalent to the specified action in the clause before the description of action category could be classed as correct. The actions in the clips included 'pushing', 'jumping', 'throwing', etc.

Speed

This category reflects whether or not the participant correctly specified the speed at which the main entity was moving. Again it is important to remember that narrations about cartoons were being analysed – and in cartoon narrations kittens can 'run' so slowly that they never seem to change position with respect to a stationary animal that is giving them instructions. In addition, the kittens can also be watching some action that is happening behind them (very difficult in the case of actual running). In other cartoons, however, characters can 'run' so quickly that they appear to be running faster than a moving car. For this reason it was decided that 'running' alone did not contain implicit speed information but that speed had to be mentioned explicitly. When the participants' answers were scored, any speed information was placed into the following four categories: 'fast', 'medium', 'slow' and 'varying speeds'.

Direction

This category reflects whether or not the participant correctly specified the direction in which the main entity was moving. Again participants had to mention explicitly, rather than implicitly, the correct direction of the movement before this category was considered to be correct. Examples of answers required in the direction category included 'upwards', 'downwards', 'spinning around', etc.

Relative position

This category reflects whether or not the participant correctly specified the position of the main entity with respect to something else. In the present corpus of gestures it seems that there were three major sub-categories contained within the relative position category. First, there was a sub-category that involved the position of the entity with respect to a particular part of another entity and this category contained 15 gestures. An example of relative position information in this category is 'moving away from the mouth'. Next there was a sub-category that involved the position of a moving entity with respect to a fixed entity and this category contained 12 gestures. An example of relative position information in this category is 'moving away from the ground'. The third sub-category involved the position of a fixed entity with respect to another fixed entity and this category contained three gestures. An example of relative position information in this category is 'the bench seat is all the way around something'.

It must also be remembered that for participants merely guessing about the information within each semantic category the chance probability of this guess being correct varied from one category to another. At one extreme was identity and description of action, where the chance probability of a correct guess was very low indeed. Next there were the categories of relative position, shape and direction. These were followed by size and speed, where the chance probability was one in four. Finally, at the other end of the scale there was the dichotomous category 'movement'. This was the category that had the highest chance probability of being guessed correctly (50 per cent chance probability).

Two experimenters independently analysed the scenes in the original cartoons, relating to each of the 30 clips, and broke the complex meaning down into the individual categories described above. We then compared these analyses with the answers of the participants who had only seen the iconic gestures produced by our narrators.

Below is an example of one participant's answer. The iconic gesture that was shown to this participant is displayed here with the segment of speech it originally accompanied, which of course was itself not shown in the present experiment:

by [pulling on his tie]

Iconic: Left hand moves quickly upwards; hand closes and a sharp downwards movement is made.

After viewing this gesture in the gesture-only condition, one participant wrote: 'Somebody is grabbing hold of a rope with their hand.' In this particular case the gesture was scored as having conveyed information to this participant about the relative position of the physical entities involved (i.e. the hand being wrapped around something) and the fact that *movement* was occurring. None of the other semantic categories, namely *identity*, *shape*, *size*, *description of action*, *speed* or *direction*, was scored as correct in the case of this particular participant, although it should be added that many participants did extract a good deal more information from this particular gesture.

This experiment found that iconic gestures in isolation from speech which were generated from a character viewpoint were significantly more communicative than those generated from an observer viewpoint. The mean accuracy score for gestures generated from a character viewpoint was 18.8 per cent and 10.8 per cent for gestures generated from an observer viewpoint.

Let us look first at the character viewpoint gesture, described above, which had originally been generated accompanying the segment 'by pulling on his tie'. When this iconic gesture was shown to participants in isolation from speech, it conveyed a great deal of semantic information – coded at 18.8 per cent accuracy overall, using the scoring scheme for deconstructing written answers into their underlying semantic categories. This gesture not only provided participants generally with information about the action involved, but also information about the *speed* and *direction of the action* and about the *size* and *shape* of the object involved and the *relative position* of the physical entities depicted in the gesture.

There were, however, still gestures in the present corpus that were generated from an observer's perspective, which were high in communicative power when presented in isolation from speech. For example:

the table can be [raised up towards the ceiling]

Iconic: Hands are resting on knee; hands move upwards, palms pointing down, forming a large gesture; hands continue moving until they reach the area just above shoulder level. Hands then clasp each other just underneath the chin.

This iconic gesture in isolation communicated significant amounts of semantic information to participants – estimated at 13.5 per cent overall accuracy. This gesture provided participants with information about the action involved (something being raised) along with the *direction of the movement* (upwards). It also provided information about the *size* of the object involved and the *relative position* of the physical entities depicted in the gesture.

When the eight different semantic categories were considered in detail in the analysis, it was found that *relative position* was communicated most effectively by character viewpoint gestures in comparison with observer viewpoint gestures. Character viewpoint gestures seem to be particularly good at this semantic category because they can directly show the position of something in relation to the actor's body, the actor's body being central to the generation of a character viewpoint gesture. The actor's body can act as a point of reference, which is not the case with observer viewpoint gestures where the actor's body is necessarily absent. Indeed those character viewpoint gestures in the present study tended to involve relative position information that fell into a particular sub-category of relative position, namely the position of the entity with respect to a particular part of another entity, and character viewpoint gestures made up 86.6 per cent of this sub-category. Observer viewpoint gestures tended to contain relative position information that fell into the following two sub-categories: the position of a moving entity with respect to a fixed entity (83.3 per cent of these were observer viewpoint gestures); the position of a fixed entity with respect to another fixed entity (100 per cent of these were observer viewpoint gestures).

This experiment demonstrated how a fundamental property of iconic gesture, namely the viewpoint from which it is generated, relates to its communicative power. However, something else was observed in the current study that may have significant implications for our understanding of how iconic gestures work in everyday talk. As mentioned earlier, McNeill (1992) had proposed that character viewpoint gestures tend to be strongly associated with transitive clauses and observer viewpoint gestures with intransitive clauses. In the present corpus we found a perfect association between the transitivity of the clause and the viewpoint of the gesture.

We also found that there was a tendency for the participants to propose transitive structures (e.g. 'he's flicking a coin') in their answers after viewing character viewpoint gestures, and these structures occurred even if the participants could not identify any specific entity involved (e.g. 'he's flicking something' or 'an object is being flicked'). On the other hand, there was a tendency for participants to propose non-transitive answers, either involving intransitive structures or partial answers about the identity of objects (e.g. 'something that is long, thin and smooth') after viewing observer viewpoint gestures. A systematic analysis was therefore carried out of the proportion of answers suggesting a transitive structure for each gesture emanating from a character or from an observer viewpoint. It was found that when participants were watching character viewpoint gestures they were significantly more likely to generate a transitive answer than when they were watching observer viewpoint gestures. This result suggests that character viewpoint gestures convey significant semantic information, particularly about the relative position and somewhat less reliably the size of the actual entities involved in the event described, but also about the syntactic structure of the clause. The transitivity of the clause in the linguistic channel, in other words, seems to be partially signalled by the accompanying iconic gesture.

This discovery hints at the complex integration between language and that form of nonverbal communication studied here, namely the movement of the hands during talk. It suggests that the claim that verbal language and bodily movement are separate languages is wrong, at least as far as the movements of the hands are concerned. The nature of the gesture accompanying speech seems to tell the listener quite a lot about the underlying structure of the speech that it is accompanying. These two channels seem to be, in fact, highly integrated rather than separate.

Of course, this last experiment has its own particular limitations. It did not try to assess the power of iconic gestures generated from different viewpoints when they are presented alongside speech, but only when they are presented in isolation from speech. So the next experiment to be carried out really suggested itself. At the same time we tried to answer the question of why we use observer viewpoint gestures at all, given that they don't appear anything like as effective as character viewpoint gestures for communication purposes, with possibly one or two exceptions that really stood out.

The same 30 iconic gestures were used as in the previous experiment and were either shown in combination with the speech that they accompanied or the speech extracts were played on their own. Again, great care was taken in the scoring of the responses of the participants. Below is an example of how a participant's answer was scored. This example was taken from the video condition (where the gesture–speech combination was played to the participant).

she starts [spewing bubbles]

Iconic: Fingers on both hands point towards mouth area, then point upwards away from mouth.

After viewing the above gesture in the video condition one participant wrote: 'Somebody begins to spew bubbles out of their mouth and the bubbles move upwards away from their mouth.' Here the gesture was scored as having conveyed information to this participant about the categories *identity* (bubbles), *description of action* (spewing), *shape* (round), *movement* (yes), *direction* (upwards) and *relative position* (moving away from the mouth). No information was provided by the participant about the *speed* at which the bubbles were moving or about the *size* of the bubbles.

This experiment found that the overall mean accuracy score in the video condition, where participants could see the iconic gestures in addition to hearing the speech, was 56.8 per cent, whereas in the speech-only condition it was 48.6 per cent. Therefore, again there was a significant increase in information obtained about the semantic properties of the original cartoon when the iconic gestures are added to the speech. The overall percentage increase from the speech-only condition to the video condition for character viewpoint gestures was 10.6 per cent, but it was only half that – 5.7 per cent – for observer viewpoint gestures. Statistical tests revealed that character viewpoint gestures and observer viewpoint gestures both added a significant amount of information to speech, but character viewpoint gestures added more.

When the analysis was deconstructed to individual semantic categories, it was found that *relative position, size, identity, movement, direction* and *description of action* were communicated more effectively by character viewpoint gestures than by observer viewpoint gestures, whereas *shape* and *speed* were communicated more effectively by observer viewpoint gestures than by character viewpoint gestures.

This experiment again demonstrated that iconic gestures contain significant amounts of information. One aspect of iconic gestures that does influence their communicative effectiveness was also identified. It was found in the previous experiment that when iconic gestures were shown without their accompanying speech, character viewpoint gestures were significantly more communicative than observer viewpoint gestures, but here it was also found that character viewpoint gestures were more communicative when they were displayed alongside speech. Character viewpoint gestures were particularly good again at conveying information about the semantic category *relative position*. Verbal clauses associated with character viewpoint gestures seem to be particularly poor at conveying relative position information, but the accompanying gestures more than make up for this.

The present study found that things like *size*, *identity*, *movement*, *direction* and *description of action* were communicated more effectively by character viewpoint gestures than by observer viewpoint gestures. However, despite the overall communicational advantage of character viewpoint gestures, observer viewpoint gestures were actually better at communicating additional information about *speed* and *shape*. This might be because observer viewpoint gestures can show speed relative to a stationary observer and observer viewpoint gestures enable the shape of something to be mapped out with the hands – as if an observer was directly looking at something. The categories *speed* and *shape* did not reach overall statistical significance, however, due to the fact that, although some observer viewpoint gestures were very effective at communicating information about these categories, this effectiveness was not consistent across all observer viewpoint gestures.

One of the most interesting findings of this study was that there was no significant correlation, across gestures, between the increase in the percentage of correct answers in going from the speech-only condition to the video condition and the amount of accurate information transmitted in the gesture-only condition. The fact that there were no significant correlations here suggests that there is an important interaction between speech and gesture in the communication of meaning, rather than a fixed amount of information contained in the iconic gesture. In other words, speech and gesture clearly interact in complex ways in the communication of meaning.

A more detailed analysis of the data reveals that there are some gestures which are highly communicative in the absence of speech, but once speech is added their contribution to the communication of meaning becomes almost redundant. In addition, there are gestures that do not communicate in the absence of speech but do communicate effectively once the speech has signalled the current theme that is being articulated. There are also some gestures that are consistently effective in terms of communication in both situations, and others that are consistently ineffective in both.

Let me try to give you some idea of the number of gestures falling into each of these four categories. In order to do this, I rank ordered the communicative effectiveness of each gesture on its own and in terms of what it added to speech. I found that five gestures were good communicators in the gesture-only condition but poor communicators when they were added to speech; three of these gestures were produced from an observer viewpoint. There were also five gestures that were poor communicators in the gesture-only condition but good communicators when they were added to speech (again three of these were produced from an observer viewpoint). There were ten gestures that were good communicators in both conditions, and seven of these were produced from a character viewpoint. In the final cell there were ten gestures that were poor communicators in both conditions, and six of these were produced from an observer viewpoint.

An example of the category containing gestures that work better in the gesture-only condition than they do when they are added to speech is:

bouncing the ball [on the ground]

Iconic: Palm of right hand points downwards; hand moves rapidly downwards and upwards three times.

When this character viewpoint gesture was shown in the gesture-only condition it was found to convey a good deal of information about six semantic categories (namely identity 'a ball', description of action 'bouncing', shape 'round', movement 'yes', direction 'up and down', relative position 'the ball moving up and down between the hand and the ground'). Once speech was added to the gesture, however, the gesture became redundant with respect to all six of these semantic categories (although interestingly speed, i.e. the fact that the ball was being bounced very quickly, only tended to be mentioned in the video rather than in the gesture-only condition). In neither the gesture-only nor the video condition did participants get the size of the object correct; it was, in fact, a large ball. The overall percentage accuracy score for this gesture was 50.5 per cent in the gesture-only condition, whereas it was 75 per cent in the speech-only condition, increasing to 82.5 per cent in the video condition. The gesture therefore only added 7.5 per cent additional information to the speech.

Here is an example of an observer viewpoint gesture that was good at communicating information about shape (44 per cent accuracy) in the gesture-only condition, but once the speech was added the gesture becomes redundant (zero per cent additional information about *shape* and only 2.5 per cent overall additional information).

it's got two [long bench either side]

Iconic: Hands are close together, palms are pointing towards each other, hands move apart in a horizontal direction.

In the gesture only condition, this communicated to participants that the object being described was long (with very little information about what the object actually was), but when the speech was added the information provided by the gesture was clearly redundant.

On the other hand, some gestures can only successfully communicate about certain semantic categories once the speech has first provided some basic information. Below is an example of an observer viewpoint gesture that was relatively poor at communicating information about speed, or any of the other semantic categories, in gesture only. However, once the speech was added, the gesture then became more than just a flick of the hand – it became a male running very quickly out of his house, thus demonstrating the importance of the global meaning of the gesture in determining the meaning of the individual components of the gesture.

[runs out of his house] again

Iconic: Thumb of right hand is pointing upwards, other fingers are curled together. Hand moves upwards slightly and then to the right in a rapid movement.

In the gesture-only condition 14 per cent of the participants correctly identified the speed of this action, whereas in the video condition 90 per cent got this right (with zero per cent in the speech-only condition).

There are also a number of cases where the gesture conveyed a good deal of information both in isolation from speech and working alongside speech. For example:

[and gets covered in soup]

Iconic: Hands move to a position in front of the face; they then move apart and follow the curve of the face.

When this gesture was added to its accompanying speech, it provided participants with information about the *relative position* of the soup with respect to the character – it is the character's face that gets covered in soup. The gesture also demonstrated the *direction* in which the soup was moving and the *size* of the area that gets covered in soup. In the gesture-only condition the gesture conveyed information to participants about the same semantic categories, even though in this case they do not know what it is that is actually covering the face.

So this gesture not only conveyed important information both in isolation from and alongside speech, but also conveyed information about the same semantic categories in both cases. However, there are other gestures that are very effective at communicating when they are presented both alongside and in isolation from speech, but they convey information about quite different semantic categories in the two different cases. This relationship is exemplified by the following character viewpoint gesture:

by [pulling on his tie]

Iconic: Left hand moves quickly upwards; hand closes and a sharp downwards movement is made.

This gesture provided participants with information over and above that conveyed by the speech, particularly about the *speed* of the action (fast) and the *relative position* of the physical entities (the hand being wrapped around the tie). In the gesture-only condition, however, the gesture provided participants with information that mainly concerned the *size* (small) and the *shape* of the object involved (thin).

Some gestures are relatively poor at communicating information in isolation from speech and are still poor when they are added to speech. The observer viewpoint gesture below is an extreme example of this.

the [roof starts cracking]

Iconic: Index finger of left hand points vertically upwards, other fingers and thumb are slightly curled. Index finger moves to his left and then to his right.

It seems that when this type of gesture is presented without speech the gesture is simply too abstract for a participant to glean much information from it. Once the speech is added, it is clear to participants what the gesture is referring to, but now the gesture does not add any additional information to that already contained in the speech.

In summary, these experiments have found that iconic gestures do indeed have a significant communicative function. Although both character viewpoint gestures and observer viewpoint gestures are communicative, character viewpoint gestures have a communicational advantage over observer viewpoint gestures, particularly about *relative position*. It was found that the speech associated with character viewpoint gestures is particularly poor at conveying *relative position* information, but that the character viewpoint gesture more than adequately makes up for this and enables *relative position* information to be communicated very successfully to participants. It was also observed that there were no significant correlations between the amount of information that gestures add to speech and the amount of information they convey in the absence of speech, which suggests that there are a number of quite different relationships between the linguistic and gestural codes. In some cases the communicative effectiveness of the gesture depends wholly on the presence of the speech; in other cases the speech is much less necessary. The relationship between gestural viewpoint and the communication of individual semantic features was discovered to be a good deal more complex than a number of psychologists had anticipated. The strength of these experiments is that it is now more precisely known what semantic information is actually received by decoders from speech and from gesture, and hence it is felt that the current analyses provide a much better insight into how the linguistic and gestural codes interact in the communication of meaning.

The implications of this set of experiments are, however, quite clear. Gestures are a window on the human mind, because there is now detailed experimental evidence that there is a great deal of important information in these iconic gestures which is never articulated in speech itself. As McNeill (2000: 139) states: 'Utterances possess two sides, only one of which is speech; the other is imagery, actional and visuo-spatial. To exclude the gesture side, as has been traditional, is tantamount to ignoring half of the message out of the brain.'

This research has also demonstrated that some people seem to miss out on this information in the gesture channel almost completely; others are tuned in to it and quite unconsciously process this important information along with the speech itself. The difference in terms of the amount of information received between those who use the gestural information and those who do not is quite staggering.

Postscript: A number of amusing depictions of gestural communication and miscommunication can be seen in Quentin Tarantino's *Pulp Fiction*. In the 'overdose scene' Vincent (played by John Travolta) misinterprets the character viewpoint stabbing gesture of Lance to comic effect. Vincent thinks that Mia has to be stabbed through the heart with adrenaline three times because Lance makes a total of three stabbing gestures to show how Mia's breastplate has to be penetrated to resuscitate her with a shot of adrenaline. Of course, she did not have to be injected three times; Lance was just a little stressed and wanted to make clear what had to be done here.

In the second example, Jules misinterprets what Vincent is telling him about him being asked to 'take care' of Mia while her husband, the Big Man, is away. 'Take care of' can, of course, mean (when gangsters are talking) 'to kill someone'; in other more mundane spheres of life it more commonly means 'to look after'. Jules asks for clarification when he hears this expression by using a character viewpoint iconic gesture representing a gun being pointed to the head (accompanying 'take care of her?') and Vincent responds immediately to this iconic gesture ('No, man . . .'). Quentin Tarantino is obviously a film director who understands the communicative power and significance of iconic gestures.

Lance: Uh (0.4) you're giving her an injection of adrenaline (.)

Straight through her heart (.) but she's got (.) ah breast plates

You gotta (.) pierce through that

So what you gotta do is [you've got to bring the needle down (.) in a

<u>STABBING</u> motion]

Vincent: I go- I I: I gotta stab her <u>THREE</u> times?

Lance: NO YOU DON'T HAVE TO FUCKING STAB HER

THREE TIMES

YOU JUST HAVE TO STAB HER ONCE

BUT IT HAS TO BE HARD ENOUGH TO GET THROUGH (.) HER BREAST PLATE

INTO HER HEART (0.2) ALRIGHT?

Figure 9.1 Overdose scene from *Pulp Fiction* (for transcription conventions see Table 1.1, p. 5).

Vincent: What's her <u>name</u> again?

Jules: MIA

Vincent: Mia

Jules: Why are you so interested in <u>Big Man's</u> wife?

Vincent: Well he's going out of town to Florida and he asked

me if I (0.4) would take care of her while he's gone

Jules: [Take c:a:r:e of her?]

Vincent: <u>No</u> man (0.4) just take her out you know (0.4) show

her a good time make sure she don't get lonely

Figure 9.2 Jules gesturally showing his interpretation of Vincent saying 'take care of her' (for transcription conventions see Table 1.1, p. 5).

SUMMARY

- There are two different viewpoints that appear in the gestures people perform during narratives: observer viewpoint and character viewpoint.

- An observer viewpoint gesture displays an event from the viewpoint of an observer of the scene, with their hands playing the part of the character as a whole.

- A character viewpoint gesture incorporates the speaker's body into the gesture space, with the speaker's hands representing the hands of the character in the story.

- Certain semantic features, namely *relative position, size, identity, movement, direction* and *description of action*, are communicated more effectively by character viewpoint gestures, whereas *shape* and *speed* are communicated more effectively by observer viewpoint gestures.

- Some people seem to neglect the information in the gesture channel almost completely; others are tuned in to it and quite unconsciously process this important information along with the speech itself.

- The difference in terms of the amount of information received between those who use the gestural information and those who do not is genuinely staggering.

10

HOW OUR EYES
ARE DRAWN TO THE
GESTURES OF OTHERS

The research that I have described so far seems to be consistently showing that the spontaneous gestures that accompany speech can both represent and convey meaningful information to an addressee, and that addressees process this gestural information and combine it with the information in the speech itself. This research has also clearly demonstrated that many iconic gestures are highly communicative but it also shows that some gestures are significantly more communicative than others. The experimental evidence suggests that the particular semantic properties captured by the gestures are one crucial feature in determining the communicational value of the individual gesture – gestures that represent the 'relative position' of objects or the relative position of objects and characters and gestures that represent the 'size' of characters or objects are particularly communicative. Another significant variable, as we have just seen, is the particular viewpoint from which the gesture is generated.

The factors that affect the communicative power of individual gestures are obviously a crucial issue in communication research for both theoretical and practical reasons. In terms of theory, it is crucial because McNeill (1992) argues that human semantic communication *habitually* proceeds through both speech and iconic gesture working together. But why then are only certain gestures communicative? How general is the claim that iconic gestures are crucial to semantic communication? Why do some gestures appear to be much less significant? Is it because they are expressing essentially the same things as the speech itself and are therefore redundant? Or, is it because there is critical non-redundant information embedded within them but the listener/addressee/judge is failing to notice this information, perhaps because he or she is not attending to the gestures? In other words, is it something to do with the fundamental semiotic organisation of the two systems of speech and gesture, or merely to do with the psychological vagaries of how people attend, or fail to attend, to gesture, when they are in conversation? In terms of practical implications, the communicative power of individual gestures is also important because if we were ever to try to design more effective communications (such as TV ads or scripted and choreographed political presentations) involving this new theoretical perspective, then we might well need to know which iconic gestures to include in our messages and which to omit. And if we were to include specific gestures, what properties should they have to maximise their effectiveness?

One way into this question is to study the visual attention of listeners when they watch someone talk. Which particular types of gestures do they actually notice and why? And, how is this attentional focus reflected in their uptake of information from the accompanying gestures? We can now do this research using the latest eye-tracking technology to analyse the individual gaze fixations of listeners, 25 times every second, as they watch someone talk and gesture. The patterns of fixation of listeners could be highly revealing for this new theory of multi-modal communication.

But first we need a little bit of background about eye movements. It turns out that when we look at a scene our eyes move around continually, locating interesting points and building up a corresponding mental image. These small, rapid movements of the eyes are known as saccades. 'Between the saccades, our eyes remain relatively still during fixations for about 200–300ms' (Rayner 1998: 373). These fixations are thought to reduce image blur, allowing the visual system time to process the image (Turano et al. 2003: 333). Research has shown that little or no actual visual processing occurs during saccades (Fuchs 1971). We make saccades so frequently because the visual field is divided into three regions: foveal, parafoveal and peripheral; only the foveal region has very good acuity due to its high concentration of colour-sensitive photoreceptor cells called cone cells. So, we move our eyes in order to reorient the fovea on that area of the stimulus that we want to see accurately. The less central parts of the retina are mostly made up of rod cells, which are particularly good at motion detection.

Several studies have looked at gaze patterns in relation to gestures but few have directly investigated the relationship between fixation and the uptake of information from gestures. Gullberg and Holmqvist (1999, 2002) found that in face-to-face interaction with naturally occurring gestures, addressees fixated the speaker's face 96 per cent of the total viewing time. Only 0.5 per cent of the total viewing time was spent actually fixating gestures and only 7 per cent of all gestures were fixated. However, in another study, Nobe (2000) and Nobe et al. (1998) presented an anthropomorphic agent (instead of a real speaker) on a computer screen and found that addressees in this situation fixated the majority of gestures (as much as 75 per cent of the total). The authors suggested that these results may be due to the fact that using an anthropomorphic agent removes the social constraint of focusing attention on the speaker's face (see, for example, Argyle 1967) and allows greater fixation on other areas of the stimulus that might not be acceptable in face-to-face interaction. In an attempt to resolve these apparent contradictory results, Gullberg and Holmqvist (2006) investigated whether attention is modulated by changes in social situation (actual partner vs partner on video with fewer social obligations about focusing almost exclusively on the face) and display size of the stimulus. In all conditions, the face dominated as the addressees' fixation target and only a minority of gestures drew fixations. In another study, Gullberg and Kita (2009) attempted to establish whether the location of the gesture performance had an effect on the pattern or frequency of fixation. Gullberg (2003) noted that it is often presumed that those gestures performed in the speaker's peripheral gesture space attract overt visual attention. This is because the majority of a speaker's gestures are performed in the central gesture space, so if the addressee naturally fixates the speaker's face (Gullberg and Holmqvist 1999, 2002), then these centrally performed gestures will already be in the peripheral vision of the addressee and will not require any overt head movements or eye movements in order to interpret them. If, however, the speaker performs a gesture in their peripheral gesture space this gesture will only appear in the addressee's extreme peripheral vision and therefore may well attract more direct visual attention. However, Gullberg and Kita (2009) actually found that the location of gesture performance had little discernible impact on the addressees' fixation.

Although Gullberg and Holmqvist's (2002) study found that participants' tendency to fixate the gestures was very low, certain types of gestures were found to reliably attract higher levels of fixation. These were termed 'holds', those momentary cessations in the movement of a gesture, and 'auto-fixations', those gestures that were fixated by the encoder themselves.

During 'holds', the movement of a gesture comes to a stop and thus the peripheral vision is no longer sufficient for obtaining information from that gesture, thus necessitating a degree of fixation. 'Autofixations', on the other hand, serve as a powerful social cue to joint attention in an interactive setting. The authors attributed the low frequencies of gesture fixation generally to the fact that peripheral vision is sufficient for detecting broad gestural information, such as location, direction and size, provided that the gestures are moving.

Although this research on gesture fixation is quite illuminating with respect to the frequency with which people attend to gestures in face-to-face communication, it does not test the relationship between the fixation of gestures and the amount of information received from them, and indeed whether gestures that attract the highest levels of fixation are those that are most communicative.

We therefore decided to investigate the levels of fixation of gestures with different properties, and the relationship between the level of fixation and the uptake of information from those gestures (although Gullberg and Kita 2009 did consider information uptake from gestures, their study was solely concerned with directional information, i.e. left or right). The gestures in the present study were designed to encode core semantic features like size, relative position, shape and movement and not just directional information. In order to measure clearly the information picked up by participants from the target gestures, the participants were asked questions after watching the clips; the information needed to answer these questions was only encoded in the gesture and not in the speech itself.

The study was based on a sample of ten college students. A remote eye tracker was set up in a laboratory, in front of a computer monitor on which the stimulus material was to be shown. The eye tracker employed a camera surrounded by infrared-emitting diodes to illuminate the eye of the participant looking at the screen. Each participant's point of gaze on the screen was determined by the camera combining the position of the pupil and the corneal reflection. The remote camera in the eye tracker fed into a screen for the experimenter's observation of the positioning of camera observing the eye. From a separate computer, the experimenter was able to adjust the illumination of the infrared camera and the 'Pan/Tilt' of the camera in the eye tracker to enable recognition of the pupil and corneal reflection. The stimulus material consisted of 12 short video clips, each lasting between 5 and 20 seconds. Each video clip contained one scripted gesture (based on real examples but re-enacted for the experiment), and there were three clips for each of the four gesture categories. Each short video clip was followed by two 'Yes/No' questions. For example, one of the video clips showed the actor saying:

'There's a guy, you can only see one of the guys but he's obviously playing beach ball with somebody or something um on the edge of a pier and he goes to hit it and is just about to fall off the end of it into the [water], um and just about catches himself and doesn't fall.'

Iconic: Left hand is low at left side of body with palm facing down and fingers spread; hand moves slightly towards the right in front of body.

The gesture in this clip coincided with the word 'water'. The two questions following the clip, which related to the information encoded in the gesture alone, were:

'Is the man quite far away from the water? (Y/N)' and

'Is the water still? (Y/N)'

We decided on four categories of gesture, varying on two dimensions – first, 'viewpoint' (either 'observer viewpoint' or 'character viewpoint'), and second, 'span' (or duration). After studying a number of naturally occurring gestures, and marking the trajectories of their stroke phases on gesture space diagrams (derived from McNeill 1992), two categories of gesture *span* were identified. 'High Span' gestures refer to those gestures that cross at least two major boundaries (solid lines) on the gesture space diagram (see Figure 10.1) and 'Low Span' gestures are those that cross no major boundaries on the diagram. This meant that we ended up with four categories, which our actor had to perform:

'Observer-Viewpoint' and 'High Span' (high span O-VPT)

'Observer-Viewpoint' and 'Low Span' (low span O-VPT)

'Character-Viewpoint' and 'High Span' (high span C-VPT)

'Character-Viewpoint' and 'Low Span' (low span C-VPT)

Figure 10.2(a)–(d) shows the spans of the 12 gestures scripted for the video clips. Some gestures were produced in the central space, others in the peripheral space and others crossed between both spaces.

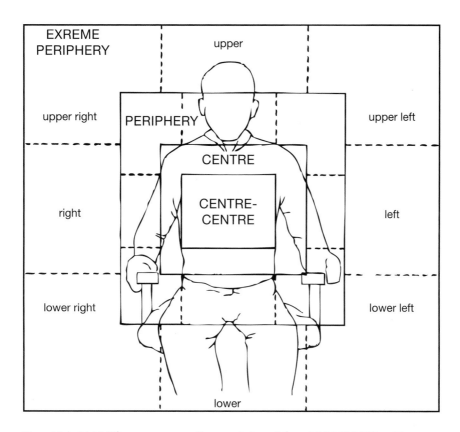

Figure 10.1 McNeill's gesture space diagram (adapted from McNeill 1992, with permission from University of Chicago Press).

The order of the clips was selected for the participant by the experimenter and each participant was reminded that, in order to answer questions during the experiment, they had only to press the 'Y' and 'N' keys on the keyboard, so if possible they should try to keep their hand resting over the keys so that they did not have to look down every time they answered a question. Participants were then asked to start the experiment in their own time by pressing the 'space bar'.

The output was in the form of a video-recording of the computer screen as the participant had seen it during the experiment, with a small black fixation marker overlaid, which told us where the participant had been looking whilst they were attending to the video clips. The fixation marker shown in the output moved around the screen to represent the participant's point of gaze on their screen as they watched the video clips. Gaze fixations,

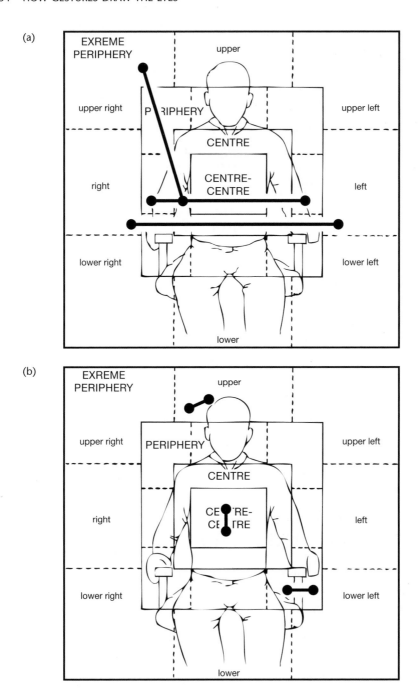

Figure 10.2 (a) Spans of the three O-VPT, High span gestures (b) Spans of the three O-VPT, Low span gestures (c) Spans of the three C-VPT, High span gestures (d) Spans of the three C-VPT, Low span gestures.

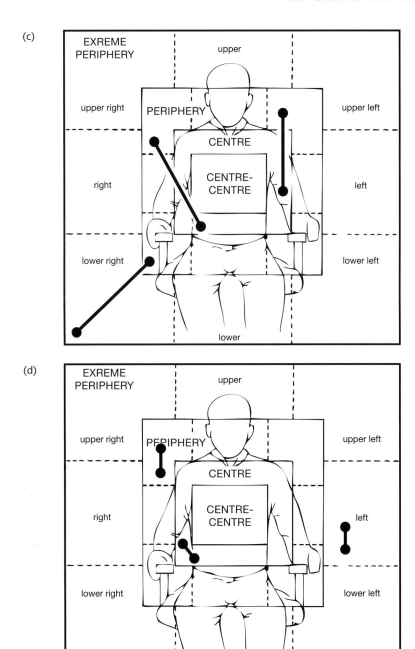

Figure 10.2 continued

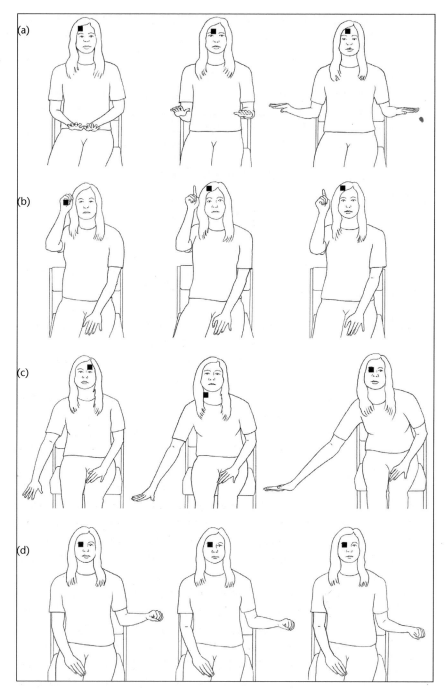

Figure 10.3 (a) O-VPT, High span gesture (b) O-VPT, Low span gesture (c) C-VPT, High span gesture (d) C-VPT, Low span gesture (taken from Beattie *et al.* 2010).

blinks, saccades and other eye movements could all be distinguished from the output for each individual. Figure 10.3(a)–(d) shows examples of the output from four of the clips presented to the participants; the frames selected illustrate the stroke phases of one gesture from each of the four gesture categories, indicating the differences between high span and low span gestures. The black fixation marker can be clearly seen on each frame, indicating fixation of the face, the gesture and so on.

Coding areas of fixation

The full recording of each participant's eye gaze during the experiment was converted into individual frames of 25 per second, so each frame represented a time span of 40 milliseconds (or 0.04 seconds) from the original data. The 12 gestures scripted for presentation to participants contained an assortment of different gesture properties other than span and viewpoint. Some gestures were performed in the peripheral gesture space, whilst others were performed centrally. Some gestures included 'holds' and 'speaker fixation', both of which have been found to increase levels of decoder fixation (Gullberg and Holmqvist 2002: 209).

The first stage of coding involved the scoring of each different area fixated by the participants whilst they were watching the 12 video clips. Before coding of the fixation areas began, it was necessary to identify different areas that could potentially be fixated. We came up with six categories here: face, torso, hand gesturing, other body, background, hand still (not gesturing); these were labelled 1–6 for ease of scoring. The frame numbers marking the beginning and end of each of the 12 clips were recorded in detail for each participant, as were the frames that marked the beginning and end of each of the 12 gestures (focusing on the stroke phase only, using McNeill's classification, 1992: 25), and the frame numbers at the beginning and end of each period of fixation on any of the six areas determined above. For example, the scoring for one gesture viewed by Participant 1 is illustrated in Table 10.1.

An area was counted as fixated if the fixation marker remained on that same area for at least three frames (representing a time of 120 milliseconds, or 0.12 seconds), following Gullberg and Holmqvist (2002: 209).

It is clear from the example in Table 10.1 that there was a slight delay between the beginning of the video clip and the participant's gaze moving to the first area of fixation (in this example, the interval between frame numbers 7153 and 7165). As the gaze moved between different areas of fixation, the fixation marker was in motion and so was not counted as

Table 10.1 An example of the scoring of fixation areas for one participant

Gesture type	Start and end of clip	Frames	Area fixated	Gesture	Gesture fixated?
C-VPT	7153–7376	7165–7168	Background	7244–7287	Y
		7169–7244	Face		
		7247–7269	Gesture		
		7273–7376	Face		

Source: Taken from Beattie et al. 2010

fixating any particular area until it had settled to a clearly defined black marker. Figure 10.4 is an illustration of one participant's fixation behaviour during their viewing of a single video clip. Their sequence of fixations began on the face (1), moving to background (2), then back to face (3), then to torso (4), and leg (5), then back to face (6), then to hand gesturing (7) and then back to face (8).

Next, the frame numbers were converted to time durations, with each frame representing 40 milliseconds of real time. This enabled the

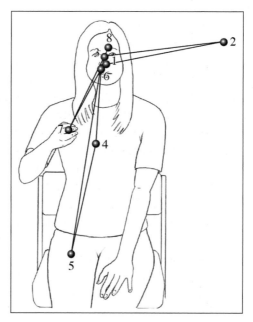

Figure 10.4 The pattern of gaze fixation of a participant during the viewing of one video clip (taken from Beattie et al. 2010).

experimenters to work out the length of each video clip, the proportion of time participants spent fixating different areas in each clip, how long the stroke phase of the different types of gestures themselves lasted for, and so on. Information is only extracted from a scene during fixations. Short deviations from the area of fixation, caused by saccades or eye blinks lasting just a few frames, were not coded. Therefore, the time intervals represented general time spent fixating one particular area before the eye gaze moved to a distinctly different area, regardless of small divergences such as blinks and saccades. If the tracker was absent from the original area of fixation for longer than a few frames and if it moved in a different direction far away from the area, not just straight down and back up (as for a blink), the area was coded as 'Other' and the frame numbers were marked so that these times could be taken into account for working out average fixation times.

Coding participants' answers

Each participant answered 24 'Yes/No' questions in total, two questions following each video clip and relating to the information encoded by the gesture presented in the clip. Answers for the four different categories of gesture (O-H, O-L, C-H and C-L) were separated. Each participant viewed three examples of each category of gesture in the 12 video clips. The percentage of correct answers for the questions (six in total) relating to the three gestures of each category was calculated for each individual participant, rendering ten percentage scores for each gesture category. These percentages of correct answers could then be compared with the percentage of time participants spent fixating the gestures in the different categories.

We found that, overall, participants spent most time fixating the speaker's face (an average of 84.9 per cent of participants' overall looking time was spent fixating on the face), followed by other regions of the body (2.7 per cent), and followed by the gestures (2.1 per cent) and lastly the background (0.5 per cent). On average, 9.8 per cent of the overall time was coded as participants looking at 'Other'. Figures 10.5 and 10.6 show the areas actually fixated by participants (i.e. removing the 'Other' category from the calculations), first divided into facial and non-facial fixations, and then showing a breakdown of all non-facial fixation averages.

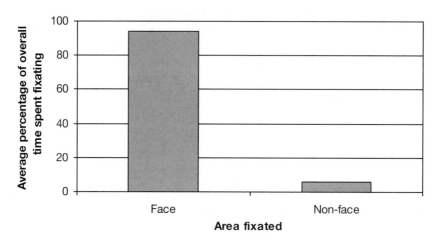

Figure 10.5 The average percentage of time spent fixating different areas of the visual scene (taken from Beattie *et al.* 2010).

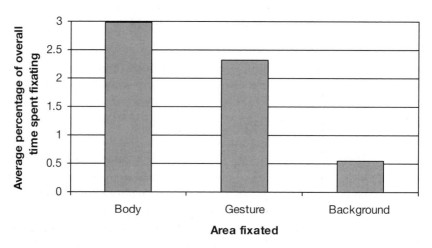

Figure 10.6 The average percentage of time spent fixating non-facial areas (taken from Beattie *et al.* 2010).

Which gestures are looked at most?

Of the small percentage of time spent fixating the gestures, there was a degree of variation in the way in which the gestures were fixated. Some gestures were not fixated at all, and some types of gesture were fixated more than others. The low span C-VPT gestures attracted more fixations than any of the other categories of gestures (32.7 per cent of fixations of all gestures

Table 10.2 How C-VPT gestures were fixated overall

	Fixated	Not fixated
High Span	9	21
Low Span	17	13

Source: Taken from Beattie et al. 2010

were in this category), although not significantly so. High span O-VPT and low span O-VPT gestures attracted the same number of fixations from participants (25 per cent) and high span C-VPT attracted the least fixations (17.3 per cent). With C-VPT gestures, the low span gestures were significantly more likely to be fixated than the high span gestures.

How long is spent looking at each type of gesture?

Given that the low span C-VPT gestures were fixated on more frequently than any other type of gesture, the actual time spent looking at each type of gesture was determined (see Table 10.3), and the average percentage of the stroke phases of each type of gesture that participants fixated was compared (see Table 10.4). The results show that low span C-VPT gestures were looked at for the longest percentage of their duration. Statistical analysis revealed that there was a significant main effect for span, but no significant main effect for viewpoint and no significant interaction effect between span and viewpoint. Statistical analysis of the average duration of fixation on the stroke phase, however, shows that there is a significant interaction effect between span and viewpoint but no significant main effect for span or for viewpoint. On average, participants fixated low span C-VPT gestures for 26.5 per cent of their duration, and looked for an average of 0.31 seconds. Low span O-VPT gestures received the next highest percentage-of-duration fixation, at 16.7 per cent of the stroke phase. The gestures that were fixated for the shortest percentage of their duration were the high span C-VPT gestures, which were only looked at for 9.4 per cent of the stroke phase, although on average the high span C-VPT gestures were fixated for slightly longer in terms of actual time (0.13 seconds) than the low span O-VPT gestures (0.12 seconds).

Table 10.3 The average duration of gesture fixations for each gesture category (in seconds)

	Observer Viewpoint	Character Viewpoint
High Span	0.18	0.13
Low Span	0.12	0.31

Source: Taken from Beattie et al. 2010

Table 10.4 The average percentage of the stroke phase of the gesture that participants fixated

	Observer Viewpoint	Character Viewpoint
High Span	12.2	9.4
Low Span	16.7	26.5

Source: Taken from Beattie et al. 2010

How did participants' fixation styles vary?

Of the 120 gestures presented in the video clips, 52 gestures in total were fixated by one or more of the ten participants. Naturally there was a great deal of variation when it came to the length of time that participants fixated each gesture that was presented to them. Some were quick to move their visual attention to the gesture once the stroke phase began, presumably having been attracted by the preparation phase of the gesture and coordinating their fixation perfectly with the beginning of the stroke phase, although no participants were found to begin fixating before the start of the stroke phase itself. Other participants took longer to begin fixating the gesture. Some moved their gaze away from the gesture before the stroke phase had finished, whilst others fixated the gesture for its full length, even continuing to fixate the area in which the gesture had been performed after the hand or hands had started to move away. Of course, there were those who did not fixate certain gestures or, in the case of one of the participants, any gestures at all. Figure 10.7 is a representation of Participant 5's fixation behaviour, giving an indication of the onset and offset of their gesture fixations on a selection of the gestures that they fixated. Gesture 2 is a high span O-VPT gesture, Gesture 5 is a low span O-VPT gesture and Gesture 12 is a low span C-VPT gesture. Participant 5 did not fixate any of the three high span C-VPT gestures presented to them. The words 'on' and 'off' above the gesture-accompanying speech give an indication as to the participant's onset and offset of fixation, relative to the stroke phase of the gesture, which is indicated by square brackets. Participant 5 fixated five out of the 12 gestures, which themselves varied greatly in length (between 0.56 seconds and 1.88 seconds). Of the gestures that Participant 5 fixated, the fixation onsets began at different points relative to the onset of the stroke phase of the gestures and the fixation offsets likewise corresponded differentially to the end of the stroke phases. Participant 5's fixation onsets had a range of +0.28 seconds to +0.40 seconds, relative to the beginning of the stroke phase. Their fixation offsets ranged between −0.80 seconds and 0 seconds relative to the ends of the stroke phases; in other words, each one of

Figure 10.7 An illustration of one participant's onsets and offsets of fixation relative to a selection of the gestures' stroke phases (taken from Beattie et al. 2010).

Participant 5's fixations finished either before the end of the stroke phase of the gesture, or at the same time as the end of the stroke phase. The range of onset of all fixations (for all participants) was from 0 seconds (i.e. fixation begins at the same time as the start of the stroke phase) to +1.40 seconds (i.e. fixation begins 1.4 seconds after the onset of the gesture). The range of offset of fixations was from −3.08 seconds (i.e. fixation ends 3.08 seconds before the stroke phase of the gesture ends) to +1.36 seconds (i.e. fixation ends 1.36 seconds after the stroke phase of the gesture ends).

How well did participants answer the questions and how did this correlate with fixation?

Each participant answered two 'Yes/No' questions after viewing each video clip (with a 50 per cent likelihood that the questions could be answered correctly by chance). All participants scored highly on the questions, with an average result of 78.9 per cent, and a range between 63 per cent and 92 per cent. Although none of the correlations were significant for any of the gesture categories, there were stronger positive correlations between information uptake and duration of fixation for the low span gestures. In addition, participants scored best on questions relating to low span C-VPT gestures, with an average score of 83.3 per cent, although the worst average score was 71.7 per cent for low span O-VPT gestures (the other two both had average scores of 80 per cent, see Table 10.5). However, statistical analyses revealed no significant effect of span or viewpoint on the proportion of correct answers.

These results are based around the averages for the ten participants. Table 10.6 shows an in-depth description of the behaviour of a single participant (Participant 8) during the experiment. The gestures in clip numbers 1–3 are O-H, numbers 4–6 are O-L, numbers 7–9 are C-H and numbers 10–12 are C-L.

Table 10.5 Percentage of correct answers to probe questions for the four categories and for span and viewpoint independently

	Low span %	High span %	Viewpoint %
C-VPT %	81.70	80.00	80.83
O-VPT %	71.70	80.00	75.83
Span %	79.99	76.67	

Source: Taken from Beattie *et al.* 2010

Table 10.6 The fixation behaviour of Participant 8 during their viewing of the 12 video clips

	Area fixated	Length of fixation (seconds)	Time fixating area as % of overall clip length	Length of stroke phase (seconds)	Percentage of stroke phase fixated	Onset of gesture fixation (seconds)*	Offset of gesture fixation (seconds)**
Clip 1 (8.84 s)	Face	7.96	90.0				
	Body	0.24	2.7				
	Other	0.64	7.2	1.36	0	N/A	N/A
Clip 2 (11.88 s)	Face	8.96	75.4				
	Body	1.40	11.8				
	Other	1.52	12.8	1.44	0	N/A	N/A
Clip 3 (11.88 s)	Face	11.24	94.6				
	Gesture	0.12	1.0	1.44	5.6	+1.36	+0.04
	Other	0.52	4.4				
Clip 4 (9.88 s)	Face	6.96	70.4				
	Gesture	1.08	10.9	1.00	72.0	+0.28	+0.36
	Body	0.40	4.0				
	Other	1.44	14.6				
Clip 5 (9.88 s)	Face	6.96	70.4				
	Body	0.72	7.3				
	Other	2.20	22.3	0.64	0	N/A	N/A

Table 10.6 continued

	Area fixated	Length of fixation (seconds)	Time fixating area as % of overall clip length	Length of stroke phase (seconds)	Percentage of stroke phase fixated	Onset of gesture fixation (seconds)*	Offset of gesture fixation (seconds)**
Clip 6 (15.88 s)	Face	15.36	96.7				
	Other	0.52	3.3				
				0.48	0	N/A	N/A
Clip 7 (8.92 s)	Face	5.84	65.5				
	Gesture	0.68	7.6	1.64	41.5	0	-0.96
	Body	0.88	9.9				
	Other	1.52	17.0				
Clip 8 (12.88 s)	Face	9.96	77.3				
	Body	1.12	8.7				
	Gesture	0.56	4.3	1.00	24.0	+0.76	+0.32
	Other	1.24	9.6				
Clip 9 (18.88 s)	Face	13.76	72.9				
	Body	0.68	3.6				
	Gesture	0.12	0.6	1.00	12.0	+0.08	-0.80
	Other	4.32	22.9				

Clip 10 (9.88 s)	Face	8.28	83.8				
	Body	0.12	1.2				
	Gesture	0.68	6.9	1.56	43.6	+0.04	−0.84
	Other	0.80	8.1				
Clip 11 (11.92 s)	Face	8.80	73.8				
	Body	0.36	3.0				
	Gesture	0.44	3.7	1.04	42.3	+0.40	−0.20
	Other	2.32	19.5				
Clip 12 (12.88 s)	Face	8.72	67.7				
	Gesture	0.68	5.3	0.96	70.8	0	−0.28
	Body	0.60	4.7				
	Other	2.88	22.4				

Source: Taken from Beattie et al. 2010

*Onset of gesture fixation refers to onset in relation to the beginning of the stroke phase of the gesture

** Offset of gesture fixation refers to the offset of fixation in relation to the end of the stroke phase of the gesture (− means offset occurs before the end of the stroke phase of the gesture, + means offset occurs after the stroke phase of the gesture has finished)

Table 10.7 Participant 8's average fixation times and question scores

Gesture category	Average time spent fixating gestures (seconds)	Average score in answering questions (%)
Observer VPT – High Span	0.01	66.7
Observer VPT – Low Span	0.24	66.7
Character VPT – High Span	0.35	100.0
Character VPT – Low Span	0.60	100.0

Source: Taken from Beattie *et al.* 2010

This particular study thus seemed to show that iconic gestures elicit little direct visual attention even when participants are presented with a speaker on a computer screen, which, of course, excludes the normal social conventions about where to look in actual interaction. The face seems to be the natural focus for visual attention (84.9 per cent of the total time) when viewing a person speaking, with iconic gestures attracting direct visual attention only 2.1 per cent of the time. In many ways this is a remarkable result given the demonstrated importance of the information contained within these gestures. However, the research also demonstrated conclusively that there appears to be little relationship overall between the amount of time we spend fixating these gestures and the uptake of information from them. It would appear that a good deal of information can be extracted from these dynamic, iconic movements through peripheral vision without having to change or modify our direct focus of attention for gestures as a whole.

The study also showed that a certain type of character viewpoint gesture, namely the low span variety, attracted the highest frequency of fixation out of all the gesture categories. They were also fixated for the longest duration, and fixated for the highest percentage of the duration of the stroke phase. Perhaps as a result of this increased fixation, participants scored highest when answering probe questions relating to these gestures. In other words, peripheral vision may be adequate for most purposes but central fixation may still provide an advantage in terms of information processing. As Ducrot and Grainger (2007) have suggested, 'It is a well-established fact that information available from peripherally presented stimuli is of lower quality, due to the decrease in visual acuity, than information extracted from centrally presented stimuli' (2007: 589). Although there are no significant correlation coefficients between scores on the semantic probe questions and duration of fixation, it would seem that some relationship does exist between these two variables for this category. This might partly explain previous research which appears to show that C-VPT gestures are particularly communicative. This would make perfect sense if the majority of the gestures in the previous sample were relatively low span.

The overall message would appear to be that when we listen to speech and in addition watch the speaker move in that animated way that they do when they are speaking, we are very selective about allowing our attention to move away from its natural focus of regard – the human face. Occasionally, our visual focus does move from the face and centres on the gestural movements that accompany speech, but this seems to happen more with some categories of gestural movements than others. Low span character viewpoint gestures seem to be viewed most frequently, with the greatest average duration of fixation (0.31 seconds) and with the highest proportion of the stroke phase of the gesture fixated. Presumably this occurs because these low span character viewpoint gestures require more direct visual attention to extract their essential meaning, the essential meaning that is crucial to the fully embodied utterance and ultimately to the underlying communicative intent of the speaker him/herself. Gestures are very powerful in terms of human communication, and our eyes seem to be drawn to them, but in a highly selective way that hints at some of the mysteries still to be discovered.

SUMMARY

- Iconic gestures elicit little direct visual attention even when participants are presented with a speaker on a computer screen, which, of course, excludes the normal social conventions about where to look in actual interaction.

- The face seems to be the natural focus for visual attention (84.9 per cent of the total time) when viewing a person speaking, with iconic gestures attracting direct visual attention only 2.1 per cent of the time.

- This is a remarkable result given the demonstrated importance of the information contained within these gestures.

- There appears to be little relationship *overall* between the amount of time we spend fixating these gestures and the uptake of information from them.

- A good deal of information is extracted from these dynamic, iconic movements through peripheral vision without having to change or modify our direct focus of attention for gestures as a whole.
- A certain type of character viewpoint gesture, namely the low span variety, attracted the highest frequency of fixation out of all the gesture categories.
- These gestures were also fixated for the longest duration, and fixated for the highest percentage of the duration of the stroke phase.
- Participants scored highest when answering probe questions relating to low span character viewpoint (C-VPT) gestures.
- Peripheral vision may be adequate for most purposes when processing gestures, but central fixation may still provide an advantage in terms of information processing.
- This might partly explain previous research which appears to show that C-VPT gestures are particularly communicative.
- When we listen to speech and in addition watch the speaker move in that animated way that they do when they are speaking, we are very selective about allowing our attention to move away from its natural focus of regard – the human face.
- Occasionally, our visual focus does move from the face and centres on the gestural movements that accompany speech, but this seems to happen more with some categories of gestural movements than others.
- We can hypothesise that low span C-VPT gestures require more direct visual attention to extract their essential meaning.
- Gestures are very powerful in terms of human communication, and our eyes are drawn to them, but *selectively*.
- This hints at some of the mysteries still to be discovered.

11

'THE GESTURE LIMITS ITSELF INTELLIGENTLY TO WHAT MATTERS'

So by now we know that gestures do carry significant amounts of information when they accompany speech. But (and this is a very big 'but') how do we know whether this information is *important* or not? Consider the following example. From this gesture, you can clearly see that it is a large table. But why did the speaker not say 'The large table can be raised up towards the ceiling'? Why was the size of the table encoded here in gesture

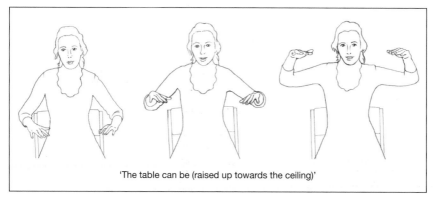

'The table can be (raised up towards the ceiling)'

Figure 11.1 A gesture showing a table moving up (redrawn from Beattie and Shovelton 2006).

rather than in the speech itself? Indeed what psychological, pragmatic or semantic factors determine which particular aspects of meaning are encoded by speech and which by gesture? In McNeill's much-quoted example ('she chases him out again'), why did the encoder use an iconic gesture to represent the weapon being used in the chasing? Why did the speaker not explicitly say 'she chases him out again with an umbrella'? Alternatively, why did the speaker not say 'she chases him out with an umbrella' and employ an iconic gesture to represent the recurrence of the action? In principle, you can imagine the relationship between what was actually said in the example and the accompanying gesture being quite different; you can even imagine no gesture at all. So what principles govern what information is encoded in which modality?

In McNeill's (1992) book *Hand and Mind* he addresses this very issue through detailed analyses of individual examples. He quotes the work of Arnheim, who wrote that 'the gesture limits itself intelligently to what matters' (1969: 117), and McNeill argues that this is exactly what his analyses here demonstrate. However, the logic of his analyses does require careful scrutiny. For example, in describing a scene in which Sylvester, a cartoon cat, goes up a pipe, McNeill writes:

> By looking at the gestures, we can discover, for each person, what was highlighted, what was relevant and what not, and from this infer the iconic side of their utterances. The five up-the-pipe gestures demonstrate how individual speakers made their own choices of what was salient.
>
> (McNeill 1992: 110)

What McNeill discovered was that all five speakers included upward movement in their gestures and all omitted any detail about the character's appearance. However, McNeill's next quote is critical: 'But each speaker also emphasized other details [in their gestures] that were not emphasized by the others' (1992: 110). So according to McNeill, for one speaker 'clambering' was salient, for another 'interiority' was important and for another both 'interiority' and 'manner of movement' were crucial. McNeill argues that iconic gestures contain information crucial to that *particular speaker* at that *particular time* for the process of communication, and that what is crucial in this story differs from one speaker to another. Indeed, McNeill claims that we can use the gestures to provide a genuine insight into the minds of the speakers to this level of specificity.

But how can McNeill support such conclusions? How can he validate the interpretations he makes – interpretations about the ongoing mental state of his experimental participants at particular points in time? What evidence do we have that the various speakers held different semantic properties to be the crucial ones in their actual communication? To go back to the example at the beginning of this chapter, the multidimensional iconic gesture here communicates a number of things when a table with people sitting around it suddenly shoots upwards. It captures *simultaneously* the size of the table, the fact that there is movement involved, the high speed of movement and the direction upwards of the table all in one single gestural movement. The action of the table at this point in the narration is undoubtedly important to the story as a whole. In other words, this is a moment of high 'communicative dynamism' (Firbas 1964), but why are certain features (both connected with properties of the object and aspects of the action) encoded in the iconic gesture? Why not other features – like the shape of the table, or the fact that there is a pole right up the middle of it, or that people are seated at the table? This might be especially important given the fact that when people are seated at a table that shoots upwards to the ceiling, this can cause chaos! Communicative dynamism is an important concept but perhaps one that is currently too broad to allow us to conclude that iconic gestures really do limit themselves to 'what matters'. How could we show that a particular gesture communicating particular features, namely size/ movement/speed/direction, was selecting the most important things for that particular speaker? This is clearly going to be very difficult but also very important. My proposed solution was to substitute a different and much simpler question. Taking the size of the table in Figure 11.1 (and ignoring temporarily all the other features), could we find any evidence that the size of the table (i.e. very large) was critical to that particular narrative by asking external judges to make an evaluation? This would not allow us to read the minds of the original speakers at the point in time but it would provide some partial evidence of potential judged 'importance'. The beauty of focusing first on *size* information is that we know that gestures are good at communicating this feature (from the experiments that I have so far described), but so too is speech. We do, after all, have a rich and varied size vocabulary ('teeny', 'minuscule', 'small', 'below average' . . .). So what examples of size information end up in gesture and what examples end up in speech?

Again this experiment involved ten encoders who were asked to narrate three cartoon stories (*Billy Whizz*, *Ivy the Terrible* and *Korky the Cat*). Ten additional participants, who were also students from the same university, were asked to be judges and score aspects of the stories. The encoders were individually invited into a room and were told that they were taking part in an experiment that investigated 'how well people could tell stories so that others could understand them'. They were then asked to narrate spontaneously the three cartoon stories that were projected, in a random order, onto a wall in front of them. The same cartoon stories were used for each encoder. One of the experimenters stayed in the room throughout the experiment acting as an interlocutor for the task, encouraging the participants to talk. The video-recorded cartoon narrations were analysed by the two experimenters. Following McNeill (1992: 78), all visible hand and arm movements produced by the encoders were put into two categories: gestures and non-gestural movements. Our method of categorisation coded 59 hand and arm movements as being iconic gestures.

For any narration, where an encoder produced one or more iconic gestures, the whole narration, including the iconic gestures, was transcribed.

Table 11.1(a) Number of times each instance of size information was encoded in speech only, gesture only or speech and gesture, or not mentioned (a sample from the cartoon *Korky the Cat* only)

Instances of size	Speech only	Gesture only	Speech & gesture	Not mentioned in speech or gesture
Size of dog's teeth	—	—	—	8
Size of dog's body	—	—	—	8
Size of fence	—	—	—	8
Size of dog's basket	—	—	—	8
Size of "ball" that is made	—	3	—	5
Size of string	—	—	—	8
Size of dog's stride	—	—	—	8
Size of bounce	—	1	—	7
Size of throw	—	—	—	8
Size of basket ball net	—	—	—	8
Size of hole in net	—	1	—	7
Size of wall	—	—	—	8
Size of dog's smile	—	—	—	8
Size of Korky the cat	1	—	—	7

Source: Taken from Beattie and Shovelton 2006

By carefully examining the three original cartoons the experimenters identified all possible instances of size information. In total there were 144 cases in which size information could be identified, which were distributed across the three cartoons. For example, in a story about Korky the Cat we identified the size of the kittens, the size of the basket, the size of the dog's mouth and so on. Some other examples of size, taken from the Korky the Cat cartoon, can be seen in column 1, Table 11.1(a) and (b).

We carefully examined the transcripts of the video-recorded narrations and marked every occurrence of size information so that we could identify how size was actually encoded. We identified whether size information was encoded just in the speech (column 2, Table 11.1(a)), just in gesture (column 3, Table 11.1(a)), in both speech and gesture (column 4, Table 11.1(a)) or in neither speech nor gesture (column 5, Table 11.1(a)). We then presented ten judges with the original cartoon stories and the list of all possible instances of size information which had been identified by the

Table 11.1(b) How the ten judges responded to each of the instances of size information (a sample from the cartoon Korky the Cat only)

Instances of size	No. of judges who rated instance in top 5	Individual judge's ratings
Size of dog's teeth	0	—
Size of dog's body	0	—
Size of fence	0	—
Size of dog's basket	0	—
Size of "ball" that is made	10	1; 2; 1; 1; 1; 1; 1; 1; 1; 3; 2;
Size of string	0	—
Size of dog's stride	0	—
Size of bounce	2	4; 3;
Size of throw	1	3;
Size of basket ball net	1	5;
Size of hole in net	2	4; 2;
Size of wall	0	—
Size of dog's smile	0	—
Size of Korky the cat	6	3; 5; 5; 3; 5; 5;

Source: Taken from Beattie and Shovelton 2006

experimenters. We asked the judges to 'Please read the cartoon story all the way through and then pick out the five instances of size information, from the list, that are most important to the story as a whole. The best way to do this is to think "If the size information was different, would it affect the nature and the outcome of the story?" Please rate these five instances of size information from 1 to 5, with 1 being the most important.'

For each possible instance of size information we had a measure of whether that example was represented just in the speech, just in gesture, in both speech *and* gesture or not mentioned. We also counted the number of judges who rated that particular instance of size information as being in the top five for the story as a whole (see Table 11.1(b), which also includes what the ratings actually were). For example, the size of Korky was rated as being in the top five most important size instances by six judges – four of these judges rated it as '5' and two judges rated it as '3'.

We found that size information was encoded in *speech only* on 20 occasions in the 20 narrations where one or more gestures occurred. For example:

'There are some little kittens in the basket.'

With no gesture accompanying the utterance.

We also found that size information was encoded in *gesture only* on 26 occasions in the same 20 narrations. In other words, size information was marginally more likely to be encoded in the gestural modality than in the speech modality. For example:

'It's on a [pole which] moves up and down.'

Iconic: Hands wide apart, palms pointing towards each other, fingers curved; hands make two large rapid movements up and down.

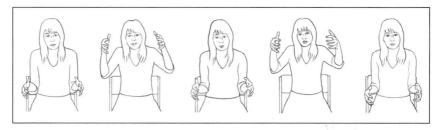

Figure 11.2 A gesture showing the moving pole (redrawn from Beattie and Shovelton 2006).

Size information was encoded in both speech *and* gesture on only four occasions in this particular sample. For example:

'There are loads of [bubbles] everywhere.'

Iconic: Both hands move to area in front of chest and form a large circle.

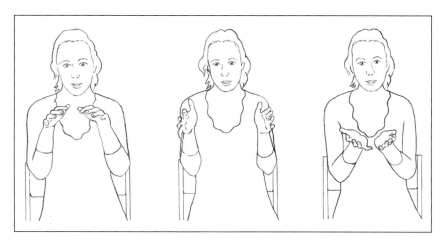

Figure 11.3 A gesture showing the size of the bubbles (redrawn from Beattie and Shovelton 2006).

To differentiate high-importance size information from low-importance size information, we defined high-importance size information as that rated by one or more judges as being in the top five most important size instances from each story. A number of examples may help illustrate how our judges came to such a decision and how the encoding of size information relates to a number of other semantic features simultaneously encoded within the complex multidimensional gestures displayed. To understand the functioning of the gestures we need to understand the basic storyline of each cartoon. In the *Korky the Cat* story a nasty dog traps the kittens inside a 'ball' (two baskets put together) and then plays with the ball in order to upset the kittens. Korky the Cat then turns up and saves the kittens and gets his revenge on the nasty dog. The size of the ball is crucial to the story, as the ball has to be big enough to fit the kittens inside – the whole point of the story was that the kittens were trapped inside the ball.

The size of the ball that was made was identified by all ten judges as being in the top five most important size instances in this story. In three cases, information about the size of the ball was encoded only in gesture;

information about the size of the ball was never encoded only in speech nor was it encoded in gesture *and* speech. Below is an example of the size of the ball encoded only in gesture – the iconic gesture shows that a large ball was made.

'He just [makes a ball] out of the two.'

Iconic: Hands are wide apart. They move towards each other, palms pointing towards each other; a round shape is formed.

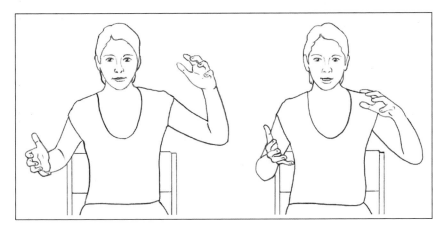

Figure 11.4 A gesture showing the size of the ball (redrawn from Beattie and Shovelton 2006).

There are other semantic features that are simultaneously encoded by this particular iconic gesture, namely *movement* (movement is involved in the event), *speed of movement* (performed quickly), *relative position of objects* (two objects moving towards each other) and *shape* (impression of roundness).

In the Billy *Whizz* cartoon story, on the other hand, Billy is always causing trouble. Billy Whizz causes a large spinning movement by jumping on a chair and causing all the chairs, the table and everything else in the room to go spinning out of control. The fact that Billy's spinning movement was a large spinning movement, rather than a smaller, less damaging one was crucial to the story as a whole, as it resulted in the family buying a different kind of table and chair set, which ended up being their ultimate downfall! The size of the spinning movement was identified by nine judges as being in the top five most important size instances in the Billy *Whizz* story. In two cases, information about the size of the spinning movement was encoded only in gesture; information about the size of the spin was never only in speech, nor in gesture *and* speech. Below is an example of an iconic gesture which shows that the spinning movement was very large.

'The table went [spinning and all the food went all over the floor].'

Iconic: Right arm moves in two large clockwise circles, while the left hand moves away from and then towards the right arm.

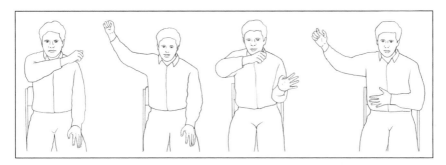

Figure 11.5 A gesture showing the spinning table (redrawn from Beattie and Shovelton 2006).

There are, of course, other semantic features that are simultaneously encoded by this particular iconic gesture, including *movement* (movement is involved in the event), *direction of movement* (clockwise rotation) and *shape* (circular).

In the *Ivy the Terrible* cartoon story, Ivy is very naughty – she causes the bubble machine to make too many bubbles and then tries to eat all the party food herself and not let any of the other children have any food. Ivy does not realise that the bubble liquid has contaminated the food, but when she eats the food many bubbles start coming out of her mouth. If fewer bubbles had been coming out of her mouth the story would not have had the same point to it – Ivy would not have had her comeuppance. The large volume of bubbles coming out of Ivy's mouth was identified by eight judges as being in the top five most important size instances in the *Ivy the Terrible* story.

In two cases information about the size (volume) of bubbles was encoded only in gesture; this information was never encoded only in speech, nor in gesture *and* speech. Below is an example of an iconic gesture which demonstrates that there is a large volume of bubbles coming out of Ivy's mouth – this is absolutely crucial to the story as a whole.

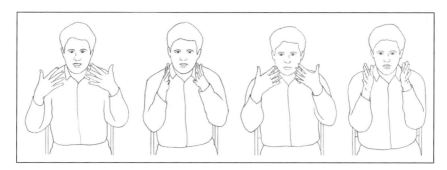

Figure 11.6 A gesture showing bubbles coming out of her mouth (redrawn from Beattie and Shovelton 2006).

'So [bubbles start coming out of her mouth].'

Iconic: Fingers on both hands are spread out and hands move rapidly backwards and forwards in front of mouth.

There are again other semantic features that are simultaneously encoded by this particular iconic gesture, namely *movement*, *speed of movement* (quickly) and *relative position* (bubbles moving away from mouth area).

Low-importance size information, on the other hand, was information that was never rated by any of the judges as being in the top five most important size instances of a story. For example, at the start of the *Billy Whizz* cartoon story, a family, which includes a little child, go into a furniture shop. This little child is Billy's brother. Although this little child features prominently in the cartoon story his size is not of crucial importance to the story as a whole. The size of the little child was never rated by any judge as being one of the top five most important size instances in this story. Information about the size of the child was never encoded in gesture, nor in gesture *and* speech. It was, however, encoded four times in the speech itself:

'It's a family, with a woman and husband and a little child.'

With no gesture accompanying the utterance.

The analysis stemming from this could not be simpler. Did gestures or speech encode the high-importance or low-importance size information? The results can be seen in Table 11.2. High-importance size information was significantly more likely to be encoded in gesture only than speech only.

Table 11.2 How 'high importance' and 'low importance' size information was represented

	Speech only	Gesture-only
High importance size information	9	22
Low importance size information	11	4

Source: Taken from Beattie and Shovelton 2006

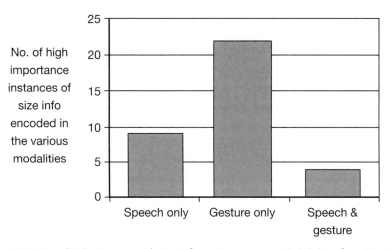

Figure 11.7 How 'high-importance' size information was encoded (taken from Beattie and Shovelton 2006).

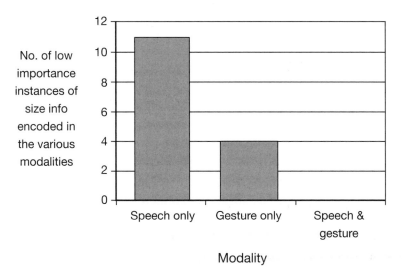

Figure 11.8 How 'low-importance' size information was encoded (taken from Beattie and Shovelton 2006).

Figures 11.7 and 11.8 summarise how high-importance and low-importance information was encoded in speech only, gesture only and in speech and gesture. For me the most surprising thing here is that the high-importance size information was *not* dually encoded in both speech and gesture. Gestures, operating on their own, really did limit themselves intelligently to what mattered with this particular semantic feature of 'size' at least.

One final point is that the original input for the size information in this experiment was almost always in the form of images in the original cartoons. There was only one instance of size information being given in linguistic form in the original stories. No one has yet attempted to tackle the question of how the linguistic and gestural modalities respond to different varieties of input, i.e. whether it is originally represented in visuo-spatial or linguistic form. Would we have obtained the same pattern of results if the original information had been represented in words alone? We cannot say. Indeed, how the brain translates from different sorts of input to linguistic and iconic output to satisfy different communicational prerogatives could well turn out to be a matter of major theoretical concern for the area of human communication in general and for research on speech and gesture in particular.

SUMMARY

- Arnheim had argued that 'the gesture limits itself intelligently to what matters'.

- McNeill had developed this argument in his analyses of gestures using Growth Point Theory. He concluded that 'By looking at the gestures, we can discover, for each person, what was highlighted, what was relevant and what not, and from this infer the iconic side of their utterances. The . . . gestures demonstrate how individual speakers made their own choices of what was salient'.

- We tried a different approach to this issue and tried to determine whether the 'important' instances of one single semantic feature (size) were more likely to be encoded in gesture, in speech or in both speech *and* gesture.

- We used independent judges to assess the 'importance' of the individual instances of the semantic feature.

- We found that when judges identified the high-importance instances of size information in the story, these were more likely to be encoded in gesture rather than in speech.
- The opposite was true for low-importance instances of size information.
- It seems that speakers pick up on crucial semantic aspects of a story and (in certain instances) encode that information into the gestural modality which operates alongside the linguistic modality.
- Iconic gestures may be multidimensional and complex but nevertheless, the gestures do represent the core dimensions of size in a sufficiently unambiguous manner such that decoders can successfully receive the information.
- The gestural modality operates effectively and efficiently to encode the most important instances of this particular dimension.
- How gesture fares with other dimensions is, of course, an equally important question and one that so far remains unanswered.

12

MANIPULATING THE SALIENCE OF INDIVIDUAL ELEMENTS TO SEE HOW GESTURES RESPOND

Imagine you meet a friend after work who you know has an important message for you. They have experienced something quite traumatic that day and they are dying to tell you about it. 'This lunchtime I was going out to the shops for a sandwich, to the usual little delicatessen on the corner – the one with the little sign outside it, just opposite that big pub O'Gradys, or whatever it's called. I was just walking across the road when this bicycle with this man on it trundled round that sharp corner and hit me head-on. He knocked me over and I was left in the middle of the road. I was just lying there. I could have been killed.' You urge them to sit down and you buy them a drink. You are, after all, a very sympathetic listener. You watch them attentively from the start of the story, part of your empathic leaning. You can see a small tear in the corner of one eye before they have even commenced. This indeed has been a traumatic day, but then you can't help noticing their hands move into position to make the stroke phase of the gesture. You feel almost guilty. Your work is interfering with your everyday life.

They are in an excited state, traumatically reliving the event. But what do they gesture about? This is a critical question in gesture research. We now have clear evidence that iconic gestures are effective at communicating a number of semantic features including size (*little* delicatessen, *little* sign, *big* pub, possibly *huge* man), relative position (*on the corner*, *outside it*, *opposite*, *across* the road, *round* the corner, *head-on*, *left in the middle of the road*, *lying on the road*), as well as other things like speed ('trundling', and therefore not that *fast*). But which semantic features are actually encoded in the iconic gestures in this short, traumatic account of what turned out to be a not very important accident? McNeill (1992, 2012), of course, has tried to answer this question. He would say that it is the important bits, those high in communicative dynamism where the new, unpredictable information is, the newsworthy bits of the story – the *size* of the man on the bicycle (big enough to knock my friend over) or maybe the fact that she was left in *the middle of the road* after the collision. These are the bits of information in context that should occasion the generation of a hand gesture. This is a very important theoretical claim about the generation of iconic gestures in speech, but for the experimental psychologist wishing to analyse and understand gesture it does create something of a problem. The examples analysed in much of the literature tend not to be like our friend's story about crossing roads. The critical bits are often less obvious in terms of their communicative dynamism or newsworthiness. However, you still have the task of trying to link the gestures with psychological salience. This can be a challenging task, as we have just seen, and can, on occasion, descend into specific reasoning that is difficult to defend. Why does a speaker produce a certain gesture at any particular point? Because, according to David McNeill, it allows the speaker to encode information that is important to them at that very moment in time. But how do we know that the information is important to the speaker at that precise moment? The answer would seem to be because the speaker produces that gesture. This might seem like a bit of an oversimplification of the detailed and painstaking analysis employed here by McNeill but there is, nevertheless, a clear possible danger of tautological reasoning.

McNeill (2012) not surprisingly rejects this accusation and criticises the evidence I marshalled in the last chapter as ignoring *speaker* context. He emphasises that he wishes to elucidate 'how the speaker differentiates the field of meaningful oppositions that she/he has at least partly constructed as part of the meaning'. McNeill (1992, 2012) has consistently argued that gestures occur at particular points in the utterance, according to what is selected by the *individual speaker* as relevant or salient in that context, where the most important feature of context is the construction of the utterance (or the unfolding of the growth point). Many of his studies clearly show that different speakers display varied gestures when talking on the same subject, hence McNeill's proposal that gestures can give an insight into what matters to the individual speaker at that point in time. McNeill argues that one of the reasons that gestures can be better than speech at showing degrees of relevance is that they have no obligatory elements or standards of form, so they are free to select only what are the most relevant attributes in context. Iconic gestures are idiosyncratic in nature, in that they are not bound by the rules of standards of good form, but are instead 'created locally by speakers while they are speaking' (McNeill and Duncan 1998: 142). It has been suggested that, due to their idiosyncrasy, the gestures that accompany speech can provide a 'window into the mind' of the individual speaker. De Ruiter (2007: 27) explains that, since gestures are not organised in syntactic sequences or need not conform to lexical and morphological conventions, they provide a direct image of the thought they arose from. This all makes perfect sense, but demonstrating it is another matter.

Of course, that was the whole point of our last analysis, to use judges other than the speaker to at least show a 'consensus' of 'importance/salience' amongst competent native language users, but this necessarily excludes the moment-to-moment cognitions of the individual speaker in that specific context at that particular time, at that particular point in his or her own narrative. Therefore, to that extent our approach is context free because it avoids being as bold as McNeill, whose aim was

> to reconstruct a speaker's momentary states of cognitive being, to show how, GP-to-GP [growth point to growth point], she differentiates psychological predicates within created and updated contexts, and how these have come to be. The goal, that is, to recover a first-person perspective.
>
> (McNeill 2012: 210)

We felt that we needed to show some relationship between what gestures capture and the elements of a story, as objectively (and therefore as 'context free' from the mind of the individual speaker) as possible.

Of course, we can extend this approach. In the last chapter we opted for judges' ratings, external and objective, of the importance of one particular semantic feature. Using independent judges to rate the importance of information is one (admittedly quite crude) way of gaining some insight into the psychological factors behind the generation of an utterance. It is not sensitive to the fact that each individual narrating the cartoon story may have a different perception of what is most important at that point in time, and cannot in the end really determine if the individual speaker is gesturing about what is truly important to them. The study is crude in other ways as well – it is correlational, showing an association between certain elements judged to be important and the probability of an iconic gesture occurring. Is it possible to move beyond correlation to produce stronger evidence of this possible association?

That was why we considered whether it might be possible to investigate this issue experimentally, by manipulating stories in such a way as to make individual elements more important for the outcome of the story. For example, say it were a story about a boy jumping a crevasse. In one version (what we might call the *neutral* version) the boy might do this quite successfully and go on to further adventures (as boys in stories often do); in other words, the size of the crevasse is not that important to the story as a whole, it is essentially 'neutral'. In a second version of the story (the so-called *consequential* version), however, he may not quite make that crevasse and may be left clinging for his life. In the second version the size of the crevasse is absolutely critical to the outcome of the story and, therefore, highly consequential. Alternatively, say it was a story about a boy playing with a ball near the end of a jetty. In one version he might hit the ball back, and in a second version he may lean back too far to hit the ball, and because he is so close to the end of the jetty he might fall in the water. In the second version the position of the boy relative to the end of the jetty is critical to the outcome of the story; the boy is now after all in the water. In this way, we can manipulate the importance of individual elements to the story as a whole.

To return to our basic hypothesis then, if iconic gestures are selective in terms of what they encode they should be more likely to encode the core semantic features – *size* of the crevasse, *relative position* of the boy relative to the end of the jetty – in the *consequential* version of the story than in the *neutral* version of the story. In other words, the experimental manipulation of the salience of certain semantic elements of the story should increase the probability of iconic gestures representing those elements, but this should not increase the probability of the features being represented in speech or speech and gesture simultaneously.

This experiment (conducted with Jamie Ross and Kate Webster) used 30 participants. Each participant was asked to narrate 12 cartoon stories and each story had two different versions, a *consequential* version and a *neutral* version. Each cartoon was made up of five pictures and the last picture was the only one that differed between the *neutral* and the *consequential* versions. The cartoons were designed specifically to manipulate the importance of either *size* or *relative position* information (six of the stories involved *size* and six involved *relative position*). In the *consequential* version of each cartoon the particular semantic feature (*size* or *relative position*) was crucial to the outcome of the story and in the *neutral* version the particular semantic feature had no real implications for the outcome of the story. The semantic feature that was crucial to the outcome in the *consequential* story has been labelled the 'critical semantic feature'.

For example, one of the cartoons that manipulated the semantic feature of *size* depicts a small child selecting a large beach ball to play with (see Figure 12.1(a) and (b)). In the *consequential* version of this cartoon the size of both the child and the ball is crucial to the outcome of the story, as in the last picture the child is squashed by the ball just as he is about to catch it. However, in the *neutral* version of this cartoon, the *size* information has no real implication for the outcome, as in the last picture the child catches the ball successfully.

An example of a cartoon manipulating the semantic feature of *relative position* portrays a boy playing ball on a jetty (see Figure 12.2(a) and (b)). The boy steps back towards the end of the jetty and teeters right on the edge as he reaches to hit the ball. In the *neutral* version of this story, the boy recovers his balance and looks relieved, but in the *consequential* version, the boy falls into the water. The salient point here is that it is because he is *right on the edge* of the jetty that he falls into the water in the *consequential* version.

The participants were told they would be taking part in an experiment that looked at story-telling and comprehension, and that they had been selected randomly to play the role of speaker and would have to narrate 12 cartoon stories to the listener (played by a confederate) who would then be tested on the content of the stories at the end of the experiment.

Each participant only saw the *consequential* or *neutral* version of each cartoon and of the 12 cartoons they were given to narrate, six were *consequential* and six were *neutral*. Every participant narrated six cartoons involving *size* information and six involving *relative position* information, meaning they saw three of each type (3 x *consequential, size*; 3 × *consequential, relative position*; 3 × *neutral, size*; and 3 x *neutral, relative position*). The order in which the stories were viewed by participants was counterbalanced, so that one participant would see a certain order of the stories, then the next participant would see the opposite version of each story but in the same order, then the next pair of participants would see a completely new order.

The first presentation of each cartoon was a paper copy which the participants held in their hands in order to familiarise themselves with the story. This was then given back to the experimenter and the cartoon was

Figure 12.1 (a) Cartoon K.i. – Neutral version.

Figure 12.1 (b) Cartoon K.ii. – Consequential version.

Figure 12.2 (a) Cartoon B.i. – Neutral version.

Figure 12.2 (b) Cartoon B.ii. – Consequential version.

projected onto a wall behind the confederate so that the participants could see it but the confederate could not. The confederate was not allowed at any point to see the cartoons.

Every instance of the participant encoding the critical semantic features (either *size* or *relative position*) in speech was transcribed. For example, in the cartoon portraying a little boy playing with a big beach ball, 'the *little boy* chose a *big beach ball*' are two examples of the critical feature of *size* being encoded in speech. For the semantic category of *relative position*, examples of this critical information being encoded in speech include 'she sat *under the beehive*' or 'they put the bag *next to the teddy*'. The experimenters did not count instances of *size* or *relative position* information encoded in speech if the aspect of the story they were describing was not critical to the narrative. For example, instances where participants described the *size* or *relative position* of objects peripheral to the core storyline such as 'the balls are in a *big crate*' or 'there's a jetty sticking *out into the sea*' were not counted, as these aspects were not felt to be critical to the outcome of the story.

The experimenters also analysed the video footage for iconic gestures specifically related to the critical semantic features of the cartoons. These gestures were recorded as either appearing with speech relative to the critical semantic features (*speech and gesture* category) or alone (*gesture only* category). Those instances of speech relating to the critical semantic features that were already transcribed but were not associated with a gesture made up the *speech only* category. Once again, the experimenters did not count instances of *size* or *relative position* information encoded in iconic gestures if the aspect of the story they were describing was not critical to the narrative, for example, an iconic gesture symbolising the size of the crate mentioned in the cartoon above would not have been counted as an iconic gesture which encoded critical semantic information. Overall there were 490 instances of critical semantic information being encoded in *speech only*, *gesture only* and *speech and gesture*. Separate totals were then calculated for all instances of critical information being encoded in the different modalities and this was also calculated for the *consequential* versions and the *neutral* versions separately.

The nature of the cartoons used in this experiment – clear, simple and easy to understand – meant that the critical points of the stories were easy to identify, as demonstrated by the fact that the majority of participants successfully encoded the critical features of the cartoons either in speech, gesture or both speech and gesture. The examples below demonstrate how the critical semantic features were encoded differently by participants in the two conditions (*consequential* and *neutral*). One of the stories, mentioned above, involves a boy playing with a ball on a jetty. One participant, seeing the *consequential* version, used only speech to encode the critical semantic feature (*relative position*), contrary to our basic hypothesis:

(1) 'He's quite close to the edge.'

No gesture.

Another participant, also seeing the *consequential* version, used both speech and gesture together to encode the critical information, again contrary to our basic hypothesis:

(2) 'He's heading back [to the edge of the dock].'

Iconic: Right hand is positioned in front of body in vertical position with palm open and facing to the left, left palm faces right palm and makes two motions pushing inwards towards right palm.

Another story involves a jogger running over crevasses in the ground. He comes across a small crevasse and leaps over it, but then comes to a bigger crevasse in the ground. In the *neutral* version he jumps the bigger crevasse and makes it to the other side, whilst in the *consequential* version he attempts the jump but doesn't reach the other side and is left clinging to the rock. The descriptions of this cartoon story again demonstrate how the critical information is encoded in different ways by participants. One participant was presented with the *neutral* version of this story and encoded the critical *size* information using both speech ('big' hole, 'quite large') and gesture:

(3) 'He jumps over [a small crack]1 . . . Then he comes to [a big hole]2 [er]3 [quite large]4.'

Iconics:

1 Hands are close together in front of body, positioned vertically with palms facing each other, fingers spread; both hands move downwards and upwards once.

2 Hands take up same position again, facing inwards but a little further apart than before.

3 Hands move out from one another but remain parallel.

4 Hands move outwards again, remaining parallel but now quite far apart.

Another participant saw the *consequential* version of the same story and used only iconic gesture to represent the critical *size* information:

(4) '[He sees a gap]1, it's like [a crack in the]2, I'm assuming it's like a cliff or something. . . He gets a bit further and there's like [a. . .]3 it just looks like a drop.'

Iconics:

1 Hands are close together in front of body, positioned vertically with palms facing each other, fingers spread; each hand moves alternately up and down, hands remaining parallel.

2 Left hand remains facing inwards in vertical position, right hand moves up and down at an angle to left hand, producing a narrow gap between the fingers of both hands, which nearly meet.

3 Hands start off with palms facing each other in front of body, then both hands move rapidly outwards but palms remain facing each other.

The same participant then went on to describe the final outcome of the story using both speech and gesture:

(5) '[He tries to jump over this gap]1 [but it's too big]2.'

Iconics:

1 Right hand makes a smooth arc in front of body, moving from left to right side of body.

2 Right hand moves back in an arc, retracing the gesture above from right to left.

Another story involves a little boy and a beach ball (semantic feature: *size*). One participant, having seen the *consequential* version of this story, represents the *size* information of the boy and the ball in speech alone:

(6) 'Unfortunately the ball is bigger than the child.'

No gesture.

Another participant, having also seen the *consequential* version of this story, represents the size of the ball in gesture alone:

(7) 'And [they choose one], it's like a beach ball.'

Iconic: Hands move outwards in a circular movement creating a large round shape in the air which represents the size and shape of the ball.

A third participant, having seen the *neutral* version of this story, encodes the *size* information in both speech and gesture:

(8) 'The man gets hold of a [really big ball that's half the size of the kid].'

Iconic: Both hands held either side of the head at head level in parallel move forwards and then back towards the head to represent the size of the ball.

In total, our participants encoded 490 examples of the critical semantic features (*size* or *relative position*) in speech, in gesture or in speech and gesture together. Of these instances, 245 occurred in the narrations of the *consequential* stories and (extraordinarily!) exactly the same number occurred in the narrations of the *neutral* stories. In other words, changing the importance of the individual semantic feature for the story did not affect the probability that these particular semantic features would be encoded in one or more modalities.

But what about the pattern of encoding? Overall there were 309 instances of critical semantic information encoded in *speech only*, 56 instances encoded in *gesture only* and 125 instances encoded in *speech and gesture*. In narrating the *consequential* stories, participants encoded the critical semantic information in *speech only* 156 times, in *gesture only* 35 times and in *speech and gesture* 54 times. In narrating the *neutral* stories, participants encoded this information 153 times in *speech only*, 21 times in *gesture only* and 71 times in *speech and gesture*. The results are presented in Table 12.1 and displayed graphically in Figure 12.3.

Statistical analyses revealed that speakers were more likely to encode the critical semantic features (*size* and *relative position*) in *gesture only* for the *consequential* version of the story rather than the *neutral* version, compared to *speech only*, as predicted (see Table 12.2). But the opposite is true of encoding in *speech and gesture* (see Table 12.3). In other words, when the semantic feature is critical to the outcome of the story, *gesture only* seems to pick this up, while *gesture* and *speech* together do not. This result is statistically reliable.

The number of gestures produced to represent the critical semantic information differed significantly between the narrations of the *consequential* and *neutral* stories, with participants producing 66.7 per cent more gestures

Table 12.1 How the critical semantic features (size and relative position) were encoded in consequential and neutral versions of a story

	Speech only	Gesture only	Speech and Gesture	Total
Consequential	156	35	54	245
Neutral	153	21	71	245
Total	309	56	125	490

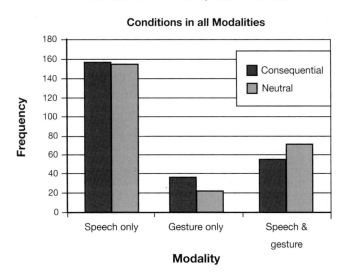

Figure 12.3 How the critical semantic features were encoded across modalities.

Table 12.2 How the critical semantic features (size and relative position) were encoded in speech only and gesture only in consequential and neutral versions of a story

	Consequential	Neutral
Speech only	156	153
Gesture only	35	21

Table 12.3 How the critical semantic features (size and relative position) were encoded in gesture only and speech and gesture in consequential and neutral versions of a story

	Consequential	Neutral
Gesture only	35	21
Speech and Gesture	54	71

on their own for *consequential* stories than for *neutral*. These results thus seem to bear out the claim that iconic gestures represent the most salient information in the context, since the same elements of *size* and *relative position* information were present in both versions of each story, but participants were more likely to encode the semantic information just in gesture only when it was critical to the outcome of the story. These results for gestural encoding contrast markedly with those for semantic information encoded through speech. Although the critical *size* and *relative position* information was encoded more frequently overall in speech than in gesture, the frequency of encoding in speech did not vary significantly across the two conditions (*consequential* and *neutral*). This would suggest that gesture, as opposed to speech, is significantly more selective in the information it encodes, tending to restrict itself to information of greater importance. Speech, on the other hand, was found to encode information of *size* and *relative position* equally regardless of the importance of the information in context in this particular study. It might be suggested, therefore, that in order to really understand what is important to any speaker, it should be the hands that we attend to rather than the speech, since the gestures they produce seem much more sensitive to the salience of individual elements. Similarly, when speech and gesture act together and both encode the same basic information, they do not cooperate in such a way as to select the most salient features of the story.

And as for our friend at the beginning of the chapter, what did she gesture about when talking about her trauma outside the delicatessen? Well, having read this chapter, it should come as no surprise that it was the size of the man on the bicycle that was depicted in the iconic gesture – he was 'huge' (although this was never mentioned in the speech). This 'huge' man nearly caused her demise, and yet she never thought to mention his size at all in the conversation, except in the movements of her hands, which articulated it beautifully.

SUMMARY

- This study attempted to determine whether speakers encode the most significant aspects of a story in gesture by experimentally manipulating the importance of individual semantic elements in the story by making them more or less relevant to the outcome of the story.

- It thus allowed a direct experimental test of the hypothesis that in stories where the individual semantic features (*size* and *relative position*) are crucial to the outcome of the story, these features should be more likely to be encoded in gesture compared with stories in which they are not crucial.

- The study found that encoding of the critical semantic information in gesture alone did differentiate between the *consequential* and *neutral* versions of the story in a way that speech or dual encoding (speech and gesture) did not.

- Participants produced 66.7 per cent more gestures on their own for *consequential* stories than for *neutral* stories.

- Participants were more likely to encode the semantic information in gesture only when it was critical to the outcome of the story.

- These results for gestural encoding contrast markedly with those for semantic information encoded through speech. Although the critical *size* and *relative position* information was encoded more frequently overall in speech than in gesture, the frequency of encoding in speech did not vary significantly across the two conditions (*consequential* and *neutral*).

- This would suggest that gesture, as opposed to speech, is significantly more selective in the information it encodes, tending to restrict itself to information of greater importance.

- One might tentatively suggest, therefore, that in order to really understand what is important to any speaker, it should be the hands that we attend to rather than the speech, since the gestures they produce seem much more sensitive to the salience of individual elements.

13

HOW METAPHORIC GESTURES AFFECT US

Of course, much of everyday communication is not confined to this concrete world of objects and actions, and much of our gestural communication is not restricted to indicating the size of an object or its position or how it moves through space (although some of it is). And yet much of the work I have described so far on how listeners interpret gesture is restricted to this very concrete domain. For this reason I became interested in how people interpret more abstract gestures, especially when their meaning does not closely match what is being said in the speech. The sheer abstractness of many gestures in everyday life might mean that they have much less of an effect than more concrete gestures. But do they have any demonstrable effect?

There has been a significant tradition in communication research, from Albert Mehrabian through Michael Argyle to those working in the Chicago gesture lab, which involves presenting participants with various conflicting communications to see how they are interpreted and this formed the basis for the present study on metaphoric gestures. One of the few early studies to have studied actual gesture–speech mismatches was conducted by Cassell *et al.* (1999). The study found that gestural messages that mismatched the information contained in the accompanying speech were often represented in listeners' subsequent retelling of the narrative and therefore that the information conveyed in the gestural channel can alter the entire underlying representation of the utterance (Cassell *et al.* 1999).

However, this experiment was quite restrictive in its scope. The only gesture categories considered were 'anaphor', 'origo' and 'manner' mismatches. Anaphor mismatches refer back to someone or something but point to the wrong part of the gestural space where it had been located previously, origo mismatches change the perspective that the action is seen from and manner mismatches provide different information regarding how a particular action was performed (Cassell *et al.* 1999). These, of course, are only a subset of the gestures that appear in naturally occurring communications and ignore the more abstract metaphoric gestures. So how would mismatches involving these more abstract gestures be responded to? We used the basic gesture–speech mismatch paradigm here with two

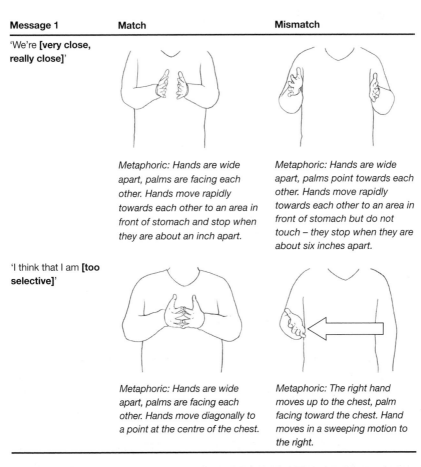

Message 1	Match	Mismatch
'We're [very close, really close]'	*Metaphoric: Hands are wide apart, palms are facing each other. Hands move rapidly towards each other to an area in front of stomach and stop when they are about an inch apart.*	*Metaphoric: Hands are wide apart, palms point towards each other. Hands move rapidly towards each other to an area in front of stomach but do not touch – they stop when they are about six inches apart.*
'I think that I am [too selective]'	*Metaphoric: Hands are wide apart, palms are facing each other. Hands move diagonally to a point at the centre of the chest.*	*Metaphoric: The right hand moves up to the chest, palm facing toward the chest. Hand moves in a sweeping motion to the right.*

Figure 13.1 Examples of the matched and mismatched versions of the speech and gesture combinations for Message 1 (redrawn from Beattie and Sale 2012, Copyright © 2012, Walter de Gruyter GmbH).

Message 2	Match	Mismatch

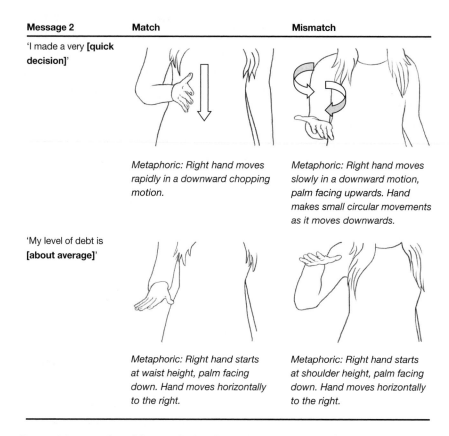

'I made a very [quick decision]'

Metaphoric: Right hand moves rapidly in a downward chopping motion.

Metaphoric: Right hand moves slowly in a downward motion, palm facing upwards. Hand makes small circular movements as it moves downwards.

'My level of debt is [about average]'

Metaphoric: Right hand starts at waist height, palm facing down. Hand moves horizontally to the right.

Metaphoric: Right hand starts at shoulder height, palm facing down. Hand moves horizontally to the right.

Figure 13.2 Examples of the matched and mismatched versions of the speech and gesture combinations for Message 2 (redrawn from Beattie and Sale 2012 Copyright © 2012, Walter de Gruyter GmbH).

independent groups of participants. The first group consisted of 33 participants; the second had 24 participants. A selection of metaphoric gestures was chosen from an extensive naturalistic corpus. The selection of the gestures informed the scripts produced, where both the speech and the movement were heavily scripted and choreographed. The gestures were then incorporated into three scripts relating to events relevant to everyday student life, including scripts about relationships (Message 1), student debt (Message 2) and work (Message 3). Three different encoders were each given a script and were recorded delivering two versions of each message. In one version, the two gestures matched the speech (matched), in the second version neither of the gestures matched the speech (mismatched), as shown in Figures 13.1–13.3.

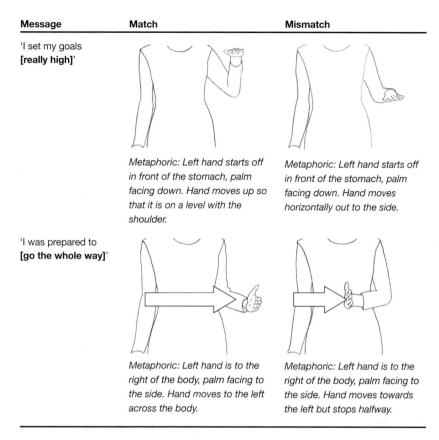

Message	Match	Mismatch
'I set my goals **[really high]**'	*Metaphoric: Left hand starts off in front of the stomach, palm facing down. Hand moves up so that it is on a level with the shoulder.*	*Metaphoric: Left hand starts off in front of the stomach, palm facing down. Hand moves horizontally out to the side.*
'I was prepared to **[go the whole way]**'	*Metaphoric: Left hand is to the right of the body, palm facing to the side. Hand moves to the left across the body.*	*Metaphoric: Left hand is to the right of the body, palm facing to the side. Hand moves towards the left but stops halfway.*

Figure 13.3 Examples of the matched and mismatched versions of the speech and gesture combinations for Message 3 (redrawn from Beattie and Sale 2012, Copyright © 2012, Walter de Gruyter GmbH).

After viewing each of the clips, participants were asked a series of questions about each of the three messages. Responses were then marked along a five-point Likert scale. For example, for Message 1 participants were asked: 'Is he selective about who he would have a relationship with?' Participants provided a rating from 1 ('not at all selective') to 5 ('extremely selective').

One group of participants were shown the three video clips where the gesture and the speech matched; the second group were shown the three video clips where the gesture and speech did not match. The results can be seen in Tables 13.1–13.3.

Of the 12 individual comparisons (four from each table), six were statistically significant in line with the prediction that the presence of a

Table 13.1 Mean scores for Message 1

Question	Mean Score (matched)	Mean Score (mismatched)
Did they have a good relationship?	2.79	2.94
Do you think he was close to his ex-girlfriend?	2.75	2.94
Does he seem quite choosy in finding a girlfriend?	2.75	3.27
Is he selective about who he would have a relationship with?	2.67	3.49

Source: Taken from Beattie and Sale 2012, Copyright © 2012, Walter de Gruyter GmbH

Table 13.2 Mean scores for Message 2

Question	Mean Score (matched)	Mean Score (mismatched)
Does she have a normal amount of debt for a student?	2.46	1.83
Does her level of debt seem about average?	2.46	1.75
Did she make a fast decision about taking out a loan?	3.67	3.50
Was her idea to take out a loan a spur of the moment thing?	4.21	2.92

Source: Taken from Beattie and Sale 2012, Copyright © 2012, Walter de Gruyter GmbH

Table 13.3 Mean scores for Message 3

Question	Mean Score (matched)	Mean Score (mismatched)
Does she seem driven to achieve goals?	4.39	3.54
Did she set her goals very high when working at the bank?	3.91	2.88
Is it likely that she would do anything to get to the top?	4.21	3.17
Is she prepared to go the whole way in whatever she is doing to show she is a good employee?	4.15	2.92

Source: Taken from Beattie and Sale 2012, Copyright © 2012, Walter de Gruyter GmbH

metaphoric gesture–speech mismatch will affect the interpretation of the message. The combined probability of obtaining six significant results like this in line with the major hypothesis is itself highly statistically significant. In other words, it seems that not only are mismatches attended to, but furthermore, the content of the mismatch has an influence on how the message is interpreted. For example, when participants were asked, 'Does she seem driven to achieve goals?' for the person in Message 3, the participants who were shown the video where the speaker's gesture and speech matched thought she seemed much more driven to achieve her goals (mean score = 4.39) than the participants who were shown the video where her gesture and speech did not match (mean score = 3.54). It is important to emphasise, however, that all of the results from Message 1 were either statistically non-significant or in one case statistically significant in the *opposite* direction to what we would expect.

Thus, the hypothesis that participants will integrate information from both speech and metaphoric gesture, even in the case of a gesture–speech mismatch, was clearly supported in this study. It demonstrated that gesture–speech mismatches influence how a message is subsequently interpreted. However, the results from Message 1 were surprising in that only one significant difference was found between the matched and mismatched versions and this was in the opposite direction to what we expected. This is probably a function of the particular gestures selected for the message. There is, of course, no lexicon to specify the form or meaning of individual metaphoric gestures, as they are movements that are generated unconsciously and spontaneously in everyday communication. The same metaphoric gesture in one context may have quite a different meaning in another and there is always the possibility that individuals may interpret the same gesture very differently. Consider one of the utterances used in Message 1 where the speaker says, 'I think that I am [*too selective*]' when talking about relationships. We had assumed that the hands narrowing (matched gesture) in Figure 13.4 indicated a degree of selectivity in terms of choosing a partner, whereas the sweeping movement (mismatched) in the second row indicated a lack of selectivity. However, it may be the case that the gesture, with the hands in motion for a greater time in the sweeping movement (our mismatched condition), could indicate the amount of time and effort that went into the process of selecting a partner. This is quite the opposite of what the gesture was intended to represent.

Whilst we assumed the positioning of the hands to be crucial, the participants might well have viewed the temporal dimension to be the crucial component of the gesture.

Gesture		Intended Meaning	Interpreted Meaning
Matched	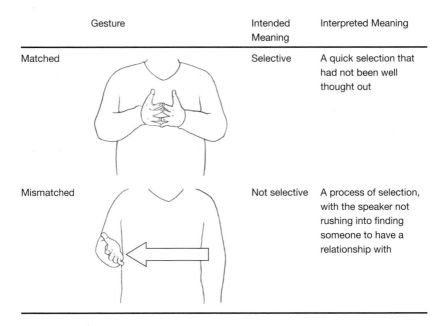	Selective	A quick selection that had not been well thought out
Mismatched		Not selective	A process of selection, with the speaker not rushing into finding someone to have a relationship with

Figure 13.4 Interpretations of matched and mismatched gestures (redrawn from Beattie and Sale 2012, Copyright © 2012, Walter de Gruyter GmbH).

Of course, so far we have only considered the effects of gesture–speech mismatches on how the underlying message is perceived, but there is also the strong possibility on the basis of previous research that such mismatches will also affect aspects of social judgement, including how the speaker is actually perceived. Speakers who display gesture–speech mismatches, for whatever reason, might well be perceived in a more negative light than those who display gestures and speech that match. Is it the case that speakers who display gesture–speech mismatches are less likeable? And does the presence of a gesture–speech mismatch influence how confident people are in the speaker's message? These simple ideas form the basis of the second study.

Again we used two independent groups of university students, with 20 participants in the first condition and 20 participants in the second condition. The metaphoric gestures used in this study again were based on examples from an actual corpus. From this corpus, five metaphoric gestures that matched the speech and five corresponding gestures that mismatched the speech were selected and incorporated into two scripts about relationships, both delivered by the same female actor. The actor was filmed as she delivered the script to a camera, incorporating the staged gestures. Although the wording was exactly the same for each script, they only differed in the

(a)

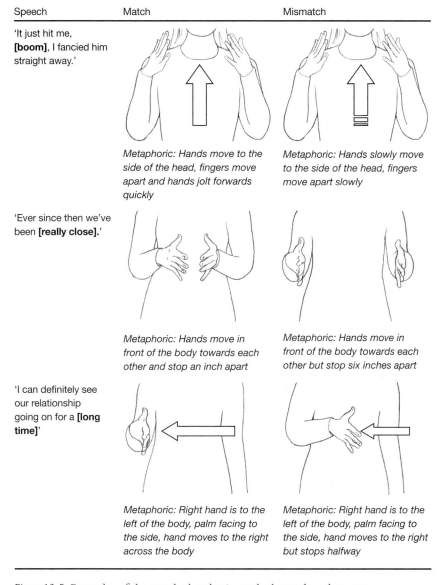

Speech	Match	Mismatch
'It just hit me, **[boom]**, I fancied him straight away.'	*Metaphoric: Hands move to the side of the head, fingers move apart and hands jolt forwards quickly*	*Metaphoric: Hands slowly move to the side of the head, fingers move apart slowly*
'Ever since then we've been **[really close]**.'	*Metaphoric: Hands move in front of the body towards each other and stop an inch apart*	*Metaphoric: Hands move in front of the body towards each other but stop six inches apart*
'I can definitely see our relationship going on for a **[long time]**'	*Metaphoric: Right hand is to the left of the body, palm facing to the side, hand moves to the right across the body*	*Metaphoric: Right hand is to the left of the body, palm facing to the side, hand moves to the right but stops halfway*

Figure 13.5 Examples of the matched and mismatched speech and gesture combinations for Study 2 (redrawn from Beattie and Sale 2012, Copyright © 2012, Walter de Gruyter GmbH).

(b)

Speech	Match	Mismatch
'I only ever ring him [once].'	*Metaphoric: Right hand moves towards the temple with the thumb and little finger extended, turns once*	*Metaphoric: Right hand moves towards the temple, both the thumb and little finger are extended, making repeated turning movements*
'I would say in terms of niceness there was [Paul], then [Luke], then some of [the proper idiots] that I regret going out with.'	*Metaphoric: Raises left hand, thumb is extended, index finger on left hand is extended, then right hand rises, thumb is extended*	*Metaphoric: Raises left hand, thumb is extended, raises right hand, thumb is extended, then the index finger on right hand is extended*

Figure 13.5 continued

gestures used, so that in one version the gesture and speech matched and in the other version, the gesture and speech did not match (see Figure 13.5).

The tone of the script was casual, with the intention that it would appear to the receiver as though the speaker had been asked to describe her relationships with her current and previous boyfriends. A questionnaire was created in which participants were asked how much they liked the person talking, which was measured on a scale from −3 ('extremely dislike') to +3 ('extremely like'), and were also asked how confident they were that everything the person said was true, which was measured on a scale from −3 ('not at all confident') to +3 ('extremely confident').

The first set of participants was shown the video clip where the gesture and speech matched. The clip was projected onto a screen in front of the

Table 13.4 Ratings for matched and mismatched scripts

Question	Mean Score (matched)	Mean Score (mismatched)
How much do you instinctively like this person?	1.00	−0.90
How confident are you that everything the person said was true?	0.05	−1.05

Source: Taken from Beattie and Sale 2012, Copyright © 2012, Walter de Gruyter GmbH

participants and afterwards they were asked to fill in the questionnaire. The same procedure was repeated for the mismatched version of the clip, which was shown to the second group of participants. Although the classic studies on social judgements about mismatching communications conducted by Argyle *et al.* (1970) used a within-subjects design, we felt that it was necessary to avoid this type of experimental design, as it is not realistic to watch someone in a video clip make a social judgement about that person and then watch the same person perform the same speech, only this time with different gestures, and then provide a 'new' social judgement. The demand characteristics in this situation would be clear to any participants and for this reason, we used a between-subjects design.

The analyses revealed that participants intuitively liked the speaker less when the speech and gesture did not match (mean score = −0.90) compared to when the speech and gesture did match (mean score = 1.00). In addition, participants were less confident that everything the speaker said was true when the speech and gesture did not match (mean score = −1.05) compared to when the speech and gesture did match (mean score = 0.05), as shown in Table 13.4.

Clearly the presence of mismatches did influence subsequent social judgements, in that participants liked the speaker less and were less likely to believe what the person was saying when the gestures did not match the speech. Of course, the experimental design was very limited in that there were five gesture–speech mismatches in one version of the message and five gesture–speech matches in the other version. Whether participants would be as sensitive to one or two mismatches in the general context of gestures and speech that did match remains to be seen. It does appear though that people seem to sense that there is something not quite right when gesture–speech mismatches are generated.

In other words, if you are going to fake it, then you had better get it right.

SUMMARY

- Metaphoric gestures, despite their abstract nature, are processed alongside speech.

- When the metaphoric gesture does not match the accompanying speech, this seems to have a significant effect on how the message is perceived.

- High goals not accompanied by an appropriately high gesture, for example, are not perceived as that high after all.

- Furthermore, we are not that favourably disposed to gesture–speech mismatches, at least when they are frequent in a message.

- This might well mean that we all know intuitively that there is something wrong about gesture–speech mismatches and things do not seem quite right when gesture and speech fail to match in the ways that we might naturally expect.

14

PUTTING ICONIC GESTURES INTO TV ADVERTISEMENTS

I like to watch TV, and study the gestures of the actors, and try to work out what they are doing with their hands. So many of the gestures of actors on TV do not fit the speech that they are designed to accompany. This is especially true in TV ads. Actors seem to have been told to do something with their hands, to give the ad more life, so they do. And the ad looks both 'alive' and curiously 'wrong' in so many ways. The preparation phase of the gesture is often missing, so the timing is out, the gesture is in the wrong quadrant of the gestural space, the post-stroke hold is too quick or non-existent, the division of meaning between the two channels does not occur, the same gesture is repeated for effect with a different verbal utterance. Imagine if we could get it right.

We now know that iconic gestures do communicate, particularly about core semantic features, in our everyday interactions and our brains have evolved to notice this information and combine it with speech. The gestures rely on their iconicity to encode certain meaningful parts of the message and we, as listeners, receive a fuller version of the speaker's message as a consequence. And yet, only now are we starting to understand how this process actually works. So can we use this theory to make messages more effective? One would surely want to argue that the design of effective communications depends critically upon an accurate and adequate model of the communication process. The traditional model of communication (discussed in Chapter 1), which has dominated psychology (and related disciplines), is that speech conveys semantic information and that bodily movement conveys information about emotion and interpersonal attitudes. This model originated with Wundt in 1921 when he wrote that 'the primary cause of natural gestures does not lie in the motivation to communicate a concept, but rather in the expression of an emotion' (Wundt 1921/1973: 146). But in this book we have been challenging this idea. The primary cause of many natural hand gestures does lie in the motivation to communicate a whole range of concepts. So what are the implications of this new communicative model of iconic gesture and the consequent reconceptualisation of the whole process of communication for the design of effective message delivery?

There are many domains that one could consider here – political persuasion (and perhaps a new type of oratory guided by science rather than just passion), religion as a unique form of persuasion, public appeals, selling, and advertising. Out of this list, we chose to start with advertising for a number of reasons. First, small margins here would make a great difference. Second, you can make an advert and test it on an audience to see if it does work. And third, advertisers, it seems, are crying out for some real guidance; the gestures in ads do not currently persuade us of anything, except that the actor is desperate to please the director.

TV ads are ubiquitous. Research in the USA has suggested that the average US child will have seen a staggering 350,000 commercials by the age of 18. But, the advertisers complain, of the 1,500 opportunities that people have to see advertisements each day, only between seven and ten are remembered by a consumer (Brierley 2002). Many argue that TV advertising is extremely successful compared with its competitors (radio, newspaper and magazine advertising), but, of course, the costs of TV advertising are proportional to this perceived effectiveness, and TV advertising accounts for approximately 32.2 per cent of all advertising expenditure (Advertising Standards Yearbook 2000).

But can we be confident that such advertising is really effective in terms of what it sets out to deliver? I am reminded of Alexander's (1927) comment that 'Advertising is neither a science, art, nor manufacture. It has no general standard, no root principles, no hard and fast rules, no precedents, no foolproof machinery' (from Bradshaw 1927: 140). Some argue that little has changed in the last 80 years (see Brierley 2002) and if we can demonstrate that TV is effective, why is it effective? Can we explain its efficacy in terms of how the brain actually processes the informational content of advertisements that rely on both speech and images accompanying the speech?

Part of the function of advertising is to provide information about the distinct features of any product, to build brand image and identity, and, of course, to create some need or desire in the customer, to be satisfied only with a purchase. Brierley (2002) identified a number of core features of the language of advertisements used first to attract attention and then to build brand image. He writes, 'In the early days of advertising, grabbing attention meant departing from formal rules of grammar and language, misspelling words, mispronouncing them on TV, or inventing new words' (Brierley 2002: 184). In time, a number of distinct rhetorical techniques were added to this list including contrast, repetition, juxtaposition, ambiguity and the punchline. But research in this area is guided by a traditional theory of human communication, which holds that language is the primary or sole medium of semantic communication. Hence the focus is clearly on rhetorical techniques like 'contrast', 'repetition', 'juxtaposition', 'ambiguity' and 'punchline', all verbal techniques without any mention of that other great carrier of semantic information, namely gesture.

But does the new model of human communication outlined here, which maintains that semantic communication depends upon both speech and accompanying image in the form of iconic gesture, have any implications for the design of more effective advertisements? And does this new model have any implications for helping us understand how different forms of media might compare in terms of relative effectiveness, and why? I wanted to test this by focusing on one important aspect of advertising, namely the transmission of core semantic information about products, necessary for brand identity. We examined the effectiveness of this transmission where this information is divided between speech and iconic gesture, possible in a TV message, compared with radio and text messages, where the inform-ation resides solely in the speech.

We began as usual by studying the most basic aspects of communication, people merely chatting about certain products, in order to see how they gestured. A sample of natural iconic gestures and speech was obtained by video-recording 50 people discussing cars, holidays and mobile phones, a variety of products and services it has to be said chosen more or less at random. Based on these recordings three messages were scripted – one for each product. Next, TV messages were constructed using an actor who was filmed narrating the script and performing six iconic gestures per message.

The physical movements and the exact timings of the gesture with regard to the speech had to be strictly choreographed. This was difficult for the actor because the start point of the preparation phase of the gesture had to begin in advance of the associated speech, so the stroke phase of the gesture would coincide with the right section of the speech. Successful delivery of the message here relied on a very detailed script, not only specifying what to say, but how exactly to move the hands, and when to start moving the hands in the preparation phase to get the hands into the appropriate part of the gestural space (a much more detailed script than actors are used to). For the radio message, only the audio soundtrack was used; for the text message, a verbatim transcription was produced.

Below is one of the three examples of the scripted messages and the six scripted corresponding iconic gestures, based on our own observation of actual gestures used for these semantic features:

Gesture/speech script for the holiday

Beach Holidays Ltd is a new holiday company designed to help you get the kind of relaxing beach holiday we all dream of.

All our holiday destinations are situated in extremely beautiful locations and yet they are only a [short flight] away.

Iconic: Right hand is by the side of the head; fingers are close together and palm is pointing downwards; hand moves horizontally away from the head in a rapid, short, steady movement.

You can relax and sunbathe on long golden beaches, where there is a [clear blue sky and the sun is out].

Iconic: Right hand is in a vertical position; fingers are pointing straight upwards; hand moves in a straight line from the left to the right. Hand then stops and fingers move apart. Fingers then curl up before stretching open again and this is repeated three times.

If you need to cool down you can go [swimming] in the sea

Iconic: Hands are touching at the front of the body; hands and arms move slowly forward away from the body. Hands and arms then move slowly away from each other before beginning to come together again so that a slow circular motion is made by each arm.

and you needn't worry about the children, as the sea is particularly [safe] in the holiday destinations we choose, plus there are twenty-four-

Iconic: Right hand is in front of the body, palm is pointing downwards. Hand moves slowly to the right and produces very slight, smooth up and down movements as it does so.

hour-a-day lifeguards. In fact your only worry will be what factor suntan cream to put on.

You will be able to [eat local delicacies],

Iconic: Right hand is in front of body, palm is pointing upwards; fingers and thumb are slightly curled. Hand then moves towards the mouth; it then remains there for a second before returning to a position in front of the body.

which are cheap yet of good quality. You can wander around markets and observe the local customs.

If you wish you [can dance the night away]

Iconic: Both arms are bent at the elbows. Right hand is slightly curved and above the head; left hand is slightly curved and is in area in front of the thighs. The two hands then swap positions before returning to their original position.

or you can continue to relax and enjoy the entertainment we provide for you.

We are sure that any holiday with Beach Holidays Ltd will be a dream come true.

We then developed a series of multiple-choice questionnaires to measure communicative effectiveness. The questions related to semantic properties such as 'manner' (e.g. style of dancing in the holiday advertisement), 'size' (e.g. size of the wheels in the car advertisement) and 'speed' (e.g. speed of vibration in the mobile phone advertisement) among others. Each question had four alternative answers, and there were 12 questions in which the information required was in gesture and/or speech (complementary gestures) and six questions in which the information was in both gesture and speech (co-expressive gestures). We used 150 participants, random members of the public, 50 in each of the conditions. After each message had been played or read the participant completed the questionnaire.

The results were very revealing – more questions were answered correctly in the TV condition (speech and gesture) than in the radio or text conditions and there was no significant difference between the text and radio conditions. Participants in the TV condition gained 10 per cent more information than participants in the radio condition and 9.2 per cent more information than participants in the text condition (see Figure 14.1).

At first sight these differences, although statistically reliable, might not seem particularly large. However, it is important to remember that multiple-

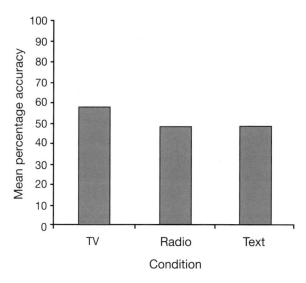

Figure 14.1 Mean percentage accuracy obtained in the TV, radio and text conditions (taken from Beattie and Shovelton 2005).

choice questionnaires with four possible alternatives were used to measure communicative effectiveness. These allowed 25 per cent correct responses through guessing alone. When we allow for chance guessing we find that, in the case of the TV condition, the increase from chance to the percentage of correct answers obtained is 33.2 per cent and for the radio and text conditions combined it is 23.6 per cent. Therefore, the participants in the TV condition gained 40.7 per cent more information than the participants in the radio and text conditions. In other words, the effect is not just statistically reliable, it is also a fairly large effect.

The holiday message was particularly well communicated in the TV condition. To appreciate the size of this effect, we need to think again about the chance probability. The increase from chance to the percentage of correct answers obtained for this message in this condition is 39.3 per cent and for the radio and text conditions combined it is 18 per cent. Therefore, the participants in the TV condition gain 118.3 per cent more information about the holiday message than the participants in the radio and text conditions combined.

Thus far, the results suggest that some iconic gestures do convey significant amounts of information, but what happens when we focus exclusively on co-expressive gestures in which all the information is represented in both the gesture and the speech? These co-expressive gestures were randomly distributed across the three products; the statistical analyses revealed the main effect of condition (TV/radio/text) was still significant and that, overall, significantly more questions were answered correctly in the TV condition than in the radio and text conditions. There was no significant difference between the radio and text conditions. Participants in the TV condition gained 9.3 per cent more information than the participants in the radio condition and 12 per cent more information than those participants in the text condition. When we allow for chance guessing, as before, we find that in the case of the TV condition the increase from chance to the percentage of correct answers for co-expressive gestures is 49.3 per cent and for the radio and text conditions combined it is 38.7 per cent. Therefore, the participants in the TV condition gain 27.6 per cent more information than the partici- pants in the radio and text conditions combined. All of the percentage correct scores, and the percentage increases, are higher in the case of co-expressive gestures than gestures as a whole because the required information was more easily accessible, as it was present in both the speech and gestural modalities.

In the case of complementary gestures, where the information presented in the gesture is different to that presented in the speech, statistical analyses revealed that the main effect of condition was highly significant and that overall significantly more questions were answered correctly in the TV condition than in the radio and text conditions. There was no significant difference between radio and text conditions. Participants in the TV condition gained 10.3 per cent more information than participants in the radio condition and 7.8 per cent more information than those in the text condition. When we allow for chance guessing, we find that in the case of the TV condition the increase from chance to the percentage of correct answers for complementary gestures is 25.2 per cent and for the radio and text conditions combined it is 16.1 per cent. Therefore, the participants in the TV condition gain 56.5 per cent more information than those in the radio and text conditions combined.

The conclusion, therefore, is that iconic gestures, both complementary and co-expressive, do significantly assist in the transmission of core semantic information about a product. We also identified at least one feature of gestures that make them particularly effective in this respect. We found that the span of the gesture, the distance travelled by the gesture in its stroke phase, appears to be absolutely critical. But so far our analyses have focused on differences between TV and radio/text with simply one exposure, but advertising depends on multiple exposures (repetition) as a fundamental principle of effectiveness. Therefore, in a second study we compared the effectiveness of TV vs radio and text across five consecutive trials to investigate whether the differences in communicative effectiveness were maintained or whether the differences start to diminish with repeated exposures. Here, we focused exclusively on the most effective TV advertisement, namely the holiday advertisement. The approach was identical to that in the first study in that we played the holiday advertisement in either TV or radio form or showed it in text form to participants, and we used the multiple-choice questionnaire already employed in that first study. However, after the participants filled in the questionnaire following the first exposure there was a one-minute delay and then the advertisement was played or shown to them again. This was repeated for five exposures. One hundred and fifty participants again took part in this study – 50 in each condition.

The analyses revealed that the main effect of condition was still significant and that overall significantly more questions were answered correctly in the TV condition than in the radio or text conditions. There was no significant difference between the text and radio conditions (Figure 14.2). The main effect of trial number was significant, and there was a significant linear trend, as participants generally gained higher percentage accuracy scores as the number of trials increased. But there did seem to be a ceiling effect of around 72.7 per cent for the TV condition. This ceiling was determined partly by the difficulty of the questions posed. The ceiling was much lower for the other two conditions – without the presence of the iconic gestures the

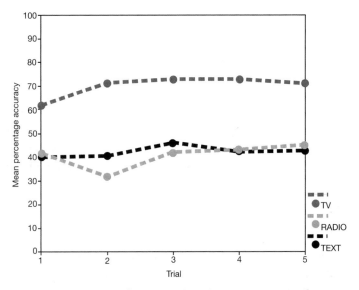

Figure 14.2 Percentage accuracy for the holiday advertisement across five consecutive trials (taken from Beattie and Shovelton 2005).

participants found some of the questions very difficult. There was also a significant trial-by-condition interaction, but only because the radio and text conditions showed significant variation with respect to each other. This new study thus demonstrated conclusively that the influence of iconic gestures is maintained across consecutive trials.

We have discovered that TV advertisements seem to be a highly effective way of communicating information about a product, compared with radio or text presentations. But is the effect due to the presence of iconic gestures in these advertisements or could the significant differences be attributable to a non-specific effect of simply more attention being devoted to a TV image? This question formed the basis for our third study, which compared two TV conditions, one with gesture and one without. A London advertising agency (Cartwright) created two broadcast standard TV advertisements for a non-existent fruit juice drink (although it was one that subsequently came to be made), one involving speech and image and one involving speech and iconic gesture. The agency was advised on what iconic gestures to use for particular properties of the product in one version of the advertisement. The images used in the alternative version of the advertisement were generated on the basis of the agency's own professional experience.

Fifty further people were video-recorded as they described core properties of this product and three iconic gestures were selected for use in the speech–gesture advertisement. The gestures represented three core properties of the product, namely that the fruit used was 'fresh' (hands are together in front of chest, then they move away from each other abruptly as fingers stretch and become wide apart), that 'everyone' was drinking it (right hand and arm move away from the body making a large sweeping movement) and the 'size' of the bottle (hands move towards each other until they represent the size of the bottle).

The advertisements were spoof gangster-style interactions. Two green-grocers were seen to be interrogating the inventor of 'F' as to how he managed to cram five portions of fruit into a little bottle. The greengrocers were worried that people would no longer need to buy as much fruit from them.

Speech and gesture ad for 'F'

Grocer 1: Come on, son, you invented 'F' so fess up, how's it done?

Grocer 2: Mango, pear, cranberries, banana and orange. Five fruit portions [crammed into every tiny little bottle].

Iconic: Right hand is above left hand. Palms are pointing towards each other. Hands move towards each other until they are about five inches apart – this represents the size of the bottle.

Grocer 1: Look, we're not monsters.
Grocer 2: No, we're greengrocers.
Grocer 1: [Everyone's drinking it.]

Iconic: Right hand and arm move away from the body making a large sweeping movement.

Grocer 2: Delicious, [fresh], you're muscling in on our patch.

Metaphoric: Hands are together in front of chest, then they move away from each other abruptly as fingers stretch and become wide apart.

Voiceover: 'F', five daily portions of pure fruit in one.

Figure 14.3 Iconic gestures representing 'freshness', 'everyone' and 'size' in the TV ad for 'F'.

For the speech–image advertisement the advertising agency created their own images to convey these same three properties (freshness – juice sparkling on the fruit; everyone – *The Stun* newspaper displaying the headline

'Everyone's drinking it'; size – image of the actual bottle with respect to the hand). The images here can be seen in Figure 14.4:

Speech and image ad for 'F'

Grocer 1: Come on, son, you invented 'F' so fess up, how's it done?

Grocer 2: Mango, pear, cranberries, banana and orange. Five fruit portions
  [crammed into every tiny little bottle].

Image of the actual bottle with respect to the hand.

Grocer 1: Look, we're not monsters.

Grocer 2: No, we're greengrocers.

Grocer 1: [Everyone's drinking it.]

The Stun newspaper displaying the headline 'Everyone's drinking it'.

Grocer 2: Delicious, [fresh], you're muscling in on our patch.

Juice sparkling on the fruit.

Voiceover: 'F', five daily portions of pure fruit in one.

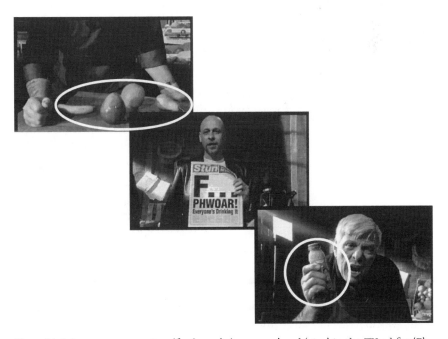

Figure 14.4 Images representing 'freshness', 'everyone' and 'size' in the TV ad for 'F'.

These ads were played twice to two independent groups of 50 participants. The participants were again a convenience sample of members of the public, and a multiple-choice questionnaire was used with five alternatives for each of these core properties.

In terms of these three core properties, we compared the proportions of 'correct' answers and 'wrong' answers – those answers deemed most undesirable for this particular product. The 'wrong' answers here were not simply all residual responses other than correct; rather they were the responses that the advertising agency considered most damaging for this particular product. For example, in the case of freshness, the 'correct' answer was 'fresh', the 'wrong' answer was 'not at all fresh' (the other three possible responses represented degrees of freshness) (see Table 14.1).

Table 14.1 Speech and image vs speech and gesture: a comparison

	Percentage choosing the correct answer		Percentage choosing the 'wrong' answer	
	Speech and image	Speech and gesture	Speech and image	Speech and gesture
Fresh	86	94	14	6
For everyone	26	50	28	12
Bottle size	32	46	20	4

Source: Taken from Beattie and Shovelton 2005

The analyses revealed that significantly more participants reported that the product was 'fresh', 'for everyone' and the 'right size' compared with the 'wrong' answers when these properties were represented with gestures rather than with images. In other words, iconic gestures are particularly effective at communicating core semantic properties of products compared with other images which are not gestural. In the world of small margins in advertising this could all be very important.

The research in this chapter seems to suggest that the effectiveness of communication, in this case advertising, can be increased using this new theory. We found that advertisements in which the message was split between speech and iconic gesture, which is possible on TV, were more effective than those in which the core information about a product resided purely in speech, as occurs in radio or in text form (newspaper/magazine advertisements). This was true for both co-expressive gestures and complementary gestures.

Allowing for chance guessing in a multiple-choice questionnaire, we found that the participants in the TV condition gained 40.7 per cent more information about the core dimensions of the products than the participants in the other conditions. Some TV advertisements were particularly effective – participants in the TV condition gained 118.3 per cent more information from the holiday advertisement about aspects of the holiday than the participants in the other conditions.

Our first study here used a single exposure of the various advertisements, but advertising in the real world depends on repetition as a fundamental principle of increasing effectiveness. Therefore, in a second study we compared the effectiveness of TV vs radio and text presentations, for the holiday message, across five consecutive trials to investigate whether the differences in effectiveness observed in Study 1 were maintained. We found convincing evidence that they were indeed maintained across all five trials. In the third study we compared the communicative power of iconic gestures with a number of contemporary images generated by professional advertisers in two comparable TV advertisements. We found that the iconic gestures were particularly effective at communicating the three core properties of the product that we focused on (the 'freshness' of the fruit, that the product was for 'everyone' and that it came in a 'small', conveniently sized bottle). These results are extremely interesting because they suggest that the effects that we have observed throughout this series of studies are not simply attributable to the general effects of TV per se, but rather that iconic gestures are particularly effective at transmitting core information about a product and better (in some cases at least) than the images generated by a professional agency. One possible explanation as to why iconic gestures are so effective is that these hand movements illustrate just the core semantic properties of a product. For example, the iconic gesture representing the 'size' of the bottle just displays the size dimension, and nothing else, with the hands moving closer together to uniquely identify the size of the bottle. There are no other aspects of the bottle communicated through this gesture, like for example, colour, texture, the shape of the bottle or width at the top, to distract from the core communication. Complex visual images of the kinds used in TV advertisements have many properties; iconic gestures, by contrast, are able to isolate just the core dimensions that one wishes to communicate. This could well be why they are so effective.

The results of these three studies have potentially significant implications for how we might think about the design of effective communication and particularly about the construction of powerful TV advertisements. They suggest that speech and gesture together are better at semantic

Woman: You went into the back of my <u>NEW CAR</u>

Michael: [Calm down dear.]

[it's a <u>commercial</u>]

Woman: °ooh°

Michael: I'm really a very good driver. That's why I'm with <u>esure</u>

Woman: Hello mum(.) I'm on the <u>telly</u>

Figure 14.5 Michael Winner esure commercial (for transcript conventions see Table 1.1, p. 5).

communication than speech alone. They suggest that iconic gestures are particularly effective in TV advertisements and significantly better than the kinds of images that are traditionally used. Some TV advertisements have used iconic gestures, for example, Michael Winner in the esure insurance advertisement (shown in the UK from 2002 onwards), but these iconic gestures possess few of the semantic or temporal properties of natural iconic gestures. They simply do not start and stop at the right points with respect to the speech, and the form of the gesture is completely unchanged with a new syntactic clause.

Our new research suggests that the effectiveness of TV advertisements could be improved by incorporating spontaneous images of the hands with the right temporal and semantic properties. Given that speech evolved in the context of (Goldin-Meadow and McNeill 1999; McNeill 2012) and possibly through (Allott 1992) these gestures, this research suggests intriguingly that aspects of our evolutionary past may have significant implications for the content of our most modern advertisements. The brain has, after all, clearly evolved to deal with speech in the context of the spontaneous images created by the human hand.

One way of making TV advertisements more effective, therefore, is to find exactly the right iconic gestures to communicate the properties we want to convey. The fact that such gestures are usually generated without any conscious awareness on the part of the speaker might also give them extra 'credibility' in the communicational task. This again could make a very significant difference in politics, in religion, in charity appeals, in selling, in advertising and in life.

SUMMARY

- Speech and gesture together are more effective at semantic communication than speech alone.

- Iconic gestures are particularly effective in TV advertisements at communicating particular semantic properties.

- Some TV advertisements have traditionally used both iconic and metaphoric gestures, but these gestures have possessed few of the semantic or temporal properties of natural iconic gestures.

- Such gestures look artificial and are less effective because of this.

- Given that speech evolved through gestures, this research suggests intriguingly that aspects of our evolutionary past may have significant implications for the content of our most modern advertisements.

- The fact that iconic gestures are usually generated without any conscious awareness on the part of the speaker might also give them extra 'credibility' in carefully constructed communications of this type.

15

HOW ICONIC GESTURES CAN LEAK THE TRUTH

We all lie, and only a liar would really try to deny this. Men, it seems, like to boast quite a bit in their daily interactions, according to a lie diary study. They often extend the truth when they are boasting, sometimes to breaking point. The same study suggests that women tell lies more frequently than men do (with some female samples telling double the number that males did), but they often tell lies to make others feel better.

'Of course you don't look fat in that dress.'

'You are just as attractive as the day I met you.'

'Eating that will not put on the pounds.'

'That dress really suits you.'

Lie diaries, where you record each and every lie told in the day relative to each interaction, reveal these findings and much more besides (DePaulo et al. 1996). Many lies are routine parts of our everyday life, designed for self-presentation and self-enhancement, or designed to smooth our interactions with others, to promote harmony, by allowing others to feel better with us, as we feed them some porky-pies. Lies are a part of the great social function of everyday talk, and we do most of this without any planning at all. In the words of Erving Goffman:

> The legitimate performances of everyday life are not 'acted' or 'put on' in the sense that the performer knows in advance just what he is going to do, and does this solely because of the effect it is likely to have . . . In short, we all act better than we know how.
>
> (Goffman 1959: 73–4)

In essence, we tell lies regularly and we are very good at it. DePaulo and her colleagues also noted that 'Consistent with the view of lying as an everyday social interaction process, participants said that they did not regard their lies as serious and did not plan them much or worry about being caught' (DePaulo *et al.* 1996: 979). In other words, they are routine and without any real consequences (although, of course, we may grow dependent on the lies told to us, and that may be quite serious enough).

However, sometimes there are much bigger lies. Lies that we need to think about and plan, lies that cause us to feel terrible guilt in the telling and sometimes acute anxiety about being discovered, lies that can tear us apart. We try to disguise these both in terms of our planning and in terms of our emotional response. We rehearse what we are going to say and then we try to control our emotions in the moment itself, and we hope we can get away with it. Lies require a degree of extra cognitive planning; it is more difficult to make up a story about why you were late and what you were doing rather than merely recounting the true version of events. Lies sometimes are associated with significant emotion in the telling – fear, guilt, anxiety, apprehension; most of these associated emotions are very negative, but occasionally we feel positive emotion – pride, relief, joy that someone is falling for it (Ekman 1985). Some individuals habitually feel positive emotion when lying; often these individuals have a personality disorder, but sometimes they do not (Ekman 1988). Lying is a complex blend of cognition and emotion that varies from lie to lie, from relationship to relationship and from situation to situation. There are no universal telltale signs of lying because of this variability in their construction, function and effects, but there are indicators of additional cognitive planning, and indicators of emotional response. Unfilled pauses increase with the demands of extra cognitive planning (Beattie 1978, 1979), but these planning pauses may not be necessary with sufficient mental rehearsal of the lie. We may feel strong negative emotions when we lie, but emotional expressions on our face can be covered quickly by a mask by efficient liars (Ekman 1988). The mask is usually a particular type of smile, called a non-Duchenne smile, characterised by a degree of facial asymmetry (stronger on one side of the face than the other side) and by its rapid onset and offset. It would be hard to find a single behavioural indicator of lying that is truly reliable given that each lie varies on the cognitive dimensions of difficulty, and degree of rehearsal (if any) and a wide variety of negative and positive emotional dimensions, where the emotional expressions may be masked or not. There may not be a single behavioural indicator but there are trends, and one interesting trend is the attempted control or inhibition of behaviour. We seem to know instinctively that our behaviour can leak a great deal, so we attempt to inhibit it, as Charles Darwin (1872) noted. After all, the most general conclusion possible about lying is that people do not want to give the game away, even in the routine lies of everyday life, where there really is no consequence, except perhaps losing face ('Alright then, you do look fat in that dress. Are you happy now?'). Therefore, we try a strategy of general behavioural control – keep normal eye contact (people usually watch our eyes), smile as naturally as possible (they watch our faces), look relaxed, do not fidget too much, try to move the hands less, keep the feet still.

Darwin (1872) had actually very little to say about either deception or lying in his seminal work on nonverbal behaviour *The Expression of Emotions in Man and Animals*. But what he did have to say was that such nonverbal behaviours 'reveal the thoughts and intentions of others more truly than do words, which may be falsified' (1872: 359). But he also wrote that

> when movements, associated through habit with certain states of the mind, are partially repressed by the will, the strictly involuntary muscles, as well as those which are least under the separate control of the will, are liable still to act; and their action is often highly expressive.
>
> (Darwin 1872: 54)

In other words, people try to repress or inhibit certain expressive movements when they are lying, but they will not always be successful. Some behaviours are harder to inhibit than others. Ekman (2003) refers to this as the inhibition hypothesis – 'if you cannot make an action voluntarily, then you will not be able to prevent it when involuntary processes such as emotion instigate it' (2003: 206). Therefore, it follows that certain emotional expressions that cannot easily be inhibited may be powerful indicators of felt emotion. Ekman (2001, 2003) calls this 'nonverbal leakage'. However, Darwin, of course, is also implying that other movements will be inhibited during deception (those that are under volitional control, like hand movements and gesture, for example), and that their form and morphology will not be so revealing of the real underlying state. Although, of course, we should note that the inhibition (or attempted inhibition) of these behaviours may be itself highly revealing.

Ekman adds one major complication to this argument, namely that although hand movements, for example, through the medium of gesture, or foot movements

> would be easy to inhibit . . . most people do not bother to censor their body actions. Because most of us do not get much feedback from others about what our body movements are revealing, we do not learn the need to monitor these actions; and so, we hypothesized, when people lie, they usually do not fine-tune their body actions.
>
> (Ekman 2003: 208)

In other words, he is arguing that although gestures could be inhibited they often are not and that therefore 'the body will be a good source of deception cues – exactly the opposite of what Darwin predicted' (Ekman 2003: 208). Elsewhere Ekman has explicitly criticised Darwin because he 'failed to note the existence of gestural slips (Ekman 1985), which leak concealed feelings and intentions, and other forms of body movement that can betray a lie' (Ekman 2009: 3451).

Therefore, if we consider the arguments of these two great pioneers in the field of nonverbal communication we end up with a number of specific hypotheses. First, when it comes to deception, there may well be an attempt on the part of those trying to deceive to suppress or inhibit certain behaviours that are potentially highly expressive, and a decrease in the frequency of certain behaviours may itself be one potential indicator of deception. Second, because the conventions of everyday talk shape our awareness of our bodily actions, then we may not monitor sufficiently certain behaviours that we could volitionally control (like gesture, which, after all, we can volitionally control quite easily by locking the hands). Some behaviours like gesture (potentially controllable but not always monitored) may, therefore, be quite revealing in terms of their manner of execution.

There is research evidence to suggest that whereas people generally think that many behaviours *increase* when people are telling lies, meta-analyses of various research studies reveal that only a small number of behaviours change reliably during deception, and these behaviours tend to *decrease* when lying as a function of behavioural inhibition. Sporer and Schwandt (2007) conducted just such a meta-analysis of the published literature on deception and found that only three forms of behaviour were reliably associated with

lying, and they were 'nodding', 'foot and leg movements' and 'hand movements'. All three were found to *decrease* in frequency. It is worth remembering
that in their classic 1969 paper on 'Nonverbal Leakage and Clues to
Deception', Ekman and Friesen predicted that because people are generally
unaware of the behaviour of their feet and legs, they should be 'a good
source for leakage and deception cues'. They predicted *more* movements in
the feet and legs during deception (things like 'abortive restless flight
movements . . . frequent shift of leg posture, and in restless or repetitive
leg and foot acts', Ekman and Friesen 1969). This prediction has been proven
wrong in the vast majority of studies (including in Ekman's own research,
see Ekman 2003: 211). People do seem to inhibit their behaviour during
deception, even the feet and legs.

The hands, of course, are particularly interesting in this regard for one
very important reason. I would argue that it is really quite difficult to fake
the form of iconic gestures when you are lying and make it accurate. It is
also very complicated to split meaning into the verbal and gestural channels
in a way that might look natural or normal. You would have to get the
division of meaning between the two channels just right, as well as the
precise iconic form of the gesture and the right degree of anticipation of
the associated part of the verbal message by the preparation phase of the
gesture. In Chapter 13 on metaphoric gestures, you can see what could
happen if you get it wrong. This would all be quite demanding, and it seems
that many people do not attempt this and opt for a safer (and easier) strategy.
People tend to inhibit their hand movements when telling lies, and gesture
frequency decreases in deception (Cody and O'Hair 1983; Davis and Hadiks
1995; Ekman 1988; Ekman and Friesen 1972; Ekman *et al.* 1976; Ekman
et al. 1991; Greene *et al.* 1985; Hofer *et al.* 1993; Kalma *et al.* 1996; Mann
et al. 1998; Vrij *et al.* 1999; but see Bond *et al.* 1985; DeTurck and Miller
1985). Indeed, a decrease in gestural frequency would seem to be one of
the more reliable indicators of deception. It suggests perhaps that at some
unconscious level, liars do not want to risk giving the game away through
revealing hand movements. Therefore, they try to inhibit this form of
behaviour by clasping their hands or using similar kinds of strategy. Aldert
Vrij (2000) has a useful summary of this research in his book *Detecting Lies
and Deceit*. He also summarises the empirical evidence that most people believe
that gesture frequency actually increases during deception, which shows that
most people have a false belief here, as in so many other areas when it comes
to deception.

Below is an interesting case of gestural inhibition recorded in the run-
up to the General Election in 2005 in the UK. The speaker is the then Prime

Minister, Tony Blair, meeting a group of young mothers in the weeks before the election. This was a core demographic group for the Prime Minister that he was attempting to reach out to. The child sitting on his knee belonged to one of the young mothers. He gestures throughout this conversation except interestingly when he says that looking after his children when his wife Cherie was at work was 'the toughest thing you ever do'. It is only during this particular utterance (and a similar one where he repeats the same basic proposition) that his hand gestures are inhibited; his hand movements occur quite freely the rest of the time.

```
If I (.) If I was looking after them (0.2) sort of
1.  [Frida::y](0.4)
2.  [Saturda::y]
3.  [Sunday and]
4.  [Cherie was away] doing something (0.4)I would go back
in(.)on
5.  Monday morning and
6.  I was (0.6)
7.  I was [completely wiped out](0.4)
```

```
8.  It's the toughest thing you ever do (0.2)
9.  It's also what you've got to do and I think (0.2)
```

```
10. actually now they they're [at this stage] I think they've
become (0.2)
11. [really really](0.4)
12. [interesting] as well(0.2)
13. they're. they're.they're fa. they're faci
14. coz you can just see them [developing all the time]
```

Figure 15.1 Behavioural inhibition – Prime Minister Tony Blair.

Description of gestures

Line

1–3.	Left arm extending along left thigh. Hand perpendicular to leg makes a beat which coincides with 'Friday'. This beat is repeated on lines 2 and 3, coinciding with 'Saturday' and 'Sunday'.
4.	Left arm moves slightly away from body. Palm facing up. A metaphoric gesture representing Cherie being away.
6 and 7.	Hand comes up, palm faces out to the interviewer (preparation phase of gesture). Palm facing down and moves out to the side away from the body, then stops on left thigh (metaphoric gesture coinciding with 'completely wiped out').
8.	Hand now stationary and in rest position on the left leg (coinciding with 'It's the toughest thing you ever do').
9.	Palm of hand facing body raises to chest level. Elbow rests on arm of the chair (start of deictic gesture)
10.	Points to child on his knee and looks at her. Fingers are stretched and open (deictic gesture referring to the child and others 'at this stage').
11 and 12.	Palm of hand facing body, fingers outstretched, moves hand forward in a beat motion away from body, corresponding to 'really, really interesting'.
13.	Palm of hand facing chest, fingers outstretched, hand rotating in a circular motion once outward from the body, gesture seems to be assisting in word finding (unsuccessfully), becomes de facto preparation phase of next gesture.
14.	Fingers outstretched, palm facing child moving towards and away from child in short, quick motion. Metaphoric gesture corresponding to 'developing all the time'.

Given that Tony Blair had invaded Iraq, revised the constitution of the Labour Party in the face of considerable opposition, abandoned the socialist traditions of his Party, won three General Elections, etc., looking after the kids for the day might not have actually been 'the toughest thing' he ever had to do. However, I am sure that the sentiment worked well with his audience that day. Gestural inhibition, however, on this occasion seems to have passed largely unnoticed.

It would seem to be a reasonable hypothesis that if the hands are not prevented from gesturing in this way, then the precise form of the gesture could *potentially* be highly revealing when people are lying. I have a number of specific examples here to support this idea (but they are largely anecdotal). The first example comes from a meeting at a Public Relations company where one of the executives was talking about the sales of a particular product after their campaign had finished. She said:

the sales after that campaign [started to soar]

Iconic: Right hand makes upward trajectory but falls fractionally at the top most part of the trajectory. The slight fall depicted in the gesture corresponds to the word 'soar'.

The iconic gesture seemed to contradict what she was saying in her speech. I actually interrupted the meeting at this point to query whether sales had indeed soared as she had said or instead had declined, as I suspected because of the gesture. She hesitated, slightly embarrassed, and admitted that I was in fact correct. Sales had declined immediately after the campaign, 'but they picked up again' she added defensively. I was 'praised', if that is the right word, for my perceptiveness.

Here is another anecdotal example. A female friend was telling me about her experiences at a party where a close friend's boyfriend had kissed her. Here is what she said:

and he [kissed me] on the cheek

Iconic: Fingers of right hand outstretched and close together, thumb curled in towards palm. Hand moves towards mouth and fingertips touch right-hand side of lips.

Since the person who kissed her was the boyfriend of a very close friend, she did not want to admit that this kiss was in any way intimate. The speech was under strict editorial control; she said exactly what she intended to. The iconic gesture was under much less strict editorial control and indicated the *relative position* of both sets of lips. This was not a kiss on the cheek, no matter what she said. I queried this and she looked astonished to be challenged in this way. 'You weren't there,' she said. 'How do you know?' I pointed out her gesture to her and she said that she did not even realise that she had made a gesture in the first place.

Another example comes from *Celebrity Big Brother* from November 2002. *Celebrity Big Brother* is a reality TV programme where a number of celebrities go into the *Big Brother* house to live for a period of ten days for charity (and be observed whilst they are there). I was the psychologist on this particular show analysing the behaviour of the housemates. One of the most striking features of this particular show was the behaviour of the comedian and game show host Les Dennis. Les had been called into the Diary Room and because he gained a score of zero in a quiz set by *Big Brother*, he was the only housemate who had to do the nominating for the forthcoming eviction. He was explaining why this nomination process was so difficult for him.

Les: We [are all six of us, very, very, close]

Metaphoric: Left hand is in front of left shoulder, palm is pointing forwards and fingers are straight and apart. Hand moves quickly to the left away from the body and then moves quickly back to its position in front of shoulder. This whole movement is repeated twice. The first half of the movement is then produced for a third time and the hand now remains away from the body.

[really close]

Metaphoric: Hands are wide apart, palms point towards each other. Hands move rapidly towards each other to an area in front of stomach but hands don't touch – they stop when they are about six inches apart.

He said that the housemates were all 'very, very close', so you would expect the gesture to be moving towards the body to represent 'closeness' in the form of an image in the gestural space, but the first gesture is actually away from the body. Then when he says 'really close', the distance between his hands tells us how close the housemates actually were – which was not close at all. If the housemates had been close the hands should have been drawn together. My interpretation here is based on the premise that speakers do use the gestural space (the space in front of the body) in a meaningful and consistent way. This particular interpretation of the mismatch was supported by an interview with Les Dennis that I conducted after the series finished. He put it very succinctly: 'I wasn't close to any of them'.

```
I can't [explain] why (0.1)

no ehm (0.8) wh (hhh)
```

```
.h YES I WILL

eh but just let me say that it's been very difficult

it sounds

[like a cliche cause judges say this at (.) ta talent contents
and things like that] .hhh
```

```
                     It's been [very
                          difficult]
```

```
              [WE ARE ALL SIX OF
           US VERY VERY CLOSE](.)
```

```
              [REALLY CLOSE]
```

Figure 15.2 Les Dennis describing his relationship with his housemates with a mismatching gesture.

The hypothesis that the precise form of iconic gestures may give the game away when people are trying to deceive formed the basis for one experiment in our lab. Here participants had to narrate a story from a static cartoon, which we projected onto a screen in front of them. They had to do this twice – once as accurately as possible (truth condition) and once with some details of the story changed (deception condition). They had to attempt to persuade another person sitting in the room that these changed details were actually part of the real story. For example, in one picture a boy was dribbling a football around an opponent in a circle. In the deception condition, the participant had to change critical details, like the fact that the boy was dribbling the ball around the other player, but doing so in the shape of a square. This was an attempt to mimic some of the cognitive aspects of lying in the real world. Reasonably good liars are often found to base their false accounts partly on things that have actually happened to them, while changing certain core details, rather than making up a completely false account from scratch. As Samuel Butler (1903) said: 'The best liar is he who makes the smallest amount of lying go the longest way' (1903:163). The question was whether the form of any iconic gestures would give some hint as to the real nature of the events at these critical points in the story.

In a simple task like this, our participants found it relatively easy to change the story in their speech ('the boy dribbles round the other player in a square shape'). The form of their gestures was, however, a different matter. Thus, one participant narrating the story about the boy dribbling the football said:

and he runs around him [in a square]

Iconic: Right hand in space in front of body, index finger straight, other fingers curled, makes a series of anti-clockwise circular movements.

The iconic gesture here still depicted the original 'true' circular movement of the boy and the ball, rather than the changed 'false' version. This is exactly what Ekman and Friesen called 'nonverbal leakage' in their classic paper back in 1969.

Simple stress-timed beats, on the other hand, would be a good deal simpler to fake than iconic gestures. Indeed, there appears to be good (and well-viewed) documentary evidence for this. When Bill Clinton was interviewed by the American Senate back in 1998 and accused of having 'sexual relations' with Monica Lewinsky, his protests of innocence contained quite a number of beats:

<u>Bill Clinton: I did [not have sexual relations] with that woman, Miss Lewinsky.</u>

Beat: Index finger of right hand pointing away from body, other fingers curled up. Hand makes four sharp, rapid downwards movements. Each downward movement begins at the start of each of the four words accompanied by the gesture.

<u>Bill Clinton: The allegations (audible swallow) are false (audible swallow)</u>

Beat: Fingers on the right hand are straight and apart; hand is positioned vertically to the body. Hand moves downwards twice – first time on the word 'allegations' and second time on the words 'are false'.

However, there is an important point to make here. President Clinton was determined to use a very precise form of words in defending himself during these accusations of sexual misconduct. At the Senate Hearings, President Clinton was asked a series of quite specific questions about his sexual relationship with Monica Lewinsky. The written statement he had provided was that 'These meetings did not consist of sexual intercourse.' He was then asked a series of highly embarrassing, more detailed questions including: 'If Miss Lewinsky says that while you were in the Oval Office area you touched her genitalia would she be lying? That calls for a "yes", "no", or "revert to your former statement".' President Clinton replied: 'I will revert to my statement on that.' He was quite determined to stick to a certain form of words.

During his verbal answers there were quite a few beats actually displayed. So does this mean that he was lying or telling the truth? What he actually said in the Senate Hearings, and in a number of interviews at the time, is very important here because the words he used repeatedly were 'sexual relations' or 'sexual intercourse'. It has since been pointed out to me that there is a saying in the Southern States of the USA that 'eatin' ain't cheatin''. In other words, oral sex does not constitute 'sexual relations'. If President Clinton had managed to persuade himself of the truth of this proposition, then it would allow for the presence of the beats in his speech as an index of truth because he only engaged in oral sex with Miss Lewinsky (as a recipient not as a giver – this is critical; see the above question put to him) and not actual sexual intercourse. He might have been using beats in his speech because strictly speaking, in his mind at least, he was actually telling the truth. Alternatively, of course, it could be that President Clinton was a well-rehearsed liar who had become an expert in the control of most aspects of his body language, except the odd micro-expression and swallow that did occasionally slip out rather noticeably. He included the easy to fake beats rather than the more difficult to fake iconic gestures in his speech for effect. Research into the ability of people to fake iconic gestures and beats while they lie is still very much in its infancy, but my bet is that a careful study of these behaviours will always reveal a great deal more than mere attention to speech itself.

However, could we uncover the effects of deception on gesture production more systematically than in the sorts of observations reported so far? This formed the basis for a new study that Doron Cohen, Heather Shovelton and I conducted. It was a very simple study (and similar to the previous one conducted in our lab) but with potentially important implications because of the detail in the analysis. As before, we instructed participants to narrate a story from a comic book to another person. In one condition, they simply had to tell the story as it was (truth condition). In the second condition (the deception condition), they had to change some critical details in three semantic events in the story and they were given explicit instructions as to what those changes had to be. Participants were provided with as much time as they required to learn the modifications to the three semantic events and a projector continually displayed the cartoon story on a wall in front of them (in an attempt to minimise the cognitive demands placed on the participants).

The study was designed to test a number of basic experimental hypotheses. First, we assumed that in line with previous research there would be a significant decrease in the relative frequency of iconic hand gestures when people are lying compared to when they are telling the truth. Second, we predicted that those gestures that do still occur during deception would have significantly shorter durations than those produced during truth-telling (a further attempt at behavioural inhibition by those involved in deception). Finally, we predicted that some of the gestures that do arise in the deception condition would display elements of the real state of affairs shown in the original story. This would constitute evidence of nonverbal leakage in Ekman's sense – the truth leaking out through the precise form of the gestural movement.

Our stimulus material consisted of a static cartoon story – Ivy the Terrible comic taken from the Beano. Each of our 30 participants was invited into an observation room and informed that they were taking part in an experiment which investigated 'how well people tell truths and lies in order to further our understanding of how the brain processes and copes with misinformation and deceit'. All the participants were told to narrate the comic story both honestly and deceptively, with the order of lying vs truth-telling being fully counterbalanced. So as not to interfere with their gesture production, the story was projected onto a wall directly in front of the participants (as in our previous research). This ensured that the participants' hands were free to move naturally. In order to obtain as natural a sample of behaviour as possible, participants were filmed by an unobtrusive video camera (see Beattie 1982). In the truth condition, the participants were simply instructed to narrate the story in their own words 'as clearly and in as much detail as possible' to a confederate. At the outset of the deception condition, the participants were told that some critical details in three semantic events in the story had to be changed (it was explained to them exactly what these changes were). They would then have to tell this altered version of the story to another person who had never seen the comic before (in other words, this version did not correspond to what was up in front of them). In addition, they were informed that at the end of the experiment this other person would have to guess whether they were telling the truth or lying, and consequently that they should try to be 'as convincing as possible'. All participants were told that if they managed to convince their interlocutor that they were telling the truth when in fact they were lying, they would be rewarded. At the end of the experiment, all participants (irrespective of their actual lying ability) were given a chocolate bar (a great motivator for many students!).

The third frame of this particular story clearly depicted Ivy, the central character, pushing a DJ into the boot of a car and slamming the boot lid by pushing it downwards, whilst her speech bubble reveals her intention to 'lock him in the boot'. In the deception condition the participants were instructed to lie by claiming that in this semantic event Ivy locks the DJ in the back seat of the car (not the boot) by pushing him through the side-door, thus involving a sideways rather than downward movement. In the seventh frame of the story, Ivy is shown pouring the contents of a bottle of extra strong washing-up liquid into a bubble machine in an attempt to produce more bubbles. The participants in the deception condition were told to say that she accidentally spills some of the washing-up liquid on the floor, making a horrible and sticky mess. In the final (twelfth) frame of the story, bubbles are shown emerging from Ivy's mouth. In the deception condition, the participants were told to say that the bubbles were coming out of her ears.

As there is some evidence that producing bodily actions can result in interlocutors increasing their own bodily movements, especially in the context of lie detection (see Akehurst and Vrij 1999), the experimenter did not 'act out' the changes (i.e. did not gesture himself) when describing them to the participant. Instead, the changes were read off a standardised script. After the three changes had been explained to the participants, they were asked to confirm that they had understood them and could remember those parts of the story that required modification.

We found that 17 of our 30 participants produced spontaneous iconic gestures in their stories. This resulted in 34 narratives (17 speakers by two conditions – truth vs deception) to be analysed. Although iconic gestures are according to McNeill 'typically large complex movements, performed relatively slowly and carefully in the central gesture space' (1985: 359), it is important to point out that sometimes gestures can be small or fast, and operate outside the central gesture space, but nevertheless still be in possession of iconic properties. In total, 351 iconic gestures were analysed in this experiment.

Before comparing the relative frequency of iconic gestures that encoded aspects of the three modified details (frames 3, 7 and 12) across the two conditions, the initial analysis examined the gesture production rate of *all* iconic gestures in both the truth and deception conditions. This analysis aimed to establish whether changing just three specific events in a story had an impact on the *overall* frequency of iconic gestures in the deception condition.

Of the 351 iconic hand gestures that were identified across the 34 narratives, 169 were produced in the truth condition and 182 in the deception condition. Table 15.1 shows the frequency distribution (in percentage terms) of the participants' hand movements as a function of condition.

Despite a greater number of gestures occurring in the deception condition than in the truth condition, Table 15.1 reveals that over half of the participants (52.9 per cent) actually executed *more* iconic gestures when

Table 15.1 Percentage frequency of participants' hand movements by condition

Frequency of iconic gestures	Percentage of participants
Increases during deception	41.2%
No difference between conditions	5.9%
Decreases during deception	52.9%

Source: Taken from Cohen *et al.* 2010, Copyright © 2010, Walter de Gruyter GmbH

telling the truth than when lying, whilst 41.2 per cent demonstrated the reverse trend (i.e. increased hand movements during deception); 5.9 per cent of participants produced the same number of gestures in both conditions. Statistical analyses revealed that the differences in the frequency of gestures between the conditions were not significant and it was also not significant when the number of words produced was controlled for. Therefore, in other words, people having to 'lie' about specific incidents in a story had no impact on gesture production in the story as a whole. Any effects of deception on gesture must be more localised than that.

The second analysis thus examined the relative frequency of iconic gestures only in relation to the three specific semantic events that were modified (the three 'lies'). In order for a gesture to be included in the second analysis, it had to satisfy a number of specific inclusion criteria. First, we had to be able to interpret the actual semantic event depicted in the speech and in the gesture. Take the first semantic event, for example. Participants would either have to describe a scene in which Ivy locks the DJ in the boot of his car (truth version), or else claim that she locked him in the car using the side-door (deception). In order to be included in this particular analysis, participants would have to execute a gesture that depicted Ivy pushing the DJ and explicitly state verbally that he entered the car through either the boot or the side-door, respectively. Alternatively, the morphological structure of the gesture would need to discriminate between the act of closing a boot (downward movement) and that of shutting the door of a vehicle (sideways movement). Consider the example below (see Figure 15.3) in which a speaker is describing the first critical detail in the deception condition:

'so she [locks him in the car]'

Iconic: Both hands rise slightly, palms facing each other and away from speaker, while arms are bent at elbows. During stroke phase elbows rotate slightly and extend forwards, pushing out into the gesture space. Palms momentarily flick outwards before returning to rest.

Here the gesture provides insufficient information to be included, as Ivy pushes the DJ into the car in both conditions, and the gesture only signals that an agent is pushing some object, but fails to disambiguate between the two competing possibilities (boot vs side-door). Interestingly, in the next example, despite an identical clause structure, the form of the gesture here explicitly reveals that the DJ has been locked in the boot of the car, and therefore this would be coded as a 'truthful gesture'.

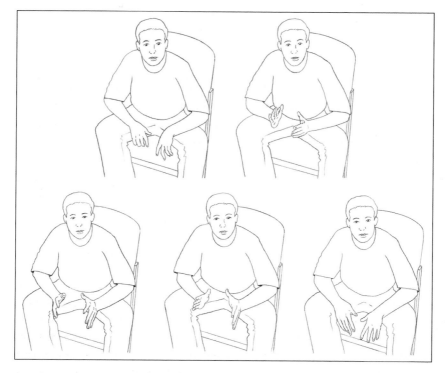

Figure 15.3 A gesture describing the DJ being locked in the car (deception condition) (redrawn from Cohen *et al*. 2010, Copyright © 2010, Walter de Gruyter GmbH).

'so Ivy locks [him in the car]'

Iconic: Right hand rises to above eye-level, palm faces away from speaker and is perpendicular. Entire right hand then descends rapidly, consistent with the act of shutting a boot, using a single hand. Left hand is locked in a post-hold pause from previous gesture.

In relation to the second semantic event, participants were required either to describe Ivy pouring washing-up liquid into the bubble machine (truth), or to fabricate the event by claiming that Ivy accidentally spills some of the solution, making a 'horrible sticky mess' (deception). Very occasionally, however, participants' descriptions (2/17 speakers) of this event went beyond these instructions, but these additions were not included in the analysis, even if they did consist of a complete falsification. For instance, one participant produced the following utterance: 'so she gets the bubble mix ... mixture and pours it in erm but ... but there is a ... I think a

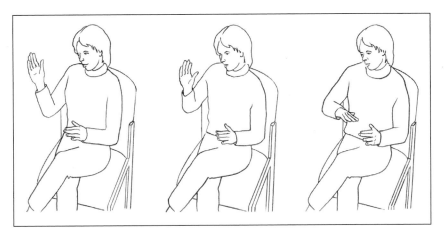

Figure 15.4 A gesture describing Ivy locking the DJ in the car (truthful condition) (redrawn from Cohen *et al.* 2010, Copyright © 2010, Walter de Gruyter GmbH).

[banana skin] on the floor . . . and she slips and . . . anyway it [spills every-where making a sticky mess].' Here only the second gesture was coded as being a 'deceptive gesture', as the first gesture represents a confabulation that the participants were not instructed to produce. To incorporate this 'extra' gesture in the analysis could bias the data towards an overestimation of gesture frequency in the deception condition.

The final semantic event required participants either to describe a scene where bubbles come out of Ivy's mouth (truth) or out of her ears (decep-tion). One difficulty encountered with this event is that a small number of narrators (3/17) in the truth condition did not specifically state that bubbles came 'out of Ivy's mouth', but rather that the bubbles had contaminated the sandwiches she ate and so they did not 'taste nice'. Again, in order not to violate the equivalence principle, gestures were only included in the second analysis if the participant described the target frame of the comic in speech (e.g. by saying bubbles 'come out of Ivy's mouth'), so that it could be compared across both the truth and deception conditions. Finally, it is important to emphasise that in line with David McNeill's 'noncombinatoric approach', participants could be 'awarded' more than one gesture per modified detail. For instance, if a participant produced the following utterance, 'So she [pushes him into the boot], and [slams it shut]', both hand movements would be coded as forming *two* independent gestures that represented the truthful properties of a *single* semantic event.

Out of a total of 351 iconic gestures, 65 gestures were directly associ-ated with the three critical semantic events (and met the inclusion criteria).

Table 15.2 Percentage frequency of participants' hand movements by condition for the three critical details

Frequency of iconic gestures	Percentage of participants
Increase during deception	17.6%
No difference between the conditions	5.9%
Decrease during deception	76.5%

Source: Taken from Cohen *et al.* 2010, Copyright © 2010, Walter de Gruyter GmbH

Of these 65 gestures, 63.1 per cent occurred in the truth condition and 36.9 per cent in the deception condition. Table 15.2 shows the frequency distribution in percentages of the participants' hand movements in relation to the critical details as a function of condition.

In contrast to Table 15.1, which reveals an inconsistent pattern in participants' gestural frequency across conditions, Table 15.2 demonstrates that when you just focus in on where the 'lies' took place, the majority of participants (76.5 per cent) produced *fewer* iconic gestures in the deception condition than in the truth condition. Only 17.6 per cent of participants produced more iconic gestures when lying than when telling the truth, whilst the remaining 5.9 per cent produced the same number of gestures in both conditions.

The mean gesture rate focusing on just those three critical semantic events revealed that, on average, participants produced nearly twice as many iconic gestures in the truth condition (2.5) than in the deception condition (1.4). The level of between-subjects variability across the truth and deception conditions was comparable. In line with the original predictions, statistical analyses revealed that participants produced significantly more iconic hand gestures when truthfully describing the three critical semantic events than when lying about them. A second gesture-to-word ratio was calculated to take into account the unequal word length across conditions – again the relative frequency of gestures between the conditions remained statistically significant.

The next analysis compared the duration of those gestures that encoded aspects of the three semantic events during both truth-telling and deception. Six of the participants only gestured in one of the two conditions and consequently were removed from the analysis, because they were unable to contribute to a direct comparison of gesture duration across conditions. As a result, only 53 of the original 65 gestures were included in this analysis (of which 31 were in the truth condition, whilst the remaining 22 occurred in the deception condition). The durations of each of the 53 gestural units (i.e. the *entire* gestures) were individually timed and broken down into their constituent phases. By definition, this included the meaningful 'stroke' phase of each gesture, as well as any preparation phase, pre-stroke hold, post-stroke hold or retraction phase. Occasionally gestures were coded as having a preparation phase when the hand appeared to be returning to a period of rest, but immediately *before* arriving at the resting position suddenly rose in anticipation of a new stroke phase.

Before presenting the timing data, it is useful at this juncture to consider the *relative frequency* of the different gesture phases for each of the 53 target gestures. Table 15.3 presents both the mean percentage distribution of the various gesture phases across the corpus, as well as the proportion of time they occurred in each of the two conditions. As stroke phases are by definition obligatory components of gestural movement they necessarily occurred in each of the 53 gestures, and so have not been reported here.

Table 15.3 reveals considerable variation in the frequency of gesture phases across the corpus. Whilst most of the 53 gestures had both a preparation (94.3 per cent) and a retraction phase (67.9 per cent), the incidence of pre-stroke and post-stroke holds was smaller, occurring in 9.4 per cent and 30.2 per cent of cases, respectively. Whilst the relative proportion of preparation, pre-stroke holds and retraction phases were comparable across the conditions (preparation: 96.8 per cent vs 90.9 per cent; pre-stroke hold: 9.7 per cent vs 9.1 per cent; retraction: 67.7 per cent vs 68.2 per cent), post-stoke holds were more than twice as likely to occur in the truth condition than in the deception condition (38.7 per cent vs 18.2 per cent). In total, 16 post-stroke holds were identified across the 53 gestures, of which 12 occurred in the truth condition and four were observed in the deception condition. This suggests that those involved in deception systematically avoid

Table 15.3 Mean percentage frequency of gesture phases across the truthful and deception conditions

Gesture phase	Overall incidence	Percentage of time occurred in Truthful Condition	Percentage of time occurred in Deception Condition
Preparation	94.3%	96.8%	90.9%
Pre-stroke hold	9.4%	9.7%	9.1%
Post-stroke hold	30.2%	38.7%	18.2%
Retraction	67.9%	67.7%	68.2%

Source: Taken from Cohen *et al.* 2010, Copyright © 2010, Walter de Gruyter GmbH

producing gestures with post-stroke holds. What is particularly interesting here is that the preparation, pre-stroke and retraction phases can, to some extent, be considered 'auxiliary' components of the gesture unit, which at best make only a very limited semantic contribution to the speaker's message. Conversely, in both its form and manner of presentation the post-stroke hold is likely to encode a good deal about the target semantic event. In line with the earlier prediction, liars may well be inhibiting them, as they have the potential to communicate information that is incompatible with the accompanying speech. Moreover, there is some evidence that post-stroke holds lead to decoder fixation (Gullberg and Holmqvist 2002: 209). Again consistent with the basic hypothesis is the idea that liars attempt to suppress the frequency of post-stroke holds, because this might well direct listener attention to their gestures, and increase the probability that their deception will be detected.

Gesture duration by condition

We turn now to a comparison of the duration of the gestures across conditions. The basic procedure for timing the data was as follows: each of the 53 gesture–speech combinations was edited onto a separate videotape and a frame-by-frame analysis was conducted in which the onset and offset times of the various gesture phases were recorded. Gesture phase duration was measured in terms of the number of recorded frames per second that elapsed between the onset and offset of the target phase. As each second of recorded material consists of 25 individual frames, one frame corresponds to 40 milliseconds (25 frames × 40 milliseconds = 1000 milliseconds). Table 15.4 compares the mean duration (in milliseconds) of the various gesture phases by condition.

Table 15.4 Mean duration of gesture phases across the truthful and deception conditions (in milliseconds)

Gesture phase	Mean duration in Truthful Condition	Mean duration in Deception Condition
Preparation	498.0	440.5
Pre-stroke	506.7	450.0
Stroke	830.3	372.1
Post-stroke	1380.0	605.0
Retraction	459.0	398.7

Source: Taken from Cohen *et al.* 2010, Copyright © 2010, Walter de Gruyter GmbH

Although it is evident that all gesture components were longer in the truth condition than in the deception condition, Table 15.4 reveals that the differences in the duration of the preparation (57.5 milliseconds), pre-stroke (56.7 milliseconds) and retraction phases (60.3 milliseconds) were at best negligible. In contrast, a marked decrease in gesture phase duration during deception was observed for the remaining two phases, which are, of course, thought to form the 'nucleus' of the gestural message (see Kendon 2004; i.e. the stroke and post-stroke hold phases). The stroke phases of the gestures were on average 458.2 milliseconds longer when they occurred in the truth condition compared to the deception condition, whilst the post-stroke holds were 775.0 milliseconds longer when executed as part of the truth condition than during deception. Statistical analyses revealed that there was no significant difference in the duration of the preparation, pre-stroke hold or retraction phases across conditions. However, participants produced significantly longer stroke phases and post-stroke holds when telling the truth than when lying. Finally, given that participants produced gestures with significantly longer stroke phases when they occurred during truth-telling than deception, we thought that it would be useful to examine stroke duration by individual speakers across the two conditions.

Table 15.5 (p. 226) reveals that whilst the majority of participants (81.8 per cent) produced gestures with longer stroke phases when telling the truth than when lying, there is again considerable variation across speakers. Overall the mean difference between the conditions was 458.2 milliseconds. What is interesting here is that whilst most participants (54.5 per cent) did produce gestures which were *at least* 458.2 milliseconds longer in the truth condition than the deception condition, two speakers actually generated gestures with longer stroke phases when lying than when telling the truth (see speakers 8 [−350.0 milliseconds] and 10 [−70.0 milliseconds], respectively). Similarly, two participants (4 and 7) showed only modest differences across conditions (183.7 milliseconds and 163.3 milliseconds, respectively).

Finally, was there any evidence of actual gesture and speech mismatches in the deception condition? We found three participants' gestures in the deception condition, which in their form appeared to contain semantic information that was incompatible with the information encoded in the speech. These participants' iconic gestures seemed to encode semantic information from the original story, whilst their speech conveyed the false information that they were instructed to include. We did not find any of these gesture–speech mismatches in the truth condition. Presented here are the three speech extracts along with their accompanying contradictory iconic gestures.

Table 15.5 Duration of stroke phases (in milliseconds) by participants across truth-telling and deception

Participant	Truthful Condition	Deception Condition	Difference between conditions
1	1100.0	400.0	700.0
2	720.0	400.0	320.0
3	1120.0	260.0	860.0
4	490.0	306.3	183.7
5	740.0	220.0	520.0
6	1460.0	240.0	1220.0
7	710.0	546.7	163.3
8	510.0	860.0	−350.0
9	793.3	200.0	593.3
10	330.0	400.0	−70.0
11	1160.0	260.0	900.0

Source: Taken from Cohen et al. 2010, Copyright © 2010, Walter de Gruyter GmbH

Consider the following example in which the participant verbally says that Ivy locks the DJ into the back of the car using the side-door:

'She like pushes the DJ into the side-door of the car and like [slams it shut]'

Iconic: Left hand is at about shoulder level, with the palm facing outward, away from speaker, fingers outstretched. Suddenly, hand descends rapidly so that the palm faces towards ground.

What is interesting about this example is that whilst the speaker verbally says that the DJ was pushed into the car using the side-door, her iconic gesture reveals that she has accurately retained a truthful mental representation of the event depicted in the original story, in which Ivy pushed the DJ into the *boot* of the car and slams the boot lid downwards (*hand descends rapidly*). The gesture in Figure 15.5 is almost identical to the gesture used by the same speaker to describe accurately the slamming shut of the boot in her truth condition (see Figure 15.6).

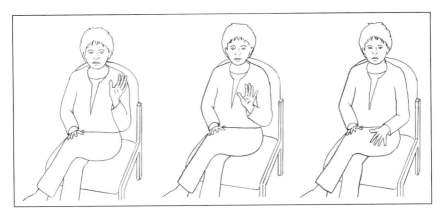

Figure 15.5 Gesture describing Ivy pushing the DJ into the car and slamming the car-door shut (deception condition) (redrawn from Cohen *et al.* 2010, Copyright © 2010, Walter de Gruyter GmbH).

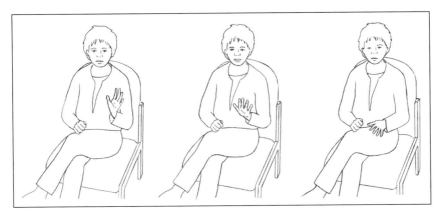

Figure 15.6 Gesture describing Ivy pushing the DJ into the car and slamming the car-door shut (truthful condition) (redrawn from Cohen *et al.* 2010, Copyright © 2010, Walter de Gruyter GmbH).

'So Ivy like [slams him into the boot of his car]'

Iconic: Left hand is slightly below shoulder level, palm faces away from speaker, fingers outstretched. Hand descends rapidly, until the palm faces towards ground. Right hand is static, and appears to be in a post-hold lock.

This provides compelling support not only for the idea that the *same* truthful idea was dominant in the speaker's mind during the production of both utterances, but critically that the underlying truthful properties of the event unwittingly found expression through a process of 'nonverbal leakage'. Furthermore, the gesture made by this participant is *completely different* from those other lie gestures executed by participants when describing pushing the DJ through the side-door. Presented below (see Figure 15.7) is a participant's gesture that typifies the 'standard iconic representation' made by the majority of participants when lying successfully with both speech and gesture:

'shoves him through the [side-door and like slams it shut]'

Iconic: Right hand appears to grip a handle (e.g. of a door). Entire arm rapidly swings sideways (from right to left). Action appears consistent with opening a car-door.

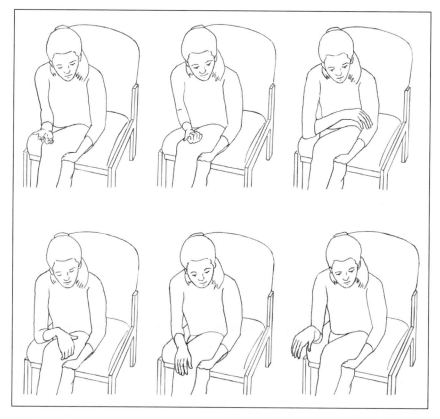

Figure 15.7 Gesture describing slamming the car-door shut (deception condition) (redrawn from Cohen *et al.* 2010, Copyright © 2010, Walter de Gruyter GmbH).

No contradictory gestures occurred that were associated with the second event in the story. Nevertheless, two participants demonstrated contradictory gestures in relation to the third event, in which they had to say that bubbles were coming out of Ivy's ears as opposed to her mouth. Given their similarity, both gestures are presented together:

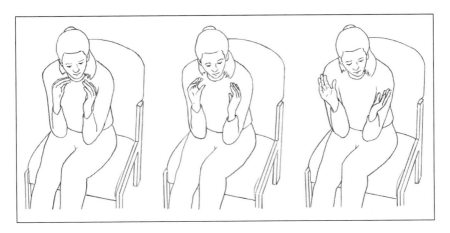

Figure 15.8 Gesture describing bubbles coming out of Ivy's ears (deception condition) (redrawn from Cohen *et al.* 2010, Copyright © 2010, Walter de Gruyter GmbH).

'so then [bubbles start coming out of her ears]'

Iconic: Both hands briefly hover less than an inch from the speaker's mouth. Fingers point inwards towards mouth. Hands then start to move away from each other, and seem to encode the motion-path of the bubbles (i.e. by capturing the idea of dispersion through space). Crucially, the gesture does not occur level with the ears.

'so in the end all the bubbles [were coming out of her ears]'

Iconic: Right hand rises to immediately below mouth, fingers curled slightly. Fingers begin to uncurl and straighten, before entire hand flicks forward into the gesture space. Again, the gesture occurs close to the speaker's mouth, but away from the ears.

Once again, it seems clear that there is a significant discrepancy between the participants' speech ('*coming out of her ears*') and the semantic information communicated by the accompanying iconic gestures (*hands briefly hover less than*

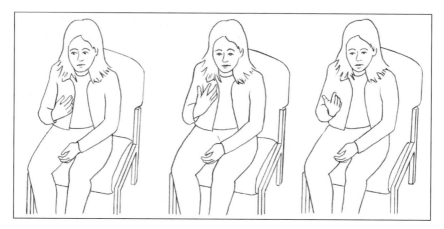

Figure 15.9 Gesture describing bubbles coming out of Ivy's ears (deception condition) (redrawn from Cohen *et al.* 2010, Copyright © 2010, Walter de Gruyter GmbH).

an inch from the speaker' mouth; right hand rises to immediately below mouth), which seems to indicate that the truth can leak out in the form of iconic gestures that accompany speech.

This particular study thus provides new insights into how gestures work alongside speech when people are consciously trying to 'lie', and having to change the description of specific semantic events in the process. It revealed that iconic gestures tend to be inhibited during deception but not throughout the whole story where some lies are taking place, but only when it comes to the description of the specific semantic events themselves that had to be changed. When iconic gestures do still occur, however, in these places, we found that the duration of the meaningful part of the gesture (the so-called 'stroke' phase) was significantly shorter. We also found that any iconic gestures that were generated about these critical semantic events in the deception condition were also less likely to include post-stroke holds as part of their execution. This all points to a degree of behavioural inhibition connected to gesture, where the nature of the inhibition and its specific effects on the structural organisation of gestures are perhaps apparent for the first time. Gestures during deception are less frequent, shorter and more quickly retracted after the stroke phase has occurred, but only when it comes to the 'lies' themselves.

One interesting question raised by my former colleague and friend, Doron Cohen, was why did only three speakers produce the telltale mismatching gesture–speech combinations, whilst the remaining participants did not? Adam Kendon had pointed out that 'Questions about how gesture usage might vary systematically by age, sex, setting, discourse circumstance and the like, although of great interest and importance, have not been explored' (2004: 110). However, a detailed re-examination of the data, focusing in particular on potential inconsistencies in the performance of the three participants who produced gesture–speech mismatches with the pattern produced by the remaining participants, can be quite illuminating. Whilst the mean gesture production rate in the deception condition was 1.4, the three participants who produced contradictory iconic gestures had the *highest* gesture rate during deception (with an overall mean gesture rate of 3.7). In other words, when lying, these three participants have a combined gesture rate which is more than two and a half times higher than the mean gesture rate during deception. Of the three speakers who made contradictory gestures, one made the same number of gestures in both conditions (four gestures in each), while the remaining two participants showed a modest reduction in their gesture frequency when lying (both producing four gestures in the truth conditions and three in the deception conditions). Conversely, almost all of the remaining participants (11/14) reduced their gesture frequency by *at least half* in the deception condition.

Additionally, we discovered that both of the participants who made gestures with *longer* stroke phases in the deception condition, and one of the participants who showed little differences across conditions (see Table 15.5, participant 7), were in fact the *same* speakers who produced the gesture–speech mismatches. It seems, therefore, that these participants in particular may have only a very limited awareness and control of their gestural behaviour. Whereas most participants reduced the frequency and duration of their gestures in deception, these three speakers did not change their behaviour in this way. By failing to adopt a strategy of behavioural inhibition, these participants appear to have placed themselves 'at risk' of being caught, and indeed went on to generate gesture–speech mismatches. Perhaps these speakers' apparent inability to regulate and constrain their gestural behaviour during deception is the principal factor mediating whether or not they manifest mismatches between speech and gesture.

Overall then, this study not only corroborates previous research findings regarding the frequency of gestures at least during the critical phases of deception, but also demonstrates that, on occasion, gestural morphology may preserve the underlying truthful properties of an event, even when the speaker is able to effectively deliver a lie verbally. This research clearly calls for more of a dialogue between those researchers investigating nonverbal cues to deceit and those interested in the semiotic value of gesture in communication taxonomies. Studies investigating bodily action during deception should therefore begin to work towards a fuller recognition of, and capitalise on, the unique placement of iconic hand movements in communication. Whilst this research supports Ekman's view that there is no universal behavioural indicator that can reliably distinguish reality from fiction, every lie has its own unique semantic structure, and it may only be through a detailed exploration of individual gesture–speech combinations, the potential inconsistencies between them and their temporal structure that deception can finally be detected. This may hold the key to documenting more fully the subtlety and complexity of nonverbal leakage.

SUMMARY

- We all lie.
- Men like to boast quite a bit in their daily interactions, according to a lie diary study.
- Women tell lies more frequently than men do, but they often do so to make others feel better.
- Lies are mostly routine and without any real consequences (although, of course, we may grow dependent on the lies told to us, and that may be serious).
- The most general conclusion possible about lying is that people do not want to give the game away, even in the routine lies of everyday life, where there really is no consequence, except perhaps losing face.
- A meta-analysis of the published literature on deception found that only three forms of behaviour were reliably associated with lying and they were 'nodding', 'foot and leg movements' and 'hand movements'. All three were found to decrease in frequency.
- We seem to know instinctively that some aspects of our behaviour can leak a great deal when we are trying to deceive, so we often attempt to inhibit them.
- Our new research has found that the frequency, duration and structural organisation of iconic gestures are all affected in deception, but the effects are often localised to the 'lies' themselves.
- All gestural phases were longer when telling the truth than in the deception condition.

- The differences between truth and deception in the duration of the preparation (57.5 milliseconds), pre-stroke (56.7 milliseconds) and retraction phases (60.3 milliseconds) are, however, negligible.

- There is a marked decrease in the duration of the stroke phase of a gesture during deception, and in the duration of the post-stroke hold (and in the probability of one occurring at all in deception). These two phases are thought to form the 'nucleus' of the gestural message.

- The stroke phases of gestures were on average 458.2 milliseconds longer when telling the truth than in the deception condition, whilst post-stroke holds were 775.0 milliseconds longer when executed as part of telling the truth than during deception.

- In terms of the form and meaning of gestures, the real underlying representation of an event can sometimes leak out when speakers are trying to deceive.

- The form and structural organisation of gestures can be a good deal more revealing during deception than their frequency alone.

- Beats are generally much easier to control and considerably less revealing in deception.

- Nonverbal leakage can become apparent in the specific form and structure of gesture.

- Tony Blair, who was once the Prime Minister of the UK, was, on occasion, quite transparent when he veered away from the truth. It is a pity that we did not appreciate this more fully at the time.

16

UNCONSCIOUS GESTURE CAN LEAK UNCONSCIOUS ATTITUDE

Many of us seem to go through life in interesting ways. We all care deeply about the planet, and do all that we can to protect it. None of us, it seems, is racist or has any types of bias against those from a different racial or ethnic group to ourselves. That is what we say and it might even be what we actually believe. Yet we sometimes notice small things about ourselves and the patterns of our everyday lives; small, telling things that we are quick to dismiss. Why do I only recycle *sometimes*? Why do I *never* seem to glance at the carbon footprint on products in supermarkets before I make my choice when I know quite well the importance of greenhouse gas emissions for global warming? Why did I not even *consider* a hybrid car (except for a few self-conscious seconds) when I was thinking about changing my car? Why, when I was on that interview panel, was the shortlist for that post so homogeneous (so White, that is) in terms of the ethnic background of the candidates? Why did I not think to *comment* on this at the time?

We all know ourselves pretty well, at least that's what most of us seem to believe, and we are quite prepared to tell others when they ask, to share our self-knowledge. 'What is my attitude to the carbon footprint of products?' we say to the earnest-looking researcher as we leave the super-market. 'Of course I'll take part in your survey. Where is the point on the scale which corresponds to "I strongly prefer low carbon footprint products to high carbon footprint products"? Where is the point on the scale which corresponds to the basic and honest proposition that "I am a True Green"? I suspect that you could tell already,' we add, 'just by looking at me what I would be ticking.'

Then when it comes to racism, we are even clearer. 'You've come to the right man,' we say to this other equally serious-looking researcher. 'Of course I don't suffer from any racial bias. How could I? I am a modern man. Just give me your attitude questionnaire, I am more than happy to help you out; I will show you how this country is changing in terms of diversity and tolerance. I'll show you that racism is a thing of the past.'

We are happy to tell the world about our underlying attitudes and ourselves, more than happy if the truth be known, and yet there does seem to be something a little strange going on. Why, if we all care so deeply about the planet, is there so little actual change to more sustainable forms of behaviour (Beattie 2010)? Why, if we are all colour blind, can we detect such clear racial and ethnic biases in employment?

I am reminded of some interesting statistics. After controlling for age, socio-economic status and number of years in education, Black and Minority Ethnic (BME) groups seem to continue to face a significant 'net' disadvantage in terms of gaining access to, and remaining in, the labour market (see Bassanini and Saint-Martin 2008). Evidence of some sort of disadvantage on the grounds of ethnicity has been reported in a wide range of different countries. It has been shown in Australia (Booth et al. 2009), Canada (Pendakur and Pendakur 1998), France (Lefranc 2010), Germany (Kogan 2011), Greece (Drydakis and Vlassis 2010), North America (Bertrand and Mullainathan 2004), New Zealand (Tobias et al. 2008), Sweden (Nordin and Rooth 2009) and the United Kingdom (Wood et al. 2009). I am also reminded of what happens if you change the apparent ethnicity of candidates on job applications, in a technique called 'correspondence testing' (see Jowell and Prescott-Clarke 1970). In a typical correspondence test for racial/ethnic bias, written job applications are randomly assigned either a traditional Anglo-Saxon-sounding name or an ethnic minority name and are then submitted for advertised vacancies. Bertrand and Mullainathan (2004), for instance, randomly assigned either Anglo-Saxon (e.g. Emily) or African-American (e.g. Lakisha) names to over five thousand fictitious CVs, which were then sent in response to a range of job advertisements in Boston and Chicago. They found that White candidates were 50 per cent more likely than non-White candidates to be offered an interview. Similarly, the results of a Swedish field study (see Carlsson and Rooth 2007) demonstrated that second-generation Swedes were, on average, ten percentage points less likely to be invited for interview if the applicant had a Middle Eastern rather than a traditionally Swedish-sounding name. In the UK, research shows that ethnic minorities not only have to send, on average, 74 per cent more applications than non-Whites to secure an interview (Wood *et al.* 2009), but that once in employment BME staff face lower hourly earnings and lower levels of occupational attainment compared to equally qualified Whites (Heath and Li 2007).

Yet, the questionnaire now firmly in the hands of the researcher clearly indicated that my attitude to race (and that of the vast majority of other people in the study) was one of extreme fairness. Indeed, it was more than just fair; it was *absolutely* colour blind. What could possibly be going on here? I am not 100 per cent convinced that it is just that we all want to appear to be more decent than we actually are. In other words, I am not 100 per cent convinced that this is just about social desirability, as we normally think about it − trying to appear better than we are to avoid sanction. If the truth be known, I'm not really sure what any of my attitudes really are but if pressed, of course, I will respond to the survey. In other words, I will generate something on the spot. This may not be the actual reporting of an attitude based on self-awareness, but more a self-conscious, self-aware construction (and all I do know is that I do not want to appear any worse than I really am, whatever that is).

Attitudes are, after all, elusive things, when you sit down and think about it. We are continually asked to report them, but what are we actually reporting? Attitude is one of the most ubiquitous and important concepts in psychology; indeed one of the founders of social psychology, Gordon Allport, wrote in the 1930s, 'The concept of attitude is probably the most distinctive and indispensable concept in contemporary social psychology. In fact several writers . . . *define* social psychology as the scientific study of attitudes.' And perhaps the single most significant contributor in the evolution of the concept of 'attitude' was Allport himself, helping to define the new science of psychology in plain opposition in both approach and theory to psychoanalysis. Indeed, Allport seems to have been repelled by how psychoanalysis dug in the dirt for the root causes of human action, in ways that could not be scientifically challenged. The emerging behavioural approaches, he thought, might reveal observable behaviour, but these often just skimmed the surface of human motivation and action. Allport himself sought a middle ground, looking inside the mind with the help of the subject him/herself, who then reported on their cognitions and attitudes (Allport

1935), sometimes on their inner conflict when it came to race and prejudice (Allport 1954), at other times on their felt discomfort with competing attitudes or thoughts (see again Allport 1954). Allport sometimes borrowed some of the concepts of psychoanalysis (repression, denial, defence and rationalisation) to explain how people could deal with this discomfort, and deal with being both racist and not racist at the same time. In his words, 'No one wants to be at odds with his own conscience. Man has to live with himself.'

What is fascinating about Allport, the man who steered social psychology on its course for the past seventy or eighty years since his work on attitudes came out, is that he liked to give us glimpses into his own life, so that we might understand why he chose one scientific course rather than another. One particular autobiographical nugget stands out from all the others. As a 22-year-old student, he tells us, he visited Freud in Vienna, and that one chance visit changed both him and almost certainly the future course of psychology. What happened in Vienna that day was that Freud tried to psychoanalyse him, because of an ice-breaking observation that Allport had made. It was a story about dirt and a little boy on a Viennese tram obsessed with dirt, just something he spotted on the tram on the way to meet Freud. Freud apparently responded by looking at Allport carefully for the first time, with his 'kindly therapeutic eyes', and asked, 'And was that little boy you?' Allport blinked uncomfortably and said nothing. Allport knew why he had told the story, he understood his own motivation, the causes of his action, but Freud was having none of it.

> I realized that he [Freud] was accustomed to neurotic defences and that my manifest motivation (a sort of rude curiosity and youthful ambition) escaped him. For therapeutic progress he would have to cut through my defences, but it so happened that therapeutic progress was not here an issue.
>
> (Allport 1967: 7–8)

Allport later wrote that the 'experience taught me that depth psychology, for all its merits, may plunge too deep, and that psychologists would do well to give full recognition to manifest motives before probing the unconscious'. This meeting encouraged Allport to develop something different, a different sort of approach to the human mind, an approach that stayed with us for some sixty years before anyone really dared challenge it in a systematic way. An approach based around conscious reflection (and the power of language) to uncover and articulate underlying attitudes, to bring attitudes into the open where they could be analysed objectively and scientifically. This was to characterise the mainstream of social psychology ever after. However, was this sort of approach ever going to reveal the whole story?

Let us consider the environmental question again. Why do people repeatedly say that they do care about the environment, but then do very little to ameliorate the effects of their own lifestyle – the so-called 'value–action' gap? This question has dominated much of contemporary social psychology. Why do people not act in accordance with their underlying attitudes? The answer might be found in the new research on implicit cognition, which suggests that many things influence us without any conscious awareness and that a major part of our attitude towards the environment, race or indeed anything might not be conscious, and therefore reportable in the normal way. This could lead us to think quite differently about the 'value–action' gap (i.e. there isn't one, there is just a gap between explicit attitudes and behaviour; in effect, we act in accordance with our implicit attitudes). If we could develop a reliable and valid measure of implicit attitudes, then we could pursue new lines of enquiry to deal with the threat of climate change. We could see whether any of our communicative or marketing strategies (government-based information campaigns, advertising, carbon footprint labelling, etc.) actually work. What do they, in fact, influence? Do they affect implicit values or just self-reported values? We could segment the population in new and innovative ways (using measures of both implicit and explicit attitudes), instead of relying just on self-report measures of attitudes (as all commercial and government organisations currently do), to work out how to target any communicational strategies. We could try to change systematically implicit values, if, that is, we can measure implicit attitudes reliably and agree that they have some predictive validity (and some plausibility).

There is currently within psychology a lot of contentious debate about implicit attitudes. Many psychologists are, it seems, hooked on the concept of infinite self-knowledge about what drives us as human beings. It is perhaps worth reminding ourselves that the classic definition of 'attitude', as introduced by Allport in 1935, was defined as 'a mental and neural state of readiness organised through experience, exerting a directive or dynamic influence upon the individual's response to all objects and situations with which it is related' (1935: 810). However, Allport had also this to say about attitudes:

The meagreness with which attitudes are represented in conscious-
ness resulted in a tendency to regard them as manifestations of brain
activity or of the unconscious mind. The persistence of attitudes
which are totally unconscious was demonstrated by Müller and
Pilzecker (1900).

(Allport 1935: 801)

He clearly did not rule out the concept of the unconscious attitude but
he focused exclusively on the measurement of attitudes with self-report
questionnaires. I have argued elsewhere (Beattie 2013) that his reasons for
this particular focus were both academic and highly personal. Academically,
he had been clearly impressed by Likert's early research on the measurement
of racial attitudes using self-reports. But at a more personal level, it is clear
from his autobiography that he was *genuinely* appalled by Freud's attempt to
psychoanalyse him on that famous visit to Vienna in 1921, and Allport later
argued that 'psychoanalytic excess' (what Freud in his view was culpable
of that afternoon in Vienna) must be avoided at all costs. Allport's legacy
was to shape our discipline. He more than shaped it, his ideas shone a light
in the darkness, gave us a path to follow; anything not in the light was
considered 'out of bounds', 'unknowable', 'beyond the pale' of civilised
scientific psychology.

The problem with possible unconscious components of an attitude was
that we had no way to access them or measure them, until Greenwald
developed the Implicit Association Test, or IAT (Greenwald *et al.* 1998). The
basic premise behind the test is that when participants categorise items into
two sets of paired concepts, then if the paired concepts are strongly
associated, participants should be able to categorise the items faster (and
with fewer errors which generate penalty scores) than if they are not
strongly associated. We therefore end up with a simple reaction time
measure (called the 'D' or difference score), which gives us a measure of
the associative links between concepts, where these associative links are built
up unconsciously over time and may influence our behaviour in various
situations. This pattern of association may function like an attitude – being
a 'mental and neural state of readiness' (Allport 1935).

In a number of domains, it has been found that there is little correlation
between the scores that derive from the usual self-report attitudinal measures
and the 'D' scores that derive from the IAT (see Greenwald and Nosek 2008;
Hofmann *et al.* 2005; Nosek 2005). This has led Greenwald and Nosek to
suggest that explicit and implicit attitudes are 'dissociated'. When it comes
to the environment and climate change, there is no significant correlation

between explicit attitudes to carbon footprint and the 'D' scores (Beattie and Sale 2009). Similarly, when it comes to race, there is no significant correlation between explicit attitudes to race and the 'D' scores (Beattie 2013). There is also now mounting evidence that the 'D' score is a better predictor of actual behaviour in many domains. This is especially true where the behaviour in question is spontaneous and unplanned, like the choice of high vs low carbon footprint products when you are in a hurry (Beattie and Sale 2011) or when the task is 'socially sensitive', like the shortlisting of candidates from different racial or ethnic backgrounds for various posts (Beattie 2013).

Some theorists have argued that implicit and explicit attitudes have structurally distinct mental representations (see Chaiken and Trope 1999; Wilson *et al.* 2000). A number have suggested that it is parsimonious to model the human mind as comprising two important subsystems: a familiar foreground, where processing is 'conscious', 'controlled', 'reflective', 'intentional' and 'slow' (the explicit system); and a hidden background, our implicit system, where processing is 'unconscious', 'automatic', 'impulsive', 'unintended' and 'fast' (see Gregg 2008; Kahneman 2011).

This concept of an implicit attitude does give us a new way of thinking about the motivational basis for human action; it could be a critical element in the fight against climate change (and racism, and many other things besides). Implicit rather than explicit attitudes may well be underpinning everyday habitual behaviours. Such behaviours may be 'sticky', in socio-logical jargon, and hard to shift, because attempts to change attitudes and behaviour often just focus on the explicit self-reported attitudes, leaving the implicit attitude intact and undisturbed.

However, the first important task for psychology must be to attempt to understand this concept more fully and to investigate how this concept relates to other aspects of behaviour. For example, how does it impact on how we process information relevant to climate change, assuming that the processing of relevant information is an important start point of the whole process of behavioural change in context? There are many persuasive messages available about climate change, including films like Al Gore's *An Inconvenient Truth*, which can produce a significant impact on how people think and feel about environmental issues (see Beattie 2010; Beattie *et al.* 2011), at least when you test these things experimentally in the lab. So why did this Nobel-prize winning film not have a bigger impact on behaviour throughout society, as it was clearly intended to do? Is part of the problem that people can choose to go to the cinema to watch *An Inconvenient Truth* or not, people can watch TV documentaries on climate change or ignore them, people can attend to images of climate change or miss them entirely (and this whole process does not have to be conscious either)? In the laboratory, it is much harder to ignore what is being shown to you. Indeed, it could potentially be the case that in the real world different individuals are drawn, or not drawn, to the same set of images, with major implications for their subsequent behaviour. What happens if you never see the evidence for climate change? Moreover, what happens if you never attend to the arguments about anthropomorphic climate change? Why should you change your behaviour if you have not seen the evidence for climate change or not attended to the arguments linking it back to people? The factors that affect attentional focus could be of immense theoretical and practical concern in this area. The question is, how important is the concept of the implicit attitude here?

That was the reason why in one study Laura McGuire and I attempted to determine how eye movements towards or away from iconic images of environmental damage and climate change are affected by different attitudinal measures (both implicit and explicit). The specific justification for our particular method derives from the early research of Kahneman (1973) on attention and effort. In Kahneman's words, 'In the absence of a specific instruction to search for visual information, spontaneous looking is controlled by enduring dispositions that determine which parts of the field of view should attract and hold the gaze' (1973: 52). So we wanted to find out whether implicit or explicit attitudes were a good measure of 'enduring dispositions' here. We did this by projecting slides onto a computer screen, each slide containing three images – one positive image of nature, one negative image of climate change and environmental damage and one neutral image (things like pictures of cups, plates and other everyday objects). We then measured the individual gaze fixations of our participants, 25 times a second, when they viewed these slides. What exactly did they focus on? And how quickly did they do this?

We found that people did not focus inordinately on the negative images of environmental damage when there were other positive images and neutral images available. They usually looked less than 40 per cent of the time at the negative images. But very importantly, those who the IAT reveals have strong positive implicit attitudes to carbon footprint were significantly more likely to focus on the negative images of environmental damage and climate change than positive images, and they focused more on these images than those who did not have such strong implicit attitudes.

However, we also found that this even occurred in the first 200 milliseconds of viewing the slide (see Figure 16.1). Those with a positive implicit attitude to low carbon footprint products (high implicit group)

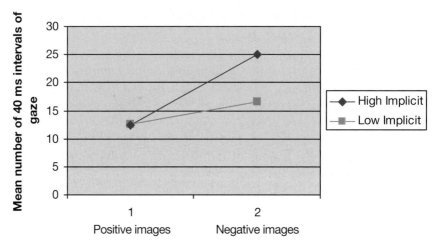

Figure 16.1 Mean number of 40-millisecond intervals of gaze at positive and negative images for high and low implicit groups (first 200 milliseconds only) (taken from Beattie and McGuire 2012, Copyright © 2012, Walter de Gruyter GmbH).

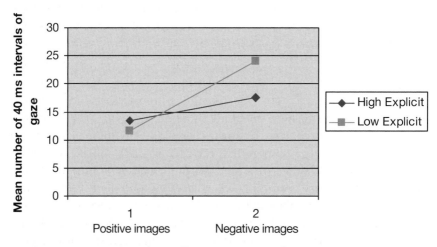

Figure 16.2 Mean number of 40-millisecond intervals of gaze at positive and negative images for high and low explicit groups (first 200 milliseconds only) (taken from Beattie and McGuire 2012, Copyright © 2012, Walter de Gruyter GmbH).

looked more at the negative images of climate change and environmental damage in the first 200 milliseconds compared with those with less strong positive implicit attitudes to low carbon footprint products (low implicit group). Measures of explicit attitude did not, however, predict patterns of eye movement towards the negative images in this way (see Figure 16.2).

It would seem that those who have strong implicit pro-low carbon footprint attitudes are primed to attend to these sorts of images, whereas those with strong explicit attitudes are not (they actually look less). Their eyes were drawn more or less automatically to these images in a minimum timeframe.

This could be important in helping us understand the diversity of people's actions when it comes to environmental matters. Some people, it seems, are doing all they can to protect our natural resources, and reduce greenhouse gas emissions. Many, however, are doing nothing. We clearly build our knowledge representations of the world using information that we gather, and some significant association between attitudes and attentional focus might give us an insight into how and why people develop quite different representations of the world and the dangers it faces. This exploratory eye-tracking research suggests that there is a significant connection between implicit attitudes and gaze fixations. However, all that we have observed here is an *association* between attitudes and behaviour (and not a causal relationship), although one that opens up intriguing theoretical and practical possibilities. We clearly do need further research to unravel the statistical association described here between implicit attitudes and attention. If we were to find that attentional focus directs implicit attitudes, then we may want to think much more strategically about how to make sure that images of climate change hit the attention of more people more of the time. On the other hand, if it is the case that certain individuals are 'primed' to notice certain things because of their implicit attitudes, then we might need to think with great urgency about the best ways of getting that information to them, in order to target this implicit and unconscious system with so much potential power. Those with positive implicit attitudes potentially direct attention to appropriate imagistic representations relevant to sustainability on products in supermarkets (like carbon footprint). But how many of these are there and where can they be found? The answer is that we do not know, but potentially we could find out and we may want to do a different kind of segmentation analysis that might look more like that shown in Figure 16.3. Carbon footprint labelling might well work for 'True Greens' (individuals with strong positive implicit and explicit attitudes to carbon footprint) and 'Hidden Greens' (individuals with a strong positive implicit attitude to the carbon footprint but who do not care to report it routinely), but it would not work for 'Surface Greens' (individuals who report strong positive attitudes but simultaneously hold non-congruent negative implicit attitudes to the carbon footprint) or 'Non Greens' (negative on both). However, what proportion of the population does each of the segments represent? How are each of these segments distributed across social classes

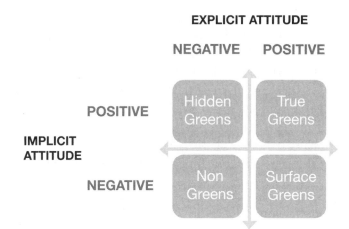

Figure 16.3 A segmentation analysis based on the concept of implicit/explicit attitudinal convergence and divergence (taken from Beattie and McGuire 2014).

and income groups? What media do they consume and how, therefore, could they be targeted? It should be remembered that Defra (and government organisations in other countries) have spent a considerable amount of time and effort engaged in segmentation analysis of the UK population as a whole, without once trying to incorporate any measure of attitude which does not rely solely on self-reports (see Defra 2008). It is easy to imagine a different sort of approach here that could prove more fruitful.

One other important point is that we know from other domains that we can induce changes to our implicit system. Researchers have managed to change automatic responses to people from different racial or ethnic groups. Olson and Fazio (2006) used 'implicit evaluative conditioning' (a form of classical conditioning) to reduce automatically activated responses to people from different races, but it would take time (and effort) to induce different emotional responses to high/low carbon footprint items through, presumably, a mixture of marketing, advertising and education. Nevertheless, importantly we can do this, and it could be a very practical proposal with some real merit in the area of green consumerism.

However, the new theoretical perspective on communication that I have been outlining in this book may be in a position to make its own unique contribution to this area. Attempts to change behaviour to make it more sustainable, more tolerant and fairer are, after all, premised on a particular concept of the attitude (it is open to introspection, it is reportable) and the concept of the attitude is premised on a particular concept of communication (we use language, and only language, to communicate our mental states to others; language tells you all you need to know here, nothing else is relevant). But what happens if there is more to an attitude than the bit that people can introspect on? What happens if some attitudes, or parts of an attitude, are unconscious and not open to introspection? Furthermore, what happens if that particular communicational concept is also wrong? What happens if there is more to communication than what people say? You can perhaps see how I am thinking here. Gestural communication can reflect aspects of thinking in a way that the speaker may well not be aware. Could this unconscious medium reflect aspects of our underlying implicit attitude? Could gesture provide us with new information here that might change how we think about this incredibly important domain?

People after all continually report their underlying attitude in surveys, focus groups and interviews. That is how we got to where we are. However, the measurement of attitudes has relied on a model in which language, the words, clauses and sentences, is the primary vehicle, no the only vehicle of communication. What secrets might the gestural accompaniments of talk hold? Could there be some hint of the dissociation between implicit and explicit attitudes in how people talk about sustainability and their role in promoting it? When we broaden communication to cover unconscious gesture unconsciously produced, could we perhaps get some hint of the complexities of holding an attitude in which not all of the elements might be conscious? We saw in the last chapter how participants sometimes allowed the real underlying representation to slip through when they tried to change certain features in story recall. Could the unconscious medium of gesture give us some insight into this much more complex issue of possible dissociation between implicit and explicit attitudes?

This formed the basis for another study in which we interviewed and studied in detail the gestural behaviour of two groups of ten participants. In the case of one group we knew from self-report measures and the IAT that their explicit self-reported attitudes and their implicit attitudes to low carbon footprint products were positive and they converged (so-called 'True Greens'). In the case of the other group, we knew that their attitudes diverged: although the participants reported a very positive attitude to low carbon footprint products, their implicit attitude (measured using the IAT) was negative, in other words, the IAT revealed that they preferred high carbon footprint products (they were the so-called 'Surface Greens').

We transcribed the interviews with both sets of participants and studied the gestures and speech in some detail. In the case of the 'Surface Greens', we noticed one small difference in the behaviour which distinguished them from the 'True Greens' – sometimes the gestures and speech in the former group that did not match.

Consider the examples below from two of our female participants talking about consumer choice in supermarkets. They both use the gestural space in front of the body to locate products that are either high or low in carbon footprint. The gesture in both cases shows the act of choice in selecting either the high or low carbon footprint product.

In the first sequence below X is talking about this choice dilemma (see Figure 16.4). She is essentially explaining how if one product had a high carbon footprint and one had a low carbon footprint, then she would buy the low carbon footprint product even if there was a difference in price and the low carbon footprint product was more expensive. The reason she gives for this is that she would feel guilty doing anything else. We know from her questionnaire that X has a positive self-reported attitude to low carbon footprint products; we also know from her IAT that her implicit attitude is very positive as well. In other words, in our terminology she is a 'True Green'.

She begins by using her right hand to represent high carbon footprint products in gesture 1, and in gesture 2 she uses her left hand to represent low carbon footprint products. She distinguishes high and low carbon footprint products by locating her right hand in the right-hand side of the gestural space and she locates the low carbon footprint products in the left-hand side of the gestural space. Gesture 3 corresponds to 'but it was the same product' and the hands move towards each other. In gesture 4 she marks the difference in price by moving the hands apart. In gesture 5 the index finger on the left hand points back towards the body and this gesture stands for 'I', which is elliptical with respect to the next part of the speech which is 'probably still feel really guilty about buying the high carbon one'. And buying the 'high carbon one' is accompanied by movement of the right-hand side of the body, palms facing upwards, fingers spread (gesture 7). The left hand also moves towards the right-hand side of the body so both hands together are referring back to where the high carbon footprint products were located in the gestural space in gesture 1. Then the speaker says 'so I'd buy the low' and here both hands flip so that they point towards the left-hand side of the body in the speaker's left gestural space. The speaker had of course located the low carbon footprint product in the left gestural space in gesture 2, so her verbal utterance that she 'would buy the low carbon product' is accompanied by a gestural movement indicating an appropriate movement towards the left gestural space where the low carbon footprint product had been located.

1. yeah if it was like [really high]

2. and something was [really low]

3. but it was [the same produ:ct] (0.2)

4. er but there was [a difference in pri:ce] (0.4)

Figure 16.4 Gesture depicting the choice dilemma in supermarkets when it comes to choosing between high carbon and low carbon footprint products.

5. [then](1.0)

6. [probably still feel (0.4) really guilty]

7. about [buying the high carbon one]

8. [so I'd buy the low]

Figure 16.4 continued

Gesture 1: Right hand moves out to the right of the body, fingers are spread, right palm is facing upwards.

Gesture 2: Right hand remains extended and the left hand moves out to the left-hand side of the body, fingers are extended, palm is facing upwards.

Gesture 3: Both hands move back into the centre of the body, index fingers on both hands are extended, pointing inwards to an area in the centre of the gestural space.

Gesture 4: Index fingers on both hands then point out, away from the body.

Gesture 5: Index finger on the left hand points back towards the body.

Gesture 6: Left hand then extends out, palm is facing upwards, fingers are spread.

Gesture 7: Right hand gestures to the right of the body, palm is facing upwards, fingers are spread. Left hand also moves towards the right with palm facing down.

Gesture 8: Both hands flip so that they point towards the left-hand side of the body.

The next example depicts a similar type of choice dilemma in a different speaker (see Figure 16.5). The speaker uses each of her two hands to represent high and low carbon footprint products. In gesture 1 accompanying 'if they were next to each other', she represents their relative position. Gesture 2 represents her perspective on perceived difference in terms of good for the environment (low carbon footprint products) or bad for the environment (high carbon footprint products). In gesture 3 she represents the product that is good for the environment (the low carbon footprint product) with her left hand and in gesture 4 she represents the product that is bad for the environment (the high carbon footprint product) with her right hand. Interestingly, in line with the previous speaker, she uses her left hand to represent low carbon footprint products and her right hand to represent high carbon footprint products. What is interesting about this speaker is that when she communicates about her actual choice 'then you'd go for the good one' she uses her right hand (which was symbolically representing the high carbon footprint product) rather than her left hand (which she had used to represent the low carbon footprint products) to signify that actual choice.

Again this is someone whose explicit attitude is very pro-low carbon footprint but whose implicit attitude is actually at odds with this (she is a 'Surface Green'). In gesture 5 you can see that the gesture does not match the speech as it did with the previous speaker. Generally speaking, people are consistent about the use of the hands in representation and the use of the gestural space. This person's speech and gesture thus constitute a mismatch. There is something else that is quite striking about the behaviour of this participant. She repeatedly makes circular movements of the hand when she has displayed her choice in the gestural space as if there was some discomfort associated with the unconscious signalling of the choice. Her intonation is also a little unusual in that it sounds incomplete, again, as if she does not want to commit herself. However, in terms of her lexical choices, and the use of specific lexical items, her choice is clear. It is just her unconscious behaviour and specifically the behaviours over which she has least control (her gestural movements and her intonation) that are sending quite a different message. The gesture seems to leak information about her underlying attitude.

1. [if they were next to each other](0.4)

2. [and it was quite obvious] that

3. [one was good and]

4.[one was bad]

5.[then you'd go for (0.6) the good one]

Figure 16.5 (facing page and above) Gestures depicting the choice between high and low carbon footprint products.

Gesture 1: Palms facing towards each other, both hands are raised in front of the chest, hands move backwards and forwards.

Gesture 2: Hands are raised in the centre of the gestural space, palms are facing away from the body, fingers are spread.

Gesture 3: Left hand then opens and closes, raised slightly above and in front of the right hand.

Gesture 4: Right hand then moves up so that it is slightly in front of the left hand.

Gesture 5: Right hand rises, left hand drops, right hand repeatedly makes smaller circular movements.

It would seem that here we have a case of nonverbal leakage in a case of self-deception (Ekman and Friesen 1969: 90), and I say self-deception because it is not obvious to me that this 'Surface Green' was aware of her actual implicit attitude. Ekman and Friesen wrote:

> During self-deception, it is likely that alter [the interlocutor or observer] may be aware of deception cues and leakage of which ego [the person him or herself] is oblivious; if ego becomes aware

of his own deception clues he may have an uncanny feeling that something is amiss, or that he has some conflicting feelings; presumably ego does not become aware of his own leakage during self-deception because to learn the information he has concealed from himself would produce severe anxiety.

(Ekman and Friesen 1969: 90)

We here are the observer.

In *The Expression of the Emotions in Man and Animals* in 1872, Darwin himself wrote:

Some actions ordinarily associated through habit with certain states of mind may be partially repressed through the will, and in such cases the muscles which are least under the separate control of the will are the most liable still to act, causing movements which we recognize as expressive.

(Darwin 1872/1955: 48–9)

Gestural movements can sometimes be inhibited (indeed we found them to be less frequent in the speech of the 'Surface Greens'), but they cannot be fully suppressed because the urge to gesture in embodying our thinking is so pronounced. They sometimes do evade the will, and their form, acutely expressive, reveals embodied action highly associated with a particular state of mind, in this case an implicit attitude influencing behaviour.

There are thus a number of possibly significant implications of this particular bit of research. The first is that what people say about their attitude to the environment (and what consumer choices they will actually make) may be a valuable resource for researchers, but on some occasions people may say one thing, but their unconscious gestural movement may tell quite a different (and potentially more accurate) story. Therefore, it may be wrong, in research on green issues, to focus *exclusively* on what people say. Explicitly people may say that they want to lead sustainable lifestyles and will make changes in their everyday lives to accommodate this, but implicitly they may actually care a good deal less about the environmental consequences of their actions. They may feel very positively about fast cars, and foreign travel, and exotic food imported from miles away, because for years advertisers and others have persuaded them that these things are highly desirable. There may even be evidence of this split between what they report about themselves in their speech and their implicit attitudes in the curious relationship between their speech and their unconscious gestural behaviour.

Given that implicit attitudes may affect our everyday 'choices' as consumers (and I put choices in inverted commas, because selection based on habit and implicit values may really be no 'choice' at all), these are clearly attitudes that we may want to understand better in order to change. These attitudes can be measured using the IAT, but they can be potentially glimpsed in everyday communication in gesture, and this could be a powerful tool. There is no point in being continually misled by our respondents in interviews and focus groups, and basing all of our prognoses about societal adaptation to the threat of climate change on their words alone, and certainly not when we may be able to 'read' people's attitudes through other means.

The second implication of this research is that there does appear to be something of a disconnect between explicit and implicit attitudes, not just seen in the lack of a correlation between the traditional measures, but in human behaviour as well, in terms of gaze fixations, visual processing and gestures, which are all often non-reflective and more or less automatic behaviours. One might well conclude that there is a conscious mind and an unconscious one. The unconscious mind may not be governed in quite the way that Freud had thought (obsessed with sexual gratification and the libido), but it is there and it does influence our everyday behaviour. It affects what we look at, the way we shop, how we talk, how we move, how we gesture and it can even produce visible signs of discomfort as we speak (with odd uncertain hand movements and strange incomplete intonation), sometimes leaving us all a little puzzled, even the 'Surface Greens' themselves.

The implication of all of this for those wishing to do something about climate change (or racism or anything else which is sensitive, difficult and pertinent to society) should be clear. It is not sufficient to rely on explicit measures of attitude to low carbon footprint products and make assumptions about how easy it will be to change consumer behaviour by merely providing carbon footprint information (as many have done), simply because our respondents tell us this is all they need – because of their reported core values. Rather, a significant proportion of individuals have implicit attitudes that are discrepant with their explicit attitudes and this may have significant implications for their 'green' choices. Moreover, on occasion, when you analyse the talk of such individuals you can sometimes glimpse the unconscious implicit attitudes of these individuals, so rigidly held and so deeply suppressed, suddenly and unexpectedly revealing themselves as the speaker lays out his or her apparently green agenda. Their sudden appearance seems to surprise everyone, even on occasion the speakers themselves.

This research could potentially change how we go about conducting research on attitudes (in terms of interviews and focus groups) in terms of what we should record, code and analyse. Words alone, the research might suggest, are never enough, as many seem to have assumed. Of course, this research itself makes many assumptions. It assumes that some types of attitude are unconscious. It assumes that speech is not the only means of semantic communication. It assumes that gestural moments can convey meaning. It assumes that gestural movements can convey such meaning with little or no conscious awareness on the part of the speaker. It assumes that gesture–speech mismatches are psychologically interesting; indeed, it assumes that such gesture–speech mismatches can be potentially revealing of internal psychological states. There are clearly many, many assumptions here, some of which (and possibly the majority) may turn out to be more than a little plausible.

However, only time (and a lot more research) will really tell.

SUMMARY

- Allport, the founder of social psychology, avoided probing the possible unconscious components of an attitude because he wanted attitudes to be observable and to be subject to scientific investigation.

- Interestingly, Freud had tried to psychoanalyse Allport when he visited Freud in Vienna when he was just 22 years old.

- Allport never seemed to have got over this experience and commented on it on many occasions.

- It seemed to have dissuaded him from speculating about the unconscious self and unconscious motivation.

- There is nothing in Allport's early definitions of attitude that excludes a possible unconscious component. Allport avoided exploring it for his own reasons.

- Allport's views have dominated the field of attitude measurement in psychology for a very significant period.

- We can easily demonstrate implicit cognition, where traces of experience affect behaviour, even though we cannot recall the influential earlier experience.

- Research on implicit cognition gave us a new way of thinking about the concept of attitude.

- Anthony Greenwald developed a reaction time technique for measuring implicit associations in the 1990s. It is called the Implicit Association Test or IAT; it seems to be reliable and robust in terms of measurement.
- In many domains, self-reported attitudes and implicit measures of attitudes (usually reported as 'D' scores) do not correlate.
- There is now mounting evidence that the 'D' score is a better predictor of actual behaviour in many domains, especially where the behaviour in question is spontaneous and unplanned or 'socially sensitive'.
- Implicit, but not explicit, attitudes can predict visual attention, including gaze fixations on images of climate change.
- Some theorists have argued that implicit and explicit attitudes have structurally distinct mental representations.
- Some suggest that the human mind comprises two important subsystems: a familiar foreground, where processing is 'conscious', 'controlled', 'reflective', 'intentional' and 'slow' (system 2); and a hidden background, our implicit system, where processing is 'unconscious', 'automatic', 'impulsive', 'unintended' and 'fast' (system 1).
- Attempts to change behaviour are based on the concept of the self-reported attitude and the self-reported attitude is based on a particular concept of communication, with language as the only conduit of meaning.
- What happens if that particular communicational concept is wrong? What happens if there is more to communication than what people say? What happens if we broaden the concept? What might we learn from a broader consideration of the nature of the communication of meaning?
- Gesture–speech mismatches appeared when explicit and implicit attitudes were not congruent; they seemed to be absent when the explicit and implicit attitudes were congruent.
- Gestures may reflect parts of our unconsciously held attitudes.
- Gestures may reflect our hidden thoughts, where such thoughts may even be hidden from our conscious self.
- Charles Darwin in *The Expression of the Emotions in Man and Animals* in 1872 seems to have suggested something similar, although he did use different language.

17

CONCLUDING
REMARKS

I hope by now that I have managed to take you on at least an interesting journey. We journeyed through some burgeoning fields of verdant academic research and into popular culture, bypassing the slick, reflective worlds of advertising, film and PR. We eventually found ourselves here, pausing temporarily, taking stock and drawing breath. Each bit of territory that we passed required a different vision, sometimes an attention to microscopic detail, sometimes a broad global scan of a horizon, sometimes we had to tread carefully, sometimes we could almost run. However, I suppose that is the point about real journeys that take them beyond the mundane, and the cliché is that they contain a varied mix of experiences and can (potentially) change how you think.

I hope that I have persuaded you that there is something interesting in those spontaneous movements of the hands that people make when they talk. This is body language, but a different sort of body language to that displayed in those catalogues of frozen behaviours captured in all the bestselling books on that topic in airport concourses. This body language is spontaneous, dynamic, imagistic and closely connected to the articulation of speech; it is part of something else, part of a whole. It is more subtle and harder to describe (as we have seen); it works around the speech. It is about semantics and meaning, minds trying to get a message across, using all human resources and modalities to achieve this. However, this is arguably how human beings naturally communicate in everyday life, whether we are describing our physical pain or mental anguish to our best friend, or describing our house to a possible vendor, or explaining our attitude to the environment to a curious researcher. We do this through words and movement simultaneously, effortlessly and effectively. The modalities help each other out, and gestures are used by speakers to resolve potential ambiguities in the verbal message (Holler and Beattie 2003b). Moreover, in everyday talk we, as listeners, 'deduce' the important meanings encoded in those movements quickly and without conscious reflection. We are, of course, never just listeners (when we can help it), we are observers as well, observers of other minds in action, articulating ideas in linear, segmented speech and articulating ideas in the accompanying global, multidimensional images. Our eyes seem to be drawn to particular types of these movements, particularly, it seems, character viewpoint gestures. Moreover, sometimes we may even notice things that do not seem quite right – images and speech that do not appear to match – and sometimes we may feel temporarily uneasy, even though it is very hard to pinpoint exactly what was wrong. And, on occasion, this sense of unease may last significantly longer and affect our social judgement (again as we have seen in the case of people viewing more abstract metaphoric gestures that did not quite match the accompanying speech). These imagistic movements of the hand do appear to change in form and manner of execution when people are lying. The image in the hands sometimes does not match what we are saying and the mismatch may jump out at us. The stroke phase of the gesture also seems to get shorter when we tell these lies and the hands are less likely to pause momentarily, in the form of a post-stroke hold. It is as if at some level of deep subconscious knowledge we are aware of how revealing our hands may be, and more often than not, when we tell lies we try to inhibit our hands altogether. These mismatches between speech and gesture may even be a more accurate indicator of an underlying or implicit attitude in a number of domains and the clash between implicit attitudes and those that people report. The power of these imagistic, spontaneous and dynamic movements should not be underestimated.

My goal in writing this book was partly to introduce the reader to a particularly vibrant area of current psychological research and partly to suggest that the time has come to rethink what body language is all about. If we recognise that bodily movement, at least in the form of hand movements, is dynamic and creative and core to the articulation of ideas, this might make us all more sensitive, as human beings, to each other. We know that the ability to 'read' other people is the key to success in many different fields of life, be it as a great leader, a caring doctor or a good partner. Understanding other minds by being even more sensitive to the movements of the hand would be a great first step in this regard. I am reminded of one study that I carried out many years ago with Heather Shovelton, which was published in the *Journal of Language and Social Psychology* in 1999. This was one of our first studies that looked in detail at how listeners extract meaning from gestures in an experimental task. We found that all of our participants gleaned some additional meaning from gestures even under these conditions. This was very much what we expected. However, we also found that our participants were not equally effective at this task. The increase in accuracy in answering questions about the original stimulus when participants saw the gestures and heard the speech in these short controlled clips, compared to just hearing the speech, ranged from 0.9 per cent to 27.6 per cent. In addition, those people who were more likely to extract accurately the meaning from the gestures on their own (that is, without sound) were better at interpreting the gestures when they accompanied speech. The range in accuracy for interpreting gestures on their own was from 6.6 per cent to 36.1 per cent, which is a very significant difference indeed. These results seem to show that we are not all tuned in to these gestural movements in quite the same way. These movements are powerful, and they are revealing, but some of us may hardly notice them. We know about decoding ability in other domains of nonverbal communication, but gestures may be different for all sorts of reasons: they may be different functionally; they may be different in terms of their connectedness with language; they may even be different in terms of requiring attentional deviations away from the natural focus of the face. Future research will have to identify what factors govern this particular decoding ability and how we might all become better at determining what hidden thoughts these movements reveal.

Towards the beginning of this book, I quoted from Cicero, who wrote that the 'action of the body' expresses 'the sentiments and passions of the soul'. Of course, Cicero was, in addition, very sensitive to the power of spoken language, but here he is adding that human actions, including hand movements, convey both 'sentiments' and 'passions', in other words, thought and emotion, and not one or the other, as so many have thought for so long within psychology and other disciplines. When you remember that souls reach out to communicate both in the voice and in movement *at the same time*, we may understand a little more about the very essence of human communication. It is not so much *homo loquens*, it is more *homo loquens et actus*.

Of course, for so long in our history we simply took spontaneous, imagistic gestures for granted. They were thought of as hand waving for

the inarticulate, crude vestiges of human evolution, noise in the communicational system with spoken language as the communicational modality par
excellence. But perhaps no longer. We can perhaps see for the very first
time what these movements do and why they matter. That, at least, was
my intention in writing this book.

And believe it or not, as I voiced aloud these final words and my hands
started to move away from the keyboard, the right hand without any
volition whatsoever made a short sweeping gesture to the right, and then
it just sat there. I suppose that it was the brevity of this movement that made
me self-consciously aware (and the many hours spent writing this book).
I was forced to glance down into that critical gestural space, and view the
gesture in its post-stroke hold, almost now a thing of beauty. I could see
what the gesture was communicating and what hidden thought was
revealed. The gesture was signalling more a temporary pause than the end;
it was not final enough for 'the end', the stroke phase was too short, the
post-stroke hold too long. I could see all that and interpret this very brief
action. It was how my mind was evidently working at that point in time
and I just laughed at this little bit of self-knowledge, obtained over the course
of this research.

REFERENCES

Aarsleff, H. (2001). *Condillac: Essay on the Origin of Human Knowledge*. Cambridge: Cambridge University Press.

Aboudan, R. and Beattie, G. (1996). Cross-cultural similarities in gestures: The deep relationship between gestures and speech, which transcend language barriers. *Semiotica* 111: 269–94.

Advertising Standards Yearbook (2000). *The Advertising Statistics Yearbook*. Henley-on-Thames: NTC Publications/Advertising Association.

Akehurst, L. and Vrij, A. (1999). Creating suspects in police interviews. *Journal of Applied Social Psychology* 29: 192–210.

Allott, R. (1992). The motor theory of language: Origin and function. In J. Wind (Ed.), *Language Origin: A Multidisciplinary Approach*. Dordrecht: Kluwer, pp. 105–19.

Allport, G. W. (1935). Attitudes. In C. Murchison (Ed.), *Handbook of Social Psychology*. Worcester, MA: Clark University Press, pp. 798–884.

Allport, G. W. (1954). *The Nature of Prejudice*. Cambridge, MA: Addison-Wesley.

Allport, G. W. (1967). Gordon W. Allport. In E. Boring and G. Lindzey (Eds), *A History of Psychology in Autobiography (Volume V)*. *The Century Psychology Series*. New York: Appleton-Century-Crofts, pp. 1–25.

Argyle, M. (1967). *The Psychology of Interpersonal Behaviour*. London: Penguin Books.

Argyle, M. (1972). *The Psychology of Interpersonal Behaviour*, 2nd edition. London: Penguin.

Argyle, M., Alkema, F. and Gilmour, R. (1971). The communication of friendly and hostile attitudes by verbal and nonverbal signals. *European Journal of Social Psychology* 1: 385–402.

Argyle, M., Salter, V., Nicholson, H., Williams, M. and Burgess, P. (1970). The communication of inferior and superior attitudes by verbal and nonverbal signals. *British Journal of Social and Clinical Psychology* 9: 222–31.

Argyle, M. and Trower, P. (1979). *Person to Person: Ways of Communicating*. London: Harper and Row.

Arnheim, R. (1969). *Visual Thinking*. California: University of California Press.

Austin, G. (1806/1966). *Chirinomia or, a Treatise on Rhetorical Delivery*. London: Bulmer and Co.

Bacon, F. (1605/1952). *The Advancement of Learning. Great Books of the Western World*, Volume 31. Chicago: Encyclopaedia Britannica.

Barakat, R. (1973). Arabic gestures. *Journal of Popular Culture* 6: 749–87.

Bassanini, A. and Saint-Martin, A. (2008). The price of prejudice: Labour market discrimination on the grounds of gender and ethnicity. In *OECD Employment Outlook*, chapter 3.

Bates, E. (1976). *Language and Context*. New York: Academic Press.

Bates, E., Benigni, L., Bretherton, I., Camaioni, L. and Volterra, V. (1979). *The Emergence of Symbols: Cognition and Communication in Infancy*. New York: Academic Press.

Bateson, G. (1968). Redundancy and coding. In T. Sebeok (Ed.), *Animal Communication*. Bloomington: Indiana University Press, pp. 614–26.

Beattie, G. (1978). Floor apportionment and gaze in conversational dyads. *British Journal of Social and Clinical Psychology* 17: 7–15.

Beattie, G. (1979). Planning units in spontaneous speech: Some evidence from hesitation in speech and speaker gaze direction in conversation. *Linguistics* 17: 61–78.

Beattie, G. (1981). A further investigation of the cognitive interference hypothesis of gaze patterns during conversation. *British Journal of Social Psychology* 20: 243–248.

Beattie, G. (1982). Unnatural behaviour in the laboratory. *New Scientist* 96: 181.

Beattie, G. (1983). *Talk: An Analysis of Speech and Nonverbal Behaviour in Conversation*. Milton Keynes: Open University Press.

Beattie, G. (2010). *Why Aren't We Saving the Planet? A Psychologist's Perspective*. London: Routledge.

Beattie, G. (2013). *Our Racist Heart? An Exploration of Unconscious Prejudice in Everyday Life*. London: Routledge.

Beattie, G. and Aboudan, R. (1994). Gestures, pauses and speech: An experimental investigation of the effects of changing social context on their precise temporal relationships. *Semiotica* 99: 239–72.

Beattie, G. and Coughlan, J. (1998). Do iconic gestures have a functional role in lexical access? An experimental study of the effects of repeating a verbal message on gesture production. *Semiotica* 119: 221–49.

Beattie, G. and Coughlan, J. (1999). An experimental investigation of the role of iconic gestures in lexical access using the tip-of-the-tongue phenomenon. *British Journal of Psychology* 90: 35–56.

Beattie, G. and McGuire, L. (2012). See no evil? Only implicit attitudes predict unconscious eye movements towards images of climate change. *Semiotica* 192: 315–39.

Beattie, G. and McGuire, L. (2014). The psychology of sustainable consumption. In A. Ulph and D. Southerton (Eds), *Sustainable Consumption: Multidisciplinary Perspectives in Honour of Sir Partha Dasgupta*. London: Oxford University Press, pp. 175–95.

Beattie, G. and Sale, L. (2009). Explicit and implicit attitudes to low and high carbon footprint products. *International Journal of Environmental, Cultural, Economic and Social Sustainability* 5: 191–206.

Beattie, G. and Sale, L. (2011). Shopping to save the planet? Implicit rather than explicit attitudes predict low carbon footprint consumer choice. *International Journal of Environmental, Cultural, Economic and Social Sustainability* 7: 211–32.

Beattie, G. and Sale, L. (2012). Do metaphoric gestures influence how a message is perceived? The effects of metaphoric gesture–speech matches and mismatches on semantic communication and social judgment. *Semiotica* 192: 77–98.

Beattie, G., Sale, L. and McGuire, L. (2011). An inconvenient truth? Can a film really affect psychological mood and our explicit attitudes towards climate change? *Semiotica* 187: 105–25.

Beattie, G. and Shovelton, H. (1998). The communicational significance of the iconic hand gestures which accompany spontaneous speech: An experimental and critical appraisal. In S. Santi, I. Guaitella, C. Cave and G. Konopczynski (Eds), *Oralitee et Gestualitee Communication Multimodale, Interaction*. Paris: L'Harmattan, pp. 371–5.

Beattie, G. and Shovelton, H. (1999a). Do iconic hand gestures really contribute anything to the semantic information conveyed by speech? An experimental investigation. *Semiotica* 123: 1–30.

Beattie, G. and Shovelton, H. (1999b). Mapping the range of information contained in the iconic hand gestures that accompany spontaneous speech. *Journal of Language and Social Psychology* 18: 438–62.

Beattie, G. and Shovelton, H. (2000). Iconic hand gestures and the predictability of words in context in spontaneous speech. *British Journal of Psychology* 91: 473–92.

Beattie, G. and Shovelton, H. (2001a). An experimental investigation of the role of different types of iconic gesture in communication: A semantic feature approach. *Gesture* 1: 129–49.

Beattie, G. and Shovelton, H. (2001b). How gesture viewpoint influences what information decoders receive from iconic gestures. In C. Cave, I. Guaitella and S. Santi (Eds), *Oralitee et Gestualitee: Interactions et Comportements Multimodaux dans la Communication*. Paris: L'Harmattan, pp. 283–7.

Beattie, G. and Shovelton, H. (2002a). What properties of talk are associated with the generation of spontaneous iconic hand gestures? *British Journal of Social Psychology* 41: 403–17.

Beattie, G. and Shovelton, H. (2002b). An experimental investigation of some properties of individual iconic gestures that affect their communicative power. *British Journal of Psychology* 93: 473–92.

Beattie, G. and Shovelton, H. (2005). Why the spontaneous images created by the hands during talk can help make TV advertisements more effective. *British Journal of Psychology* 96: 21–37.

Beattie, G. and Shovelton, H. (2006). When size really matters: How a single semantic feature is represented in the speech and gesture modalities. *Gesture* 6: 63–84.

Beattie, G., Webster, K. and Ross, J. (2010). The fixation and processing of the iconic gestures that accompany talk. *Journal of Language and Social Psychology* 29: 194–213.

Beaumarchais, P.-A. C. de (1964). *The Barber of Seville and The Marriage of Figaro*. UK: Penguin.

Benus, S., Enos, F., Hirschberg, J. and Shriberg, E. (2006). Pauses in deceptive speech. *Speech Prosody* 18: 2–5.

Bertrand, M. and Mullainathan, S. (2004). Are Emily and Greg more employable than Lakisha and Jamal? *American Economic Review* 94: 991–1013.

Birdwhistell, R. L. (1970). *Kinesics and Context: Essays on Body Motion Communication*. Philadelphia: University of Pennsylvania Press.

Bond, C., Kahler, K. and Paolicelli, L. (1985). The miscommunication of deception: An adaptive perspective. *Journal of Experimental Social Psychology* 21: 331–45.

Booth, A., Leigh, A. and Vaganova, E. (2009). Does racial and ethnic discrimination vary across minority groups? Unpublished paper, Australian National University.

Bradshaw, P. (1927). *Art in Advertising*. London: The Press Art School.

Brierley, S. (2002). *The Advertising Handbook*. London: Routledge.

Brown, A. S. (1991). A review of the tip-of-the-tongue experience. *Psychological Bulletin* 109: 204–23.

Brown, R. and McNeill, D. (1966). The 'tip of the tongue' phenomenon. *Journal of Verbal Learning and Verbal Behaviour* 5: 325–37.

Bulwer, J. (1644/1974). *Chirologia: On the Natural Language of the Hand*. Carbondale, IL: Southern Illinois University Press.

Butler, S. (1903). *The Way of All Flesh*. London: Methuen.

Butterworth, B. and Hadar, U. (1989). Gesture, speech, and computational stages: A reply to McNeill. *Psychological Review* 96: 168–74.

Carlsson, M. and Rooth, D. O. (2007). Evidence of ethnic discrimination in the Swedish labor market using experimental data. *Labour Economics* 14: 716–29.

Cassell, J., McNeill, D. and McCullough, K. E. (1999). Speech–gesture mismatches: Evidence for one underlying representation of linguistic and nonlinguistic information. *Pragmatics and Cognition* 7: 1–34.

Chaiken, S. and Trope, Y. (Eds) (1999). *Dual-process Theories in Social Psychology*. New York: Guilford Press.

Chomsky, N. (1957). *Syntactic Structures*. The Hague: Mouton.

Chomsky, N. (1972). *Language and Mind*. New York: Harcourt Brace.

Chomsky, N. (1976). *Reflections on Language*. London: Temple Smith.

Church, R. B. and Goldin-Meadow, S. (1986). The mismatch between gesture and speech as an index of transitional knowledge. *Cognition* 23: 43–71.

Cody, M. J. and O'Hair, D. (1983). Nonverbal communication and deception: Differences in deception cues due to gender and communicator dominance. *Communication Monographs* 50: 175–92.

Cohen, D., Beattie, G. and Shovelton, H. (2010). Nonverbal indicators of deception: How iconic gestures reveal thoughts that cannot be suppressed. *Semiotica* 182: 133–74.

Condillac, E. B. de (1756/2001). *An Essay on the Origin of Human Knowledge*. Cambridge: Cambridge University Press.

Darwin, C. (1859/1971). *The Origin of Species*. London: Dent.

Darwin, C. (1872/1955). *The Expression of the Emotions in Man and Animals*. London: John Murray.

Davis, M. and Hadiks, D. (1995). Demeanor and credibility. *Semiotica* 106: 5–54.

Defra (2008). *The UK Climate Change Programme*. UK: Department for Environment, Food and Rural Affairs.

DePaulo, B. M., Kashy, D. A., Kirkendol, S. E., Wyer, M. M. and Epstein, J. A. (1996). Lying in everyday life. *Journal of Personality and Social Psychology* 70: 979–95.

De Ruiter, J. P. (2007). Postcards from the mind: The relationship between speech, imagistic gesture, and thought. *Gesture* 7: 21–38.

DeTurck, M. A. and Miller, G. R. (1985). Deception and arousal: Isolating the behavioral correlates of deception. *Human Communication Research* 12: 181–201.

Diderot, D. (1751/1916). Lettre sur les sourds et muets. In H. Jourdain (Ed.) (trans.), *Diderot's Early Philosophical Works*. Chicago: Open Court Publishing.

Drydakis, N. and Vlassis, M. (2010). Ethnic discrimination in the Greek labor market: Occupational access, insurance coverage and wage offers. *Manchester School* 78: 201–18.

Ducrot, S. and Grainger, J. (2007). Deployment of spatial attention to words in central and peripheral vision. *Perception and Psychophysics* 69: 578–90.

Efron, D. (1941/1972). *Gesture and Environment*. New York: King's Crown Press.

Ekman, P. (1985). *Telling Lies: Clues to Deceit in the Marketplace, Politics, and Marriage*. London: Norton.

Ekman, P. (1988). Lying and nonverbal behavior: Theoretical issues and new findings. *Journal of Nonverbal Behavior* 12: 163–76.

Ekman, P. (2001, revised 2009). *Telling Lies: Clues to Deceit in the Marketplace, Politics, and Marriage*. New York: W. W. Norton & Company.

Ekman, P. (2003). *Emotions Revealed: Recognizing Faces and Feelings to Improve Communication and Emotional Life*. New York: Times Books.

Ekman, P. and Friesen, W. (1969). The repertoire of nonverbal behavioural categories: Origins, usage, and coding. *Semiotica* 1: 49–98.

Ekman, P. and Friesen, W. (1972). Hand movements. *Journal of Communication* 22: 353–74.

Ekman, P., Friesen, W. and Scherer, K. (1976). Body movement and voice pitch in deceptive interaction. *Semiotica* 16: 23–7.

Ekman, P., O'Sullivan, M., Friesen, W. and Scherer, K. (1991). Face, voice, and body in detecting deceit. *Journal of Nonverbal Behavior* 15: 125–35.

Ellis, A. and Beattie, G. (1986). *The Psychology of Language and Communication*. New York: Guilford Press.

Firbas, J. (1964). On defining the theme in functional sentence analysis. *Travaux Linguistiques de Prague* 1: 267–80.

Freud, S. (1905/1953). Fragments of an analysis of a case of hysteria. In J. Strachey (Ed.), *Standard Edition of the Complete Psychological Works of Sigmund Freud*, Volume VII. London: Hogarth Press.

Fuchs A. F. (1971). The saccadic system. In P. Bach-y-Rita, C. C. Collins and J. E. Hyde (Eds), *The Control of Eye Movements*. London: Academic Press.

Gardner, A. and Gardner, B. T. (1978). Comparative psychology and language acquisition. *Annals of the New York Academy of Sciences* 309: 37–76.

Goffman, I. (1959). *The Presentation of Self in Everyday Life*. New York: Doubleday.

Goldin-Meadow, S. (1999). The development of gesture with and without speech in hearing and deaf children. In L. Messing and R. Campbell (Eds), *Gesture, Speech and Sign*. Oxford: Oxford University Press, pp. 117–32.

Goldin-Meadow, S. and McNeill, D. (1999). The role of gesture and mimetic representation in making language the province of speech. In M. Corballis and S. Lea (Eds), *The Descent of Mind*. Oxford: Oxford University Press, pp. 155–72.

Goldin-Meadow, S., McNeill, D. and Singleton, J. (1996). Silence is liberating: Removing the handcuffs on grammatical expression in the manual modality. *Psychological Review* 103: 34–55.

Goldman-Eisler, F. (1968). *Psycholinguistics: Experiments in Spontaneous Speech*. London: Academic Press.

Greene, J., O'Hair, H., Cody, M. and Yen, C. (1985). Planning and control of behavior during deception. *Human Communication Research* 11: 335–64.

Greenwald, A. G. (1990). What cognitive representations underlie social attitudes? *Bulletin of the Psychonomic Society* 28: 254–60.

Greenwald, A. G., McGhee, D. E. and Schwartz, J. L. (1998). Measuring individual differences in implicit cognition: The Implicit Association Test. *Journal of Personality and Social Psychology* 74: 1464–80.

Greenwald, A. G. and Nosek, B. A. (2008). Attitudinal dissociation: What does it mean? In R. E. Petty, R. H. Fazio and P. Briñol (Eds), *Attitudes: Insights from the New Implicit Measures*. Hillsdale, NJ: Erlbaum, pp. 65–82.

Gregg, A. P. (2008). Oracle of the unconscious or deceiver of the unwitting? *The Psychologist* 21: 762–6.

Gullberg, M. (2003). Gestures, referents, and anaphoric linkage in learner varieties. In C. Dimroth and M. Starren (Eds), *Information Structure, Linguistic Structure and the Dynamics of Language Acquisition*. Amsterdam: John Benjamins, pp. 311–28.

Gullberg, M. and Holmqvist, K. (1999). Keeping an eye on gestures: Visual perception of gestures in face-to-face communication. *Pragmatics and Cognition* 7: 35–63.

Gullberg, M. and Holmqvist, K. (2002). Visual attention towards gestures in face-to-face interaction vs. on screen. In I. Wachsmuth and T. Sowa (Eds), *Gesture and Sign Language in Human–Computer Interaction*. Berlin Heidelberg: Springer, pp. 206–14.

Gullberg, M. and Holmqvist, K. (2006). What speakers do and what addressees look at: Visual attention to gestures in human interaction live and on video. *Pragmatics and Cognition* 14: 53–82.

Gullberg, M. and Kita, S. (2009). Attention to speech-accompanying gestures: Eye movements and information uptake. *Journal of Nonverbal Behavior* 33: 251–77.

Habets, B., Kita, S., Shao, Z., Özyurek, A. and Hagoort, P. (2011). The role of synchrony and ambiguity in speech–gesture integration during comprehension. *Journal of Cognitive Neuroscience* 23: 1845–54.

Hadar, U. (2001). The recognition of the meaning of ideational gestures by untrained subjects. In C. Cave, I. Guaitella and S. Santi (Eds), *Oralitee et Gestualitee: Interactions et Comportements Multimodaux dans la Communication*. Paris: L'Harmattan, pp. 292–5.

Hall, E. T. (1959). *The Silent Language*. New York: Doubleday.

Heath, A. and Li, Y. (2007). Measuring the size of the employer contribution to the ethnic minority employment gap. Consultation paper for the National Employment Panel, London.

Hewes, G. (1973a). Primate communication and the gestural origin of language. *Current Anthropology* 14: 5–12.

Hewes, G. (1973b). Reply to critics. *Current Anthropology* 14: 19–21.

Hewes, G. (1992). Primate communication and the gestural origin of language. *Current Anthropology* 33: 65–84.

Hockett, C. (1960). The origin of speech. *Scientific American* 203: 88–96.

Hockett, C. (1978). In search of Jove's brow. *American Speech* 53: 243–313.

Hofer, E., Kohnken, G., Hanewinkel, R. and Bruhn, C. (1993). *Diagnostik und Attribution von Glaubwürdigkeit*. Final report to the Deutsche Forschungsgemeinschaft. KO, Kiel: University of Kiel.

Hofmann, W., Gawronski, B., Gschwendner, T., Le, H. and Schmitt, M. (2005). A meta-analysis on the correlation between the Implicit Association Test and explicit self-report measures. *Personality and Social Psychology Bulletin* 31: 1369–85.

Holler, J. and Beattie, G. (2002). A micro-analytic investigation of how iconic gestures and speech represent core semantic features in talk. *Semiotica* 142: 31–69.

Holler, J. and Beattie, G. (2003a). How iconic gestures and speech interact in the representation of meaning: Are both aspects really integral to the process? *Semiotica* 146: 81–116.

Holler, J. and Beattie, G. (2003b). Pragmatic aspects of representational gestures: Do speakers use them to clarify verbal ambiguity for the listener? *Gesture* 3: 127–54.

Holler, J., Shovelton, H. and Beattie, G. (2009) Do iconic hand gestures really contribute to the communication of semantic information in a face-to-face context? *Journal of Nonverbal Behavior* 33: 73–88.

Iverson, J. M. and Goldin-Meadow, S. (1997). What's communication got to do with it? Gesture in children blind from birth. *Developmental Psychology* 33: 453–67.

James, W. (1893). *The Principles of Psychology*, Volume 1. New York: Holt.

Jancovic, M. A., Devoe, S. and Wiener, M. (1975). Age-related changes in hand and arm movements as nonverbal communication: Some conceptualisations and an empirical exploration. *Child Development* 46: 922–8.

Jefferson, G. (2004). Glossary of transcript symbols with an introduction. *Pragmatics and Beyond New Series* 125: 13–34.

Jowell, R. and Prescott-Clarke, P. (1970). Racial discrimination and White-collar workers in Britain. *Race and Class* 11: 397–417.

Kahneman, D. (1973). *Attention and Effort*. Englewood Cliffs, NJ: Prentice-Hall.

Kahneman, D. (2011). *Thinking, Fast and Slow*. New York: Farrar, Straus and Giroux.

Kalma, A., Witte, M. and Zaalberg, R. (1996). Authenticity: Operationalization, manipulation, and behavioural components: An explanation. *Medium Psychologie* 8: 49–65.

Kendon, A. (1972). Some relationships between body motion and speech. In A. Siegmanand and B. Pope (Eds), *Studies in Dyadic Communication*. New York: Pergamon Press, pp. 177–210.

Kendon, A. (1980). Gesticulation and speech: Two aspects of the process of utterance. In M. R. Key (Ed.), *The Relation between Verbal and Nonverbal Communication*. The Hague: Mouton, pp. 207–27.

Kendon, A. (1982). The study of gesture: Some observations on its history. *Semiotic Inquiry* 2: 45–62.

Kendon, A. (1988). How gestures can become like words. In F. Poyatos (Ed.), *Cross-cultural Perspectives in Nonverbal Communication*. Toronto: Hogrefe, pp. 131–41.

Kendon, A. (2004). *Gesture: Visible Action as Utterance*. Cambridge: Cambridge University Press.

Kennedy, G. (1972). *The Art of Rhetoric in the Roman World: 300 BC–AD 300*. Princeton: Princeton University Press.

Kogan, I. (2011). New immigrants – old disadvantage patterns? Labour market integration of recent immigrants into Germany. *International Migration* 49: 91–117.

Kortlandt, A. (1973). Comment on Hewes. *Current Anthropology* 14: 13–14.

Kortlandt, A. (1992). Comment on Hewes. *Current Anthropology* 33: 73–4.

Krauss, R., Morrel-Samuels, P. and Colasante, C. (1991). Do conversational hand gestures communicate? *Journal of Personality and Social Psychology* 61: 743–54.

La Barre, W. (1964). Paralinguistics, kinesics, and cultural anthropology. In T. A. Sebeok (Ed.), *Approaches to Semiotics*. The Hague: Mouton, pp. 191–220.

Laing, R. D. and Esterson, A. (1964). *Sanity, Madness and the Family*. London: Penguin.

Lefranc, A. (2010). Unequal opportunities and ethnic origin: The labor market outcomes of second-generation immigrants in France. *American Behavioral Scientist* 53: 1851–82.

Leroi-Gourhan, A. (1964–5). *Le Geste et la Parole*, 2 vols. Paris: Albin Marcel.

Levelt, W. J. M. (Ed.) (1993). *Lexical Access in Speech Production*. Cambridge, MA: Blackwell.

Maclay, H. and Osgood, C. E. (1959). Hesitation phenomena in spontaneous English speech. *Word* 15: 19–44.

McNeill, D. (1985). So you think gestures are nonverbal? *Psychological Review* 92: 350–71.

McNeill, D. (1992). *Hand and Mind. What Gestures Reveal About Thought*. Chicago: University of Chicago Press.

McNeill, D. (2000). *Language and Gesture*. Cambridge: Cambridge University Press.

McNeill, D. (2012). *How Language Began: Gesture and Speech in Human Evolution*. Cambridge: Cambridge University Press.

McNeill, D. and Duncan, S. D. (1998). Growth points in thinking-for-speaking. In D. McNeill (Ed.), *Language and Gesture*. Cambridge: Cambridge University Press, pp. 141–61.

Mann, S., Vrij, A. and Bull, R. (1998). Telling and detecting true lies. Paper presented at the Eighth Annual Meeting of the European Association on Psychology and Law, Cracow, Poland, September 1998.

Marler, P. and Tenaza, R. (1977). Signalling behaviour of apes with special reference to vocalization. In T. A. Sebeok (Ed.), *How Animals Communicate*. Bloomington: Indiana University Press.

Mehrabian, A. and Ferris, S. R. (1967). Inference of attitudes from nonverbal communication in two channels. *Journal of Consulting Psychology* 31: 248–52.

Mehrabian, A. and Wiener, M. (1967). Decoding of inconsistent communications. *Journal of Personality and Social Psychology* 6: 109–14.

Morrel-Samuels, P. (1990). John Bulwer's 1644 treatise on gesture. *Semiotica* 79: 341–53.

Morris, D., Collett, P., Marsh, P. and O'Shaughnessy, M. (1979). *Gestures: Their Origins and Distribution*. London: Cape.

Müller, G. E. and Pilzecker, A. (1900). Experimentelle Beiträge zur Lehre vom Gedächtniss. *Zeitschrift für Psychologie, Ergänzungsband* 1: 1–128.

Nelson, K. (2007). *Young Minds in Social Worlds: Experience, Meaning, and Memory*. Cambridge, MA: Harvard University Press.

Nobe, S. (2000). Where do most spontaneous representational gestures actually occur with respect to speech? In D. McNeill (Ed.), *Language and Gesture*. Cambridge: Cambridge University Press, pp. 186–98.

Nobe, S., Hayamizu, S., Hasegawa, O. and Takahashi, H. (1998). Are listeners paying attention to the hand gestures of an anthropomorphic agent? An evaluation using a gaze tracking method. *Gesture and Sign Language in Human–Computer Interaction* 1371: 49–59.

Nordin, M. and Rooth, D. (2009). The ethnic employment and income gap in Sweden: Is skill or labor market discrimination the explanation? *Scandinavian Journal of Economics* 111: 487–510.

Nosek, B. A. (2005). Moderators of the relationship between implicit and explicit evaluation. *Journal of Experimental Psychology: General* 134: 565–84.

Oldfield, R. (1963). Individual vocabulary and semantic currency: A preliminary study. *British Journal of Social and Clinical Psychology* 2: 122–30.

Olson, M. A. and Fazio, R. H. (2006). Reducing automatically activated racial prejudice through implicit evaluative conditioning. *Personality and Social Psychology Bulletin* 32: 421–33.

Pendakur, K. and Pendakur, R. (1998). The colour of money: Earnings differentials among ethnic groups in Canada. *Canadian Journal of Economics* 31: 518–48.

Petitto, L. A. (1988). 'Language' in the prelinguistic child. In F. S. Kessel (Ed.), *The Development of Language and Language Researchers*. Hillsdale, NJ: Erlbaum, pp. 187–221.

Quintilian, M. (100/1902). *Quintilian Institutions Oratoriae* (trans. H. Butler). London: Heinemann.

Rayner, K. (1998). Eye movements in reading and information processing: 20 years of research. *Psychological Bulletin* 124: 372–422.

Richards, I. A. (1936). *The Philosophy of Rhetoric*. New York: Oxford University Press.

Rowbotham, S., Holler, J., Lloyd, D. and Wearden, A. (2012). How do we communicate about pain? A systematic analysis of the semantic contribution of co-speech gestures in pain-focused conversations. *Journal of Nonverbal Behavior* 36: 1–21.

Ruesch, J. (1953). Synopsis of the theory of human communication. *Psychiatry* 16: 215–43.

Ruesch, J. (1955). Nonverbal language and therapy. *Psychiatry* 18: 323–30.

Sapir, E. (1927/1949). The unconscious patterning of behaviour in society. In D. G. Mandelbaum (Ed.), *Selected Writings of Edward Sapir in Language, Culture, and Personality.* Berkeley and Los Angeles: University of California Press.

Saussure, F. de (1916/1959). *Course in General Linguistics* (trans. W. Baskin). New York: Philosophical Library.

Scheflen, A. (1974). *How Behavior Means.* New York: Aronson.

Scheflen, A. and Scheflen, A. (1972). *Body Language and Social Order: Communication as Behavioral Control.* New York: Prentice-Hall.

Seidenberg, M. S. and Petitto, L. A. (1979). Signing behaviour in apes: A critical review. *Cognition* 7: 177–215.

Sporer, S. L. and Schwandt, B. (2007). Moderators of nonverbal indicators of deception: A meta-analytic synthesis. *Psychology, Public Policy, and Law*, 13: 1–34.

Streeter, L. A., Krauss, R. M., Geller, V., Olson, C. and Apple, W. (1977). Pitch changes during attempted deception. *Journal of Personality and Social Psychology* 35: 345–50.

Terrace, H. S. (1979). *Nim.* New York: Knopf.

Tobias, M., Bhattacharya, A. and White, P. (2008). Cross-classification of the New Zealand population by ethnicity and deprivation: Trends from 1996 to 2006. *Australian and New Zealand Journal of Public Health* 32: 431–6.

Trower, P., Bryant, B. and Argyle, M. (1978). *Social Skills and Mental Health.* London: Methuen.

Turano, K. A., Geruschat, D. R. and Baker, F. H. (2003). Oculomotor strategies for the direction of gaze tested with a real-world activity. *Vision Research* 43: 333–46.

Tylor, E. B. (1878). *Researches into the Early History of Mankind.* London: John Murray.

van Lawick-Goodall, J. (1971). *In the Shadow of Man.* London: Collins.

Vrij, A. (2000). *Detecting Lies and Deceit.* Chichester: Wiley.

Vrij, A., Edward, K., Roberts, K. and Bull, R. (1999). Detecting deceit via criteria-based content analysis, reality monitoring and analyses of nonverbal behaviour. Paper presented at the Ninth European Conference on Psychology and Law, Dublin, Ireland, July 1999.

Wilson, E. O. (1975). *Sociobiology.* Cambridge, MA: Harvard University Press.

Wilson, T. D., Lindsey, S. and Schooler, T. Y. (2000). A model of dual attitudes. *Psychological Review* 107: 101–26.

Wood, M., Hales, J., Purdon, S., Sejersen, T. and Hayllar, O. (2009). A test for racial discrimination in recruitment practice in British cities. Department for Work and Pensions (Research Report No. 607).

Wundt, W. (1921/1973). *The Language of Gestures.* The Hague: Mouton.

INDEX